IssueWeb

A Guide and Sourcebook for Researching Controversial Issues on the Web

Karen R. Diaz
Nancy O'Hanlon

LIBRARIES
UNLIMITED
A Member of the Greenwood Publishing Group

Westport, Connecticut • London

Library of Congress Cataloging-in-Publication Data

Diaz, Karen R.

   IssueWeb : a guide and sourcebook for researching controversial issues on the Web/
Karen R. Diaz and Nancy O'Hanlon.

     p. cm.

   Includes index.

   ISBN 1–59158–078–1 (alk. paper)

   1. Internet research. 2. Internet searching. 3. Computer network resources—Evaluation.
4. Internet research—Study and teaching (Secondary)—United States. 5. Internet
research —Study and teaching (Higher)—United States. I. O'Hanlon, Nancy. II. Title.

ZA4228.D53   2004

025.04—dc22   2003065946

British Library Cataloguing in Publication Data is available.

Library of Congress Card Number: 2003065946

ISBN: 1–59158–078–1

First published in 2004

Libraries Unlimited, 88 Post Road West, Westport, CT 06881

A Member of the Greenwood Publishing Group, Inc.

www.lu.com

Printed in the United States of America

Contents

Introduction

Rationale

What student has graduated from college without writing an opinion or position paper? We dare to venture that the number is quite small. After all, opinion papers are an avenue for teaching critical thinking skills. They can help students understand whether their opinion on a topic has a bias, is based on sufficient information, and falls within a continuum of widely held beliefs. It is a way for individuals to begin playing lifelong values and beliefs off those of society as a whole, to evaluate their own beliefs, and to determine what roles they wish to play in society. However, to accomplish all these things, one must be exposed to new and different ideas. One important route to this exposure is research.

The idea for this book came from an online Internet course in which we teach students to use the Web for research purposes. Topics that lend themselves well to our assignments are those that are controversial in nature. We have discovered in the years of teaching this course that not only do students need to learn about search techniques and tools they also require instruction in the evaluation of published or online materials. Put simply, what the student knows or believes colors his or her understanding of the significance or purpose of what he or she reads. For instance, if we ask students to judge whether a Web site is trying to sway opinion, one student might think it is not if the Web site corroborates his or her own worldview, while another student might think it is if the view stands in opposition to his or her own beliefs.

We have also found that the ease of using search engines, such as Google or AltaVista, encourages students to take a noncontextual, keyword approach to research. Spit in a word and see what comes out. Not only does this present the student with an overwhelming amount of material, it provides a haphazard lump made of pieces that are unrelated in context. An ad might appear in the same result list as a scholarly article. An extremist individual's Web page might be grouped with a student assignment posted to a course Web site.

How do we get past this? How do any of us move from being individuals who can only see controversial information we read through the lens of our own bias? And how do we find material that is grouped appropriately by type? This is the process we are attempting to address here.

Structure

First there is an information-gathering component, followed by an evaluating component. For both components there are a variety of useful tools and strategies, which we attempt to outline in the first two chapters. We also present a number of controversial topics to provide examples and ideas for individual researchers.

Each topical "issue brief" includes a summary, providing background on the topic and outlining key controversies. Suggested keyword search terms and a list of related topics within this book are provided. The Web sites listed are divided into the following categories:

- **Reference:** These are sites that provide a good starting point for research, include many links to other sites (usually organized into categories), and do not promote only a single point of view.

- **Law/legislation:** These sites provide texts of legal documents, pointers to legal information sources, or updates on federal and/or state legislative activity related to the topic.

- **News:** These sites enable the reader to keep up-to-date with new developments on the topic.

- **Data:** These sites provide factual information, primary source material, or research findings that can be used to develop sound arguments or positions on a topic.

- **Advocacy:** These sites promote a particular viewpoint on a controversial issue. We have organized these into subgroups, by position.

Finally, the book includes three appendixes that augment the sources listed in the issue brief chapters. The first two describe opinion magazines and think tanks or research institutes that are broadly useful for finding additional information on controversial topics. Because these sources are categorized as conservative, liberal, or neutral in focus, they may be used to locate opinion on all sides of a topic. Another appendix lists some proprietary databases that are useful for research on controversial issues but are available only through libraries.

Limitations

We feel the need to make some disclaimers about what this book does and does not do. First and foremost, it is an American book. The topics we have chosen are of interest to Americans, and the definitions, strategies, and tools outlined for researching the topics are given in the context of U.S. society. (See, we are bringing our own bias to the table.)

Next, although we attempt completeness in the guide and strategy portion of the book, we have been very purposefully selective in the number of topics covered and in the number of think tanks and magazines listed in our appendixes. We feel these are representative in nature, core to the types of topics students often research, and timely. If we covered every topic, group, and publication considered to be controversial to our society, we would need volumes to fit in everything. And even then someone would find that we had left something out. Somehow the number 40 presented itself as large enough to be inclusive and representative yet small enough for the authors and the readers to manage.

We have addressed the research process. We do not address reasoning methods or writing skills.

And while listed last here, the most obvious limitation is that our focus is on online research. Why? First, we see the Web as an ideal and vast venue for this sort of research. Controversial topics are often timely in nature, which the Web accommodates nicely. News and legal materials essential to this research are often available only on the Web. Organizations that advocate for social and public policy causes often have a Web presence and often have opinions that are not published in any easily identifiable printed source. Highly motivated individuals can have a voice in the midst of scholarship on the Web. These voices can be very legitimate for controversial research. And realistically, most students use the Web for research these days. The key is to steer them to the best resources and train them to critically evaluate their findings.

Audience

We envision this book being useful to high school and undergraduate college students, their instructors, and the librarians who serve all of them. Students can get ideas for research topics, help on where to start, and strategies for moving through the research process. Instructors can gain ideas on how to break down a research project. Rather than simply assigning a paper, why not create a series of assignments that provide opportunities to locate different types of information sources on the topic, and later ask students to combine their findings in a paper? Librarians can find useful resources for lost souls trying to find a position in opposition to or in support of their own or to guide a student who is in search of a topic.

PART **1**

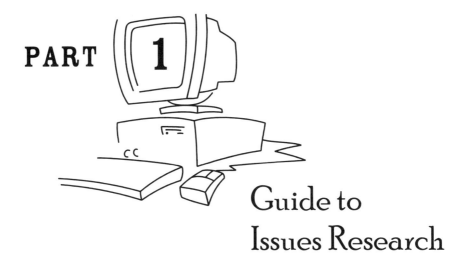

Guide to
Issues Research

1

Finding Resources

There are two basic parts to finding the right resources for a research project: topic and format. Although it may seem obvious that you need to know what (topic) you want to know about, it is equally important to understand the kind of material (format) that will most likely have the kind of information you need.

Selecting a Topic

For any type of research—including that regarding controversial issues—choosing a topic can be the greatest barrier to progress upon starting the research process. It can also be a lot of fun. Your topic is what defines your research process. The process of choosing a topic can be instructional in and of itself. It can broaden your horizons and sharpen your thinking about how some issues might be related to and be affected by others. But perhaps the most important reason for you to spend time crafting your topic is that it will *save you time* in the long run. Hours can be wasted doing unfocused and unclear research.

Your starting point likely falls somewhere on a continuum of choices. Your instructor may provide very specific projects or may allow you a lot of choice in the matter. On one end might be such strict parameters that you essentially do not have a choice. On the other are virtually limitless possibilities. (See Figure 1.1, page 4.)

Regardless of where you are beginning this process, you do need to take a little time to be sure you have a usable and appropriate starting point. Recognize also that with controversial topic research, you will have at least two components to your research: the topic itself and your position on the topic. There are a variety of approaches to topic selection and definition.

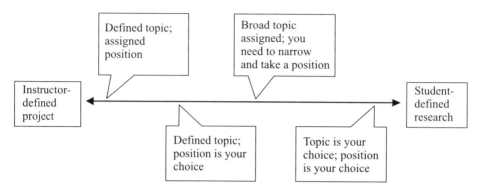

Figure 1.1. Topic Selection Continuum

Browsing

For the most undefined and broadest assignments, browsing might be the best way to begin the topic selection process. A variety of tools can be of use. Web directories tend to be the most useful tools for browsing. Directories present materials in a hierarchical subject arrangement, allowing you to browse through topics and burrow your way down to something of specific interest to you. A general interest in the environment could lead you to a topic as specific as drilling for oil in the arctic wildlife refuge. See the "All Topics" chapter of this book for references to Web directories for controversial issue browsing. Of course, another great tool for browsing is this text itself. See the "Issue Briefs" part of this book for a sampling of topics that might be of interest. We have provided some definition, context, and starting research points for you. Take a look!

Although starting cold with no defined topic can be stymieing, it can also lead you down the most rewarding path. When this is your "problem," use it for the most personal reward. If there is a topic whose research will benefit you in another class, use it. If there is an issue on a local ballot that you have not made up your mind about, choose that topic as your focus. If you've been meaning to write to your congressperson on a political concern, make that the focus of your paper. You will then have research-based facts for your letter. If your personal leanings are toward moral issues, pick a topic of moral significance. If you are a science major stuck in a required English class, pick a topic that relates to your scientific interest. There is hardly an area of our private concerns that does not take on controversial or debatable significance when moved to the public arena. Be personal in your choice and your work will be much more enjoyable.

Cruising for Ideas?
- Browse a Web directory
- Peruse the topics in this book
- Be personal!

Narrowing

If an assignment is general in nature, your challenge in topic selection might be to narrow your focus sufficiently. For instance, if you are asked to defend any position on how technology affects society, you may have to consider a specific technology or a specific impact. Browsing is still one appropriate way to begin this process. Web directories often start broadly. Clicking on a category will take you to a subset of topics. The further you "drill" through the site, the more specific the topic becomes. Library catalogs can do the same for you. While searching subject headings, you will be presented with the subject and all its subheadings.

Another approach to narrowing a topic is to do some preliminary searching in an appropriate search engine or database. By starting a search with your generalized topic, you will be taken to specific material on specific topics. Browsing through your results can give you ideas of trends and topics.

Here's an approach that does not involve using any online tools. Ask yourself some questions about the topic:

- What do you already know about this subject?

- What are some specific examples of your broad terms?

- Can you think of a particular event or issue that relates to this question?

- Ask some friends what examples they can think of related to this problem

- Chart your ideas. Let's use our example of the impact of technology on society.

Step 1: Chart Your Ideas

	Technology	Impact	Society
Think of examples	Telephones	Positive	Adults
	Computers	Negative	Children
	Televisions	Good	Schools
	PDAs	Bad	United States
	The Internet	Productive	Teens
	Cell phones	Nonproductive	The workplace
		Problem	
		Solution	
Select the narrower examples of interest to you	The Internet	Positive	Teens

Step 2: Take a Stand!

"The Internet has been a positive force in the lives of teens."

Broadening

You will usually discover that a topic is too narrow and needs broadening once you've begun the research process. If you can't find any material, chances are either your topic or your approach to searching the topic is too narrow. Here's an example of a very narrow topic:

"Remote controls destroy marriages."

Use the same charting approach in reverse. This time, in addition to thinking of examples, think of context.

Step 1: Chart It

	Remote Controls	Destroy	Marriages
Related examples	• Mice on computers • Channel surfing • Steering wheels in cars	• Implode • Bombard • Impossible • Satisfy • Better	• Divorce • Men • Women
Broader context	• Television • Computers • Technology	• Challenge • Negative • Problematic • Nonproductive • Enhance	• Personal relationships • Gender differences
Settle on a compromise	• Technology	• Challenge	• Gender differences

Step 2: Take a Broader Stand/Ask a Question

"Gender differences in the use of technology are a real challenge."

Remember that one of the constricting factors for your topic might be the point of view language you are using (too adamant or too neutral). Also, not all aspects of your topic may need to be broadened.

Academic Context

What are your own academic bents? Understanding this may help you with topic selection, topic definition, and your research strategy. From what perspective or academic discipline(s) would you (or would you like to) approach a topic?

- Humanities: religious, ethical, moral, philosophical, or cultural
- Social sciences: political, economic, sociological, anthropological, or legal
- Sciences: biological, medical, or environmental

Understanding the academic perspective of your topic will help you with the next steps of looking at search terminology and selecting appropriate search tools.

Final Touches/Checklist

☐ Do you need/have you obtained approval of your topic by your instructor?

☐ Is your topic a meaningful sentence or an interesting question?

☐ Did your preliminary browsing and searching indicate the likelihood of available materials?

☐ Did your preliminary browsing and searching indicate that your topic is debatable?

☐ Have you talked to a couple of people (friends, teachers, librarians, on-line group) about your topic? Everyone has an opinion, and if you throw a controversial topic out there you are likely to get some feedback!

☐ Have you kept a list of the terminology you have encountered during your topic selection process? This terminology will become important during the search phase of your research.

Assessing Your Information Need

Different needs call for not only differing amounts of research time but also different tools. Consider the different types of information available; this will help you understand the choice in research tools.

Reference Sites

You've already done a bit of thinking about how much you know about your topic. If it's not much, background materials, issue briefs, or overviews will give you the definition of the problem and the context in which it functions in society. Such materials will also help you with determining the vocabulary of the topic and may introduce you to the stakeholders in the issue. Examples of these materials are encyclopedia articles, political platforms, executive summaries, and topical portals. Although portals won't summarize an issue for you, they should lead to summaries as well as a host of other types of resources.

News Sites

Use news sites and databases to understand why an issue is relevant, how and why legislation is being formulated, and what real world applications exist. Use these sites to find out what the latest event(s) are that are related to your topic.

Law and Legislation

Use legislative sites, databases, and guides to find out what the current law regarding your topic is. The debate that took place before a law was enacted also provides a very good perspective on pros and cons. Determine whether your ideas fall within a legal, legislative, or administrative context. Would your ideas support pending legislation or entail changing current laws?

Data Sites

Your research need may require expert knowledge from professionals and intellectuals. Use in-depth analysis done by university professors, think tanks, documentary journalists, and scholars in a field. Such analysis is often found in scholarly journals, white papers, conference proceedings, and research papers.

To support an argument, sometimes statistics or other data are your strongest weapon. Use statistical sources, government reports, and other data tools to find the appropriate information.

Graphics and sounds are generally useful for enlivening the presentation of your work. Pictures can be powerful tools for gaining attention and shocking readers. Sound and video might be appropriate for oral presentations of your research. Use multimedia search capabilities of search engines to find alternate formats of information.

Advocacy

Use the opinions of others to formulate your own opinion or to develop your contrasting argument. Web sites of advocacy groups are very useful for understanding a point of view different than your own. Magazine and journal articles (especially from op/ed sections) are also a good way to find opposing opinions on a topic.

Needs Assessment Chart

Although you won't know all the answers to the questions presented here before you have begun your research, asking yourself these questions will prove immensely helpful in thinking through the effort that will be required and the places you might wish to begin. These answers will help you begin to realize how much information you need and how much time you will have to spend in the research process. In Table 1.1 we have indicated how the answers to some questions will affect either the resources you use or the nature of your searches.

Table 1.1. Assessing Research Needs

Question	Possible Resources	Possible Search Strategies/Search Terms
What length and type of assignment do you have to complete? (e.g., five-minute oral presentation, 3-page paper, 20-page paper)	Lots of resources vs. few resources required	One vs. several pro and one vs. several con
Is this issue currently in the news?	News sites (current vs. archival) Specific newspapers News magazines	Use of date limiters in databases/search engines
Where do you expect to find the most information? (in newspapers, on Web sites, in magazines, in scholarly journals, books, etc.)	Search engine/reference site Legislative site Data site News site or search tool Proprietary database Library catalog	
What groups are interested in this topic? Who's in favor and who's opposed?	Advocacy sites	
Who is most affected by this issue? (Who are the stakeholders?)	Advocacy groups	Names of organizations Names of people Societal groups (teens, adults, workers, children, etc.)
Is this a local, regional, or federal issue?	Local papers National papers Federal legislation sites State legislation sites	
Is this a moral issue, a political issue, or both?	Religious publications/ Web sites Political publications/ Web sites	Religious vs. political terminology
Do you know of pending, attempted, or enacted legislation on this issue?	Legislative sites/databases Current vs. archival	Names of laws and acts
Would your argument be better supported if you had statistics or other data on your topic?	Statistical sources/data sites Government sites Research organization/ think tank sites	

Selecting the Right Tool

Assessing your needs should highlight the importance of selecting the right tool. Too often beginning researchers think that all they need to research a topic on the Web is to "go to the Web." The Web is not one thing. Rather, it is lots of tools linked together. Success in finding information begins with selecting the right tool. The second portion of this book is designed specifically to outline the right tools for researching various topics. Because we cannot cover every topic there is, and because the topics we do cover cannot contain every resource available for them, we have also provided an "All Topics" chapter to highlight resources generally useful for controversial topic research. Although not a complete list, these tools will set you on the right path to finding information on a variety of topics.

Selecting the Terminology

Once you have selected the right tool(s) for your search, you need to determine how you will search. The basics of your search involve identifying the terminology you will use. Generally, your choices are browsing, searching by subject, or searching by keyword.

Browsing, Subjects, and Keywords

One simple way of "searching" that might be available is browsing. Browsing is a common method of finding information in a directory or portal. As stated previously, browsable tools are great when you don't have a topic in mind and need to find one. However, when you do have a topic that you are searching, to browse you must understand how your search term(s) fits into a broader context. For instance, a directory might place items about "education vouchers" in the following path structure:

```
EDUCATION
    SCHOOLS
        SCHOOL CHOICE
            EDUCATION VOUCHERS
```

Some search tools allow you to use subject searching, which means you are searching by subject terms predetermined by the database and assigned to items within the database. Another term for subject headings is *controlled vocabulary*. Some people have decided that one particular term will be used to describe all related documents, even if the authors used different terminology to express the same concept. (See Figure 1.2.)

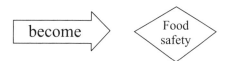

Figure 1.2. Turning Keywords into Subject Headings

Not many free Web search tools use subject headings, as this approach requires labor-intensive human intervention. The major exceptions are library catalogs. The benefit of subject heading searching is the assurance that you have retrieved all items on a topic using one search term. The drawback is needing to learn which accepted search term(s) to use.

A more common approach, particularly for the sorts of free Web tools introduced in this book, is to search by keyword. Keywords are terms that appear throughout the text of the works. No special indexing needs to be done to retrieve items by keyword, but the searcher must guess at the terminology used by authors.

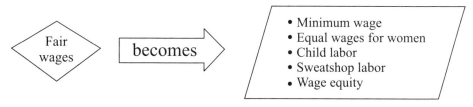

Figure 1.3. Expanding Keywords for Comprehensiveness

Keyword Search Construction

You can employ a variety of techniques to arrive at the best search strategy for a keyword approach to researching a topic. Different search engines and proprietary databases will allow different techniques to be used. Check the search help screens of the tool you are using to see which of these approaches will work.

Boolean Searching

Some databases use special connector words called Boolean operators to combine search terms. The most frequently used Boolean operators are **AND, OR, NOT:**

Search for	What Happens?
addiction AND treatment	Requires that ALL of these words be present in results; use AND to connect concepts.
cocaine OR crack	ANY of these words can be present in results; use OR to connect synonyms.
drugs NOT prescription	Excludes words from results.

From *net.TUTOR: Searching 101.* http://gateway.lib.ohio-state.edu/tutor/les4/pg3.html
(Accessed June 3, 2003).

Mathematical Symbols

Some databases allow you to use either Boolean operators (words) or mathematical operators (symbols) to combine search terms. These mathematical operators are the plus symbol (+) and the minus symbol (-):

Search for	What Happens?
+addiction +treatment	Requires that ALL of these words be present in results, like the Boolean operator AND.
+drugs -prescription	Excludes words from results, like the Boolean operator NOT.

From *net.TUTOR: Searching 101.* http://gateway.lib.ohio-state.edu/tutor/les4/pg3.html
(Accessed June 3, 2003).

Note: *Spacing counts.* When constructing search statements using mathematical operators, be sure to format them correctly, so that the search works as intended:

DON'T leave a space between the math symbol and your search word.

DO leave a space between each element (symbol plus search term).

Phrase Searching

Phrase searching lets you search for words "next to each other." This can help you be very specific:

Example: "**world trade**" will search for records in which the exact phrase **world trade** appears. It will not find where the words appear in a different order, such as "Joe wanted to **trade** his baseball cards around the **world**".

Some databases require you to use these quotation marks around your phrase; others do not but will automatically run a phrase search if you do not use AND, OR, or NOT between terms. Generally, use the quotation marks to perform a phrase search.

Truncation Symbols

Truncation broadens a search by letting you search for variations in word endings, including plurals. Different databases use different truncation symbols, so check which symbol is appropriate for the database you are searching:

> Example: If the truncation symbol is *, then, **environment*** will search for records containing environment, environments, environmental etc.

Truncation is great for longer words but can be troublesome for short ones. Cat* will retrieve *cats*, but it will also retrieve *catheter, catatonic*, and *catalyst*. You may retrieve items completely unrelated to your original word.

Wildcard Symbols

Wildcards are like truncating within a word. Use the wildcard symbol to search for variations in spelling. This strategy is especially useful when you have to search for words with British spelling variations or irregular plurals. Symbols such as ? or # or * may be used as the wildcard. Check which symbol is appropriate for the database you are searching.

> Example: **wom*n** will search for records with women or woman.
> Example: **organi?e** searches for organise or organize.

This strategy is not available in all databases.

Nesting

For complex search statements, use nesting (grouping) to organize how the search will be done. Parentheses are used to group pieces of the search together in a logical manner:

> Example: "**gun control**" and **(law or legislation)** will find items that include the phrase gun control and either the word law or the word legislation.

Done without nesting:

> Example: "**gun control**" and **law** or **legislation** could find items that contain gun control and law. Or it could simply find anything with the word legislation in it!

Nesting is most commonly used to group synonyms or related terms together:

> Example: **(guns or firearms)** and **(law or legislation)**

Putting the Pieces Together

Now that you have learned the techniques available for constructing your keyword search, beware: Getting too fancy with search techniques can greatly hamper your efforts. Start simple. If you are choosing search tools and databases carefully, you have already placed useful limits on what you will retrieve. Start with the main concept that expresses what you are looking for. If you get too few hits or too many unrelated ones, use search techniques to broaden your search with related terms. Then focus or limit as needed, with terms representing the attributes of the topic you seek.

2

Evaluating Your Resources

Introduction

Research today challenges us to navigate effectively through Internet space. At one time, knowledge of the library and skill using printed resources was sufficient preparation for finding useful information. Today, the Internet, particularly the World Wide Web, is the vehicle for most research. The sheer volume of information available through this medium is staggering. To be a successful researcher requires imagination and flexibility, well-developed searching skills, persistence, and the ability to evaluate information coming from diverse sources.

It is relatively easy and inexpensive to "publish" information on the Internet. On the one hand, this open environment often permits you to see more sides of a topic than you might when relying only on printed sources. For example, when doing research on sweatshop labor in developing countries, you may be able to locate first-person accounts and discussions of working conditions in overseas factories, reports of watchdog groups, and other kinds of information sources that are difficult or impossible to find in print.

On the other hand, because there is no real filtering mechanism to check accuracy, one cannot accept at face value the information found on the Web. In *Evaluating Internet Research Sources* (http://www.virtualsalt.com/evalu8it.htm), Robert Harris argues that on the Internet, information exists on a continuum of reliability and quality:

> Information is everywhere on the Internet, existing in large
> quantities and continuously being created and revised. This in-
> formation exists in a large variety of kinds (facts, opinions, sto-
> ries, interpretations, statistics) and is created for many
> purposes (to inform, to persuade, to sell, to present a view-
> point, and to create or change an attitude or belief). For each of
> these various kinds of purposes, information exists on many
> levels of quality or reliability. It ranges from very good to very
> bad and includes every shade in between.

Harris also notes that when evaluating information sources, there is no single perfect indicator of quality. You must make inferences from a collection of
clues. Some important variables to consider as you review and evaluate sources
are described in the following section.

Guidelines for Evaluating Web Information Sources

Determine Site Purpose:

The key to understanding and evaluating any Web site is determining its
primary purpose, the main reason for its existence. The purposes of Web sites
can be categorized as follows:

- Advocacy: to sway opinion about an issue or topic

- Reference/information: to provide access to useful information

- Commercial: to promote or sell products and services

To determine whether the primary purpose of a site is to inform or to promote an
idea or product, look at the site's mission statement or follow "about this site"
links to learn about goals.

Advocacy Sites

The Web is a key resource for learning about the different positions that
various advocates take on a hot topic. There is no clearer way of understanding
specific points of view than by hearing from the groups that actively advocate
each point of view. Many advocacy groups provide a clear mission statement for
their organizations on their Web sites. Some provide links to current legislation.
Some track how politicians have supported or opposed their efforts. Advocacy
sites also usually include membership applications or requests for contributions
of money or time. Many advocacy organization Web addresses end with ".org"
(such as www.sierraclub.org).

Sites published by advocacy groups (such as the Sierra Club or the American Civil Liberties Union) often include fact sheets, position papers, and research studies. However, these groups may present evidence to support their

cause but ignore contrary findings. Consider the purpose of the site when deciding how much weight to give information found there. If you are attempting to understand an organization's mission or find evidence that is representative of a particular viewpoint, advocacy organization Web sites can be quite useful. You will need to look elsewhere to find other sites that present opposing viewpoints, in order to understand and write about controversial issues.

Reference or Informational Sites

Universities, government agencies, publishers, or individuals may produce reference sites. Their primary purpose is to provide access to useful information. Because these sites are not designed to promote a specific viewpoint or product, they are more likely to offer a full range of information on a topic. Reference sites may offer "link collections" that are organized and annotated to provide a good jumping-off point for research on a topic. They may also offer original content, background information, articles, and reports written by site contributors. Some reference site addresses may end with ".edu" if an educational institution like a college or library produces them, or ".gov" if they originate in a government agency. Others that are created by organizations or commercial publishers may have different types of addresses.

Commercial Sites

Commercial sites are intended to promote products or services by companies. Some commercial sites also provide short articles and other useful information to draw readers to their site, and at times this information is also useful for research. Some sites that have a Web address ending with ".com" may not be truly commercial sites, according to this definition. For example, some publishers and organizations acquire site addresses ending in ".com" and yet their purpose may be primarily informational, or the commercial aspect may be secondary. Look beyond the site address when determining a site's purpose.

Examine Author Credentials

When evaluating a Web site, it is important to consider the background of its author. The author is either the person or the organization responsible for determining what information the site provides. You may have to browse around a site to determine its author.

Authors who have appropriate education, training, or life experience in a relevant field provide the most credible information. You can read the jacket blurb to find out more about the author and the scope of a printed book. On the Web, look for an "About Us" link to find biographical statements, resumes, or other background about the site author. If no individual author is named, consider the reputation of the organization associated with the site. Often the copyright statement on a Web page will indicate the name of the organization that claims responsibility for the site.

For example, the NationalIssues.com Web site (http://www.nationalissues.com) has an "About Us" page that provides the names and educational/employment backgrounds of the principal staff as well as a statement about the site's intent to provide a balanced viewpoint on issues such as gun control, school reform, and taxes. The authors appear to be individuals with substantial experience in public policy research, government, and journalism.

But inquiring minds may want to check credentials or learn more than Web site authors tell us about themselves. If the author is an organization rather than an individual, what is their reputation? You have access to the tools that will help you to locate this kind of information. Use a Web search engine like Google to find other documents that the site authors may have published. Use your library's catalog and online reference databases (of newspaper, magazine, and journal articles) to locate works written by or about individuals and organizations.

Consider Content Quality

When evaluating the content provided by a Web site, there are a number of questions to consider. These are the same questions that one would ask when evaluating the content of any information source.

Currency

It is important to note publication dates of information. What was true at one point may have been changed by subsequent events or legislation. Making sure that your information is current is particularly important when considering legal or legislative sources. To determine the currency of the information on a Web site, look for

- Page creation or revision dates,
- A "What's New" page that describes when content was updated, or
- Press releases or other dated materials.

If the site you are evaluating does not appear to have been updated during the past three to six months, you may wish to check news and legislative sites for the most recent information on a controversial topic.

Accuracy

Does the information appear to be accurate? Check other sources to verify factual information. To do accurate research, it is necessary to examine a variety of sources, and compare them against each other. You may use a Web search engine or the "What's Related" function of the Netscape or Internet Explorer Web browser to find Web sites that cover the same research topic. Be sure to include printed materials and library databases when comparing sources to determine accuracy. Although the Web is vast, there are pockets of information that do not appear online or may only be available in subscription databases from your library.

Point of View

Researchers should also learn key techniques for assessing bias. When reviewing sites that deal with controversial topics, check to determine whether the information presented is biased (one-sided) or balanced (both pro and con viewpoints provided). Does the author use a calm, reasoned tone, or resort to inflammatory language? Opposing viewpoints should be presented in a fair manner. Although there is really no such thing as pure objectivity, a writer should be able to represent opposing viewpoints without letting personal biases intrude. (See Table 2.1.)

Table 2.1. Tips for Identifying Point of View

Strategy	Explanation
Look for buzzwords	Use of certain words or phrases may indicate a conservative viewpoint (for example, free enterprise, family values, states' rights) or a liberal/progressive one (for example, equity, inclusion, sustainable development).
Scan publications	Browse at least three different publications (articles, research reports) on a site to understand whether one or several different perspectives on an issue are represented.
Check key people	Look at the listing for an organization's board of directors. These are usually prominent people who support its mission. If you don't recognize names, use a search engine or a biographical database to learn about key people.
Examine links	Many advocacy sites maintain a listing of links to other sites with a similar perspective. By reviewing the Resources links you can often get a sense of the point of view of the site you are evaluating.

Evidence

Finally, does the author cite evidence to support claims and then document (provide references to) these sources, so that they are easily available for further research? Some research experts recommend that you "triangulate" an important information source, finding at least two other sources that support it. References supplied by an author can help in this process, but you should look for other sources as well.

Good information sources not only present a chain of evidence to support any unusual or controversial claims, but they also present the other side of the issue in a fair, objective manner, so that the reader can consider all points of view.

If an argument is made in a logical, convincing manner and supported with credible sources, then the writer need not be afraid to expose readers to contradictory claims. When evaluating the content of Web information sources, consider which points of view are presented and whether claims are well-documented. If you use the grid shown in Figure 2.1, the best sources would be those that could be placed in the lower right quadrant of the figure.

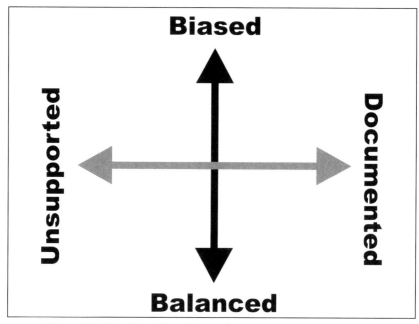

Figure 2.1. How Does Your Source Score on These Two Factors?

Verify Recognition

What do others think about the site you are evaluating? Is it recognized as an excellent information source? There are several ways to make this determination: Look for other sites that link to the site you are evaluating; look for reviews of the site. The former method is generally easier than the latter.

Several Web search engines, such as Google and AltaVista, allow searching for sites that link to a particular URL (Web address). Some online publications write reviews of Web sites, and these may be located using a search engine. Web directories select the best or most useful sites on various topics to include in their topical listings. Check research-oriented Web directories, such as *Librarians' Index to the Internet* (http://lii.org) or INFOMINE (http://infomine.ucr.edu) when evaluating a Web site to determine whether your site is included in the directory. This is another quality indicator.

Use a function built into your browser to find information about a Web site that you are viewing, such as

- Site ownership,

- Number of links to this site from other sites, and

- A list of sites offering related or similar information.

Click on the "What's Related" button in the Netscape browser's toolbar. If you use Internet Explorer, choose "Tools" from the browser menu, then highlight "Show Related Links" to see a similar display. Alexa, an Internet research company, provides this information. Another tool that provides similar information is alltheweb URL Investigator (http://www.alltheweb.com). Enter a URL in the search box to see this work. Your results will look like the screen shown in Figure 2.2.

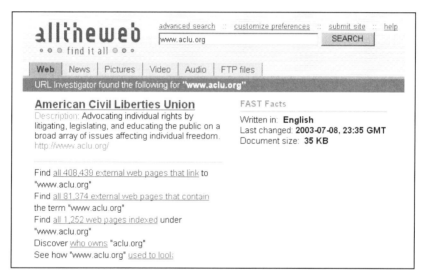

Figure 2.2. Results from *alltheweb* URL Investigator.

Notice that the URL Investigator provides a short description of the site, some "Fast Facts," including the date that the site was last updated, and a number of links that display other pages linking to the site in some manner. It also provides information about who owns the domain name of the site and links to previous versions of the site, which have been collected and stored online by a project called the *Internet Archive Wayback Machine* (http://web.archive.org).

Some Web pages cannot be "investigated" in this manner. If the page you are evaluating, such as an online article or report, is stored within a database or is generated "on the fly" by Web server software, you may not be able to use the URL Investigator to get information about that specific page. You can, however, investigate the top-level address for the site and retrieve useful information for evaluating your source. For example, investigate the URL for *American Enterprise Online* magazine rather than a specific article published in it.

Web Site Evaluation Quick Checklist

Criteria	Directions
Site purpose	Check "About this Site" to determine the type of site: advocacy, commercial, reference/information.
Author credentials	Look for information about the site author (person or organization).
Content quality	Examine some site content to determine currency and point of view. Are claims documented? Compare to other sources to determine the accuracy of the data.
Recognitions	Use a search engine to determine how many other sites have links to the site being evaluated. Is it included in Web directories?

Evaluating Online Magazine and Journal Articles

An article is defined in the *American Heritage Dictionary* (2000) as "a nonfiction composition that forms an independent part of a publication." There are many different kinds of articles. Some are published in reference sources, such as encyclopedias. Others are published in periodicals—regularly issued (or "serial") publications, like popular magazines or scholarly journals.

Popular magazines are geared toward the interests of general readers, not specialists. Articles may be written by staff writers and usually do not include footnotes or references. Print format magazines often have online Web versions as well. Popular magazines are particularly useful for keeping up with news, trends, and opinion and for obtaining background information on a controversial topic.

Scholarly journals publish reports and data aimed at the specialist or serious researcher. They are produced by commercial publishers as well as universities and research institutes. These sources always include references or footnotes. Either an editor or an editorial board of scholars reviews an article before it is accepted for publication in scholarly journals. This process, called "peer review," helps to ensure the quality of information in scholarly journal articles. Some scholarly journals are freely available on the Web, but most are only available through libraries that maintain subscriptions.

Some articles can be found using a Web search engine or by using the site search function available on a magazine's Web site. Usually the best way to locate articles is by searching a special article database, otherwise called a periodical index. Regardless of the method you use to find a particular article, it should be evaluated as an information source by considering four criteria: currency of information, author credentials, content quality, and the nature and reputation of the source it is published in. The first three criteria were discussed previously in this chapter, and the same techniques for evaluating Web sites according to these criteria apply to online articles as well.

To learn more about the goals or mission of a particular online publication, look for information on the magazine or journal's Web site. When considering the reputation of the publication itself, use a reference source called a periodical directory to learn more about the characteristics of a particular magazine or journal. One of the most comprehensive directories is *Ulrich's Periodicals Directory*. Many libraries provide either the print or online version of this directory. *Ulrich's* indicates the type of publication (trade, academic or scholarly, consumer or popular) and who publishes it, provides a brief description of content, and includes short evaluative reviews for many periodicals.

You may also refer to Appendix A, "Opinion Magazines" at the end of this book. It provides a listing and description of many popular magazines that are useful for research on controversial issues and have some or all content freely available on the Web. The sources listed in this appendix are also classified by point of view as conservative, liberal/progressive, or neutral (representing diverse viewpoints).

Evaluating Research Reports

Most research reports on Web sites are produced by either advocacy organizations or public policy research organizations—academic research institutes and think tanks. A think tank is a nonprofit organization composed of experts who do research and publish reports on topics of interest to that group. Think tanks originated in the United States in the 1960s and generally seek to assist in development of government domestic or foreign policies. Many think tanks are located in Washington, D.C., and have an explicitly partisan interest. An academic research institute, on the other hand, is generally located within a university and may be funded by that university or by grants from foundations. These organizations are less likely to be partisan in nature.

When using research reports, it is important to learn more about the viewpoint of the organization that produced or sponsored the report to evaluate the content critically. Tips for determining point of view that were discussed previously in this chapter will be helpful here as well. Refer to Appendix B, "Think Tanks" in this book to learn about the policy perspectives of some well-known research organizations.

Finding Sites That Present an Opposing Viewpoint

Research on controversial issues requires that you look at the whole spectrum of opinion on a topic before taking your own position on it. For example, if the source you are evaluating takes a liberal stance on an issue, check a conservative magazine or think tank to locate the opposing viewpoint. If an article, report or Web page reflects a particular bias or viewpoint on your research topic, you can also find advocacy organizations that present another side of the discussion by using the sites listed under "Advocacy Sites" in the "All Topics" chapter in Part 2 of this book.

3

Incorporating Your Resources

The final step in using the resources you've found in a paper or project is to successfully incorporate the sources through correct acknowledgment. It is completely appropriate to use other works in a research project, but it is not appropriate to claim those ideas as your own. To avoid "stealing" others ideas, cite the sources you use. Citing sources means listing the materials you used for your research. There are a variety of reasons that citation is used in academic research. Telling your audience which materials you consulted allows them the option of learning more about your topic through your materials. It helps your instructor determine the merits of your research process. And perhaps most important, it is a way to use information from others while giving credit to those authors and to avoid plagiarizing.

Plagiarism

Plagiarism is an interesting dilemma encountered in most academic settings. On its face, it is easy to understand. It means stealing other people's ideas and claiming them as your own. In practice, even experts can disagree on how to avoid plagiarism and have been caught (perhaps quite inadvertently) committing this sin themselves.

Your educational experience by definition should include getting ideas from others who know more about a thing than you do, and learning through reading. But a more complex part of your education must then involve synthesizing this new information and putting it in a framework that is your own. This synthesis is an essential part of controversial research and in fact is the educational reason for doing such exercises. Learning from others will help you justify your stand on an issue. It can move you from feeling something as a very personal belief to acting in a very public manner on that belief. This synthesis can also act to change your opinions on issues.

Following is a diagram of one possible process followed in presenting controversial research, which will culminate with properly cited work. In the sample text below, *italics* denote the author's original ideas. In **bold** are the statements that need to be cited. Both are essential components of controversial research.

> *I believe sample topic is true.*
>
> **Smith** agrees with me for this **reason**.
>
> **Jones** agrees with me for this **reason**.
>
> **Hughes** agrees with me for this **reason**.
>
> There are some who disagree.
>
> **Hayes** says this alternate **idea** is more the case. *I disagree because . . .*
>
> **Ford** is of the **opinion** that this negative consequence exists. But it is public knowledge that this alternate reality exists.
>
> *Therefore, I am justified in my belief and I am justified in acting in a certain manner because of it.*

Knowing how to handle some of the neutral text is the trickiest part. In particular, note the occurrence of the phrase "public knowledge." Facts, figures, and data are the bugaboo of novice (and sometimes experienced) researchers when considering what to cite. Do you cite an idea or fact that is public knowledge? If so, how do you attribute the citation?

Following are some guidelines for such situations:

Is the fact an undisputed fact?	YES—DON'T CITE NO—CITE
Is the fact a well-documented fact?	YES—DON'T CITE NO—CITE
Is the fact known because of the result of a specific study?	YES—CITE NO—DON'T CITE
Does your argument depend on this fact?	YES—PROBABLY SAFEST TO CITE NO—MAY NOT BE NECESSARY TO CITE

Following are some examples of facts that *would not* need to be cited:

• The population of Ohio is 11,353,140. (Undisputed and easily found.)

• There are over 16,000 students enrolled at the University of New Orleans. (Undisputed and easily found.)

Following are some examples of facts that *would* need to be cited:

- Only 20 percent of all criminal lawyers believe in the death penalty. (A study or survey would have had to determine this.)

- Breast cancer killed 40,200 women in the United States last year. (This figure may not be easy for the reader to find and may be an important factor in an argument.)

- The deaths of at least 240 Arizona children could have been prevented last year. (An expert study would need to determine this.)

- Green is the best color for cars. (This would have to be stated as an opinion held by someone. This is a disputable statement.)

Referencing Styles

After you have determined what you are going to cite, you must then know how to cite your research material. Think about what the text of your paper will look like, as well as what your list of citations will look like.

Quoting versus Paraphrasing

When incorporating material you are citing into your text, you must first decide whether you are going to quote the information exactly as it appears in the source you are taking it from or are going to paraphrase it. The important thing to note is that paraphrasing an idea does not negate the need to cite it! Some people think that simply picking up a thesaurus and changing a few words in a quote gives them the right to make a statement their own. Remember, an opinion or a fact taken from someone is still that person's opinion or fact.

Quotations are best used when citing an opinion, largely because of the strength of the language of an argument. (Some people just have a way with words!) When you quote something you literally place quotation marks around the statement. An example of quotation follows:

> "After a shooting spree, they always want to take the guns away from the people who didn't do it. I sure as hell wouldn't want to live in a society where the only people allowed guns are the police and the military." William Burroughs, 1992, taped conversation

This same idea paraphrased might read as follows:

> William Burroughs insightfully asserts that guns are often taken away from the people who did not commit a crime, and that there are serious implications to living in a society where only the police and military have access to them. (1992, taped conversation)

Paraphrasing will likely be used most often because it allows you to fit the opinion or fact into the point *you* are trying to make.

Imagine this: Some instructors do not allow students to use *any* direct quotations as a means of forcing students to shape the thought they are borrowing into their own framework.

Style Manuals

There is no one right way to cite references in your paper. Neither can you cite them any old way you wish. When an instructor assigns a research project, he or she will also generally indicate what *style manual* you are to use. A style manual is generally a published text that tells you the exact format to use for everything you can imagine related to citing your references. It indicates how to mark your text for cited items, where to place your list of cited items, what each citation should look like, and more. Some style manuals include information about actual writing style as well. There are several style manuals available, and they tend to be used according to academic discipline. Your academic department may dictate to instructors which style format they should have their students use, or you instructor might make that decision based on his or her own academic background. If you are not assigned one specific style to use, pick one and be consistent using it throughout your citation process. The major style guides in use are described below.

For Humanities

Turabian. *A Manual for Writers of Term Papers, Theses, and Dissertations*, 6th ed., by Kate Turabian (1996).

There is no official online site with examples for citations.

MLA. *MLA Handbook for Writers of Research Papers*, 6th ed., by Joseph Gibaldi (2003).

Online information from this style guide can be found at http://www.mla.org.

For Social Sciences

APA. *Publication Manual of the American Psychological Association*, 5th ed., by the American Psychological Association (2001).

Examples for online citations can be found at http://www.apastyle.org/elecref.html.

For Sciences

Turabian. See above.

CBE. *Scientific Style and Format: The CBE Manual for Authors, Editors, and Publishers*, 6th ed., prepared by the Council of Biology Editors Style Manual Committee (1994).

Information about online citations can be found at http://www. councilscienceeditors.org/publications/citing_internet.cfm.

> A Web site useful for a variety of citation styles showing specifically how to cite online information is *Online!,* at http://www.bedfordstmartins.com/online/.

.

PART 2

Issue Briefs

All Topics

The following resources are generally helpful for researching controversial topics. Use them in addition to the resources listed for specific topics in this book or to research those topics not covered in this book.

A variety of sources useful for finding published articles are listed in the "Data Sites" section below. However, most librarians and teachers will balk at a research process that uses *only* the freely available sources listed here. The reason for this is that there is a wealth of information only available to researchers through paid access. This is certainly the case for most published, peer-reviewed, scholarly articles. Generally, these are found by searching proprietary (subscription) databases.

Some proprietary databases are listed in Appendix C of this book. Many libraries provide access to such databases. Consider whether the information you have gathered is rich enough for your purposes. If not, consult those proprietary sources available to you through your local library.

Web Sites

Reference Sites

Almanac of Policy Issues

http://www.policyalmanac.org

Outlines major issues of public policy concern. Nine broad categories provide a simple outline of the issue with a list of related sites, issues, articles, and organizations. Subtopics under each category provide more complete detailing of the various positions and histories of those specific issues.

Google Directory—Society > Issues

http://directory.google.com/Top/Society/Issues/

A great place to browse for topic ideas as well as find appropriate Web sites with information on the topic. Most of the subtopics subdivide Web sites by pro and con bias and can be used to locate advocacy sites.

IDEA Debatabase

http://www.debatabase.org

Created for debaters worldwide, this site is an excellent place to get ideas for topics, a summary of the controversial nature of the issue, and a list of the pro and con arguments for the topic. Also included are helpful books and Web sites, as well as the option to engage in some online discussion or view what others have posted. Of added interest, many of the entries are submitted by individuals outside of the United States, thus giving a broader perspective on many topics.

NationalIssues.com

http://www.nationalissues.com

Issue briefs for a variety of public policy concerns. Gives the pros and cons of the arugment and provides an overview article.

Public Agenda Online—Public Opinion and Public Policy

http://www.publicagenda.org

For twenty-one broadly defined topics, this site gives extensive reports on public opinion research, while also placing this opinion in the context of public policy and defining the issues for the reader. Click on the "Issue Guides" button.

SpeakOut.com

http://speakout.com

An activism site that provides background information on issues grouped into fifteen broad catagories. Each category is further divided by questions or issues prompted by recent events. Each question or issue is represented with a perspective summary outlining the various points of view on a topic, links to related articles, and links to all types of advocacy organizations interested in the issue.

Yahoo! Society and Culture > Issues and Causes

http://dir.yahoo.com/Society_and_Culture/Issues_and_Causes/

Like the Google directory, this site is a great place to browse for topic ideas as well as to burrow down to appropriate Web sites on the topic. Most subtopics list the most popular Web sites first, then an alphabetical listing of the rest. Some subtopics link to a list of organizations involved in the issue and can be useful for locating advocacy organizations.

News Site

Yahoo! News: Full Coverage

http://fullcoverage.yahoo.com/fc/

Provides full coverage of topics, incorporating recent and older news on one page. Also links to related Web sites and multimedia coverage. A "one-stop shop" for news on your topic.

Law/Legislation

FindLaw

http://www.findlaw.com

Browse FindLaw to locate federal and state laws and court cases. Topical directories (adoption, education, employment, healthcare, etc.) provide links to articles, legal forms, FAQs, and related resources on these topics. Use the search feature to find resources within FindLaw, on other legal Web sites, or on government sites.

GovSpot

http://www.govspot.com

A government information portal for federal, state, and local information. This site will help you find appropriate sites for legislative information online as well as link to government news.

Thomas—U.S. Congress on the Internet

http://thomas.loc.gov

The definitive and official site for federal legislation. Search for proposed federal bills and public laws by keyword or by number. Recently considered initiatives are highlighted on the top level page. It is also possible to find how congressional members voted on the bills.

Data Sites

AllAcademic

http://www.allacademic.com/search/

Indexes over 200 freely available refereed journals and provides a browsable list of 350 academic journals listed by discipline or alphabetically. Also included are scholarly works in the form of books, magazines, convention papers, working papers, scholarly projects, editorials, and book reviews. Be sure to keep your search statements short and simple.(e.g., instead of stem cell research, try stem cells).

American FactFinder

http://factfinder.census.gov

Published by the U.S. Census Bureau, this site helps you find population, housing, economic, and geographic data.

FedStats

http://www.fedstats.gov

Portal to data and government agencies that have data on all aspects of American life.

IPoll Online Database of Public Opinion—Roper Center for Public Opinion Research

http://www.ropercenter.uconn.edu/ipoll.html

Contains survey results on hundreds of thousands of questions done for academic, commercial, and media survey organizations. The full service requires a paid subscription, but users can log in for free access. Free access users can search the database and will receive up to ten sample answers out of the total number retrieved. These results may or may not be the most current available.

LookSmart's Find Articles

http://www.findarticles.com

A searchable database of thousands of articles from hundreds of magazines and journals going back to 1998. The searching and the full text of the articles are available for free.

Opinion-Pages

http://www.opinion-pages.org

Search opinion pages, editorials, and letters to the editor from over 600 newspapers around the world. The strength of this source is in finding local ideas. The interface is a little clunky and unprofessional looking, but there is no other tool like it.

Pew Research Center for People and the Press

http://people-press.org/

The Center is an independent opinion research group that studies attitudes toward the press, politics, and public policy issues. All survey results are available free of charge. Search for keywords in questionnaires or browse surveys by broad topic: business and economics, domestic and social policy, politics, foreign policy, global attitudes.

PollingReport.com

http://www.pollingreport.com

For truly timely topics this site provides extensive information on public opinion. However, for topics of general interest that might not be currently in the headlines, results are less predictable. This site is browsable only, not searchable as is iPoll.

Advocacy Sites

Moving Ideas: An Electronic Policy Network

http://movingideas.org/

Find news and information resources from more than 130 progressive or liberal-leaning advocacy and policy research organizations. Browse sources by topic (criminal justice, education, gender, globalization, etc.) or by organization.

NIRA's World Directory of Think Tanks

http://www.nira.go.jp/ice/nwdtt/

Contains up-to-date information available on 320 think tanks from seventy-seven countries and regions. Detailed entries describe the organization's political and research focus, funding source, staff, and key publications. Published in English by the National Institute for Research Advancement (NIRA), a Japanese organization.

PolicyExperts.org

http://www.policyexperts.org/index.cfm

This is a searchable database of the conservative movement, presenting detailed information on over 300 public policy and advocacy organizations in the United States.

WebActive Directory

http://www.webactive.com/page/directory

An annotated, searchable directory of 1,250 progressive groups. Browse the list of broad topics to identify controversial issues to research or to find advocacy organizations involved in affecting change in that area.

Abortion

Summary

Abortion is defined as the termination of pregnancy and expulsion and death of the fetus, generally before it is viable (capable of independent life). Abortions may be spontaneous, or naturally occurring (these are generally called "miscarriages") , as well as deliberate. Deliberate abortions are performed through surgical means or use of medication.

Keywords
Abortion clinic violence
Abortion pill
Emergency contraception
Parental consent
Partial-birth abortion
Pro-choice
Pro-life
Roe v. Wade
RU-486

Related Topics
Adoption
Reproductive technologies
Teen pregnancy

Although abortion has been practiced since ancient times, it was not considered a crime in the United States until the nineteenth century. Some states began to legalize abortion in the 1960s. In 1973, the U.S. Supreme Court, in the landmark case *Roe v. Wade,* declared most of the state laws restricting abortion to be unconstitutional. The Court defined the various stages of pregnancy (three-month periods called "trimesters") and the conditions for abortion during each period.

Those who support abortion on demand and the individual woman's right to make this decision are called "pro-choice." Those who are against abortion in any form are called "pro-life." Some extremist pro-life groups have been associated with violence against abortion clinics and doctors who perform abortions. Between these two poles are those who support abortion under certain specific circumstances (such as for victims of rape and incest).

In the three decades that have passed since the *Roe v. Wade* decision made abortion legal in the United States, the controversy has not abated. Abortion opponents have in recent years focused on banning specific procedures and enacting new restrictions. A variety of other legal decisions concern these restrictions:

- Mandatory waiting periods

- Informed consent

- Spousal and parental notification and consent for abortions by minors

- Use of public Medicaid funds for abortions

One procedure that has attracted considerable attention by abortion opponents in Congress is "partial-birth abortion." This late-term abortion, usually in the fifth or sixth month of pregnancy, involves the extraction of the fetus into the birth canal, where the contents of the skull are suctioned. The dead fetus is then removed from the woman's body. Because of the gruesome nature of this procedure, women who have partial-birth abortions generally do so because their fetuses have severe or fatal anomalies or because the pregnancy endangers their health. Congress passed several bills banning this procedure that were later vetoed by President Clinton. A number of states also enacted bans on this procedure. However, the U.S. Supreme Court struck down the Nebraska law banning partial-birth abortions, noting that it failed to make an exception for women who want this procedure for health reasons. In 2003 Congress again passed, and President George W. Bush signed, a bill that bans partial-birth abortions. This law will face challenges at the state level and probable review by the United States Supreme Court.

Other current controversies include availability of an "abortion pill" (RU-486) that can be prescribed in the doctor's office and use of embryonic stem cells for genetic research. RU-486 (or Mifepristone) is a steroid hormone invented in France in 1980. Trade names for this medication in the United States are Preven and Plan B.

Since it first became available in the United States as a form of emergency contraception in 1998, use of RU-486 has steadily increased. Planned Parenthood, a leading provider of emergency contraception in the United States, reports that the number of women receiving emergency contraceptive pills (ECP) from their organization has grown from roughly 17,000 in 1995 to 310,000 in 2000. Supporters of emergency contraception argue that these pills do not end pregnancies but rather reduce the risk of pregnancy and the need for abortion by inhibiting ovulation, fertilization, and implantation of the fertilized egg. Opponents believe that once a human egg is fertilized, life has begun and thus by preventing implantation, the pill actually terminates a pregnancy.

Stem cell research is also a hot topic for those who oppose abortion. Stem cells are unspecialized cells that can renew themselves for long periods through cell division. Under certain experimental conditions, they can also be induced to become cells with special functions, such as heart muscle cells or the insulin-producing cells of the pancreas. Some scientists believe that stem cells may become the basis for treating diseases such as Parkinson's disease, diabetes, and heart disease.

Scientists primarily work with two kinds of stem cells from animals and humans, embryonic stem cells and adult stem cells, which have different functions and characteristics. Embryonic stem cells are controversial. They come from the blastocyst, the term for a fertilized egg four days after conception. Harvesting stem cells destroys the embryo. Many pro-life advocates are opposed to using embryonic cells for research. They argue that taking life, even if the end result is beneficial to others, is always wrong. President George W. Bush has endorsed limited federal funding of embryonic stem cell research. Under this plan, federal funds may be used for research only on sixty existing embryo stem cell lines, since the embryos for these lines have already been destroyed.

Web Sites

Reference Sites

Abortion: All Sides of the Issue

http://www.religioustolerance.org/abortion.htm

Provides an impartial look at the topic of abortion, including basic facts about pregnancy, contraception, and different methods of abortion; data; views of various religious groups; public opinion; and legal aspects of abortion.

MEDLINEplus: Abortion

http://www.nlm.nih.gov/medlineplus/abortion.html

Research guide from the National Library of Medicine organizes sites into the following categories: general overviews, research, specific conditions/aspects, law and policy, organizations, and statistics. Also provides a link to retrieve current journal articles on the topic from the MEDLINE database.

Public Agenda Online: Abortion

http://www.publicagenda.org

Select "Abortion" from the list of Issue Guides. This site is an excellent starting point for research on this topic. It provides an overview of the issues, current news stories, a detailed discussion of three points of view on abortion, along with pro and con arguments for each one, a wealth of factual information, and summary data from public opinion polls.

News Sites

Kaiser Network.org

http://www.kaisernetwork.org

See the "Daily Reports" for news summaries on health policy and reproductive health issues. The Kaiser Foundation provides brief abstracts of stories appearing in a variety of news sources on abortion, pregnancy, childbirth, family planning, and politics/policy related to these topics. These daily reports are also archived; the archive can be searched by keyword and date.

Yahoo! News: Full Coverage: Abortion Rights Debate

http://fullcoverage.yahoo.com/fc/

Search Full Coverage for the term "abortion". Select the Full Coverage Category for "Abortion Rights Debate" to view news stories, editorials, feature articles, audio/video resources, Web sites, and links to other specialized news sources on this topic.

Law/Legislation

Abortion Law Development: A Brief Overview

http://www.policyalmanac.org/archive.html

This article from the Congressional Research Service provides a brief history of abortion law in the United States. Sections include developments prior to 1973, the Supreme Court's 1973 rulings, public funding of abortions, subsequent decisions on informed consent and parental/spousal consent, and a variety of other important decisions.

Abortion Policies: A Global Review

http://www.un.org/esa/population/publications/abortion/

Online publication from the United Nations Population Division provides country profiles.

Oyez: Supreme Court Multimedia: Roe v. Wade

http://www.oyez.org/oyez/resource/case/334/

Read written transcripts or listen to audio versions of the various oral arguments presented to the Supreme Court in the 1973 *Roe v. Wade* case.

prochoiceamerica.org: Legislation

http://www.naral.org/legislation/

Follow the link to NARAL's State Tracker online database, which provides detailed information, on both federal and state levels, about legislative activity concerning reproductive rights.

Supreme Court: Historic Decisions by Topic

http://supct.law.cornell.edu/supct/cases/topic.htm

Click on the topic "abortion" to find the text of *Roe v. Wade,* the historic 1973 U.S. Supreme Court decision that made abortions legal, as well as a number of related opinions.

Data Sites

Alan Guttmacher Institute

http://www.agi-usa.org

The Institute provides publications, policy reports, and data, including state fact sheets, on abortion, teen pregnancy, contraception, sexual behavior, and diseases. Fact sheets are updated monthly.

Advocacy Sites

—*Oppose Abortion*

Family Research Council: Human Life and Bioethics

http://www.frc.org/context.cfm?c=RESEARCH

National Right to Life

http://www.nrlc.org

RoevWade.org

http://www.roevwade.org

U.S. Conference of Catholic Bishops

http://www.usccb.org/prolife/issues/

—*Support Abortion Rights*

Center for Reproductive Law and Policy

http://www.reproductiverights.org

Choice USA

http://www.choiceusa.org

National Abortion Rights Action League (NARAL)

http://www.naral.org

Religious Coalition for Reproductive Choice

http://www.rcrc.org

Adoption

Summary

Adoption is defined as the act by which a legal relation of parent and child is created. In the United States, adoption is a judicial proceeding, requiring a hearing before a judge. Although there are federal laws on adoption-related issues, adoption practice is regulated by the laws of the states. There are various types of adoptions.

One type of adoption is by relatives. The most common example of this is a stepparent adoption. When nonrelatives adopt a child, they may use an adoption agency (public or private) that is licensed or regulated by the state. Public agencies generally place children who have become wards of the state because they are orphans or have been abandoned or abused. Private agencies are often run by charities or social service organizations.

Independent or private adoptions occur when a child is placed with adoptive parents without the involvement of an agency. Some independent adoptions involve a direct arrangement between the birthparents and the adoptive parents, while others involve an intermediary such as an attorney or doctor.

As abortion has become more available, the number of infants available for adoption has declined. More prospective parents have turned to other countries to find children to adopt. In an international adoption, prospective parents adopt a child who is a citizen of a foreign country. In addition to satisfying the adoption requirements of both the foreign country and the parents' home state in the United States, the parents must obtain an immigrant visa for the child through the U.S. Bureau of Citizenship and Immigration Services.

Though few are against adoption per se, there are certainly factions in the adoption "triad." Some groups are supportive of adoptee rights (open records, search/reunion), some focus on birthparent rights (open adoption), and others on needs of adoptive and foster parents. In an adoption by unrelated adults, states

---

Keywords
Adoption triad
Agency adoption
Birth parents
Child custody
Foster care
Gay and lesbian adoption
Independent adoption
International adoption
Open adoption
Open records
Search and reunion
Single parent adoption
Special needs adoption
Transracial adoption
Unmarried fathers

Related Topics
Abortion
Gay rights
Teen pregnancy

---

have traditionally protected the privacy of the child's birth parents by maintaining confidentiality of these records. Since the 1970s, however, a growing number of adopted children have attempted to identify their birthparents through searches of adoption records, in states that permit some access to them, and by other means.

"Open adoption," in which adoptive and birthparents maintain a relationship, has also become more accepted. The National Adoption Information Clearinghouse (NAIC) notes that there are many variations in the types of relationships that occur. In an open adoption, families who adopt older children are provided with information about the birth family that they might not receive in a confidential adoption. If there was abuse or neglect in a child's background, this information will help the parents to deal with any behavioral or emotional problems that might arise.

Many states now permit adoption by unmarried adults, and some allow adoption by homosexual couples. Most adoptions are of the same race. Transracial adoptions, where the adoptive parents and the child are of different races, are also controversial. However, the Multiethnic Placement Act (1994) made it illegal for U.S. states to delay adoptions solely to match the racial or ethnic background of the child.

Web Sites

Reference Sites

About: Adoption

http://adoption.about.com

Comprehensive directory of adoption-related topics, with articles, a glossary of terminology, and links to useful sites for those wishing to adopt, adoptive and foster parents, adult adoptees, birth families, and agencies. Other topics include laws, search and reunion, support, scams and fraud, parental rights, money issues, gay and lesbian adoptions, racial and cultural issues, statistics, and studies.

Evan B. Donaldson Adoption Institute

http://www.adoptioninstitute.org

The Evan B. Donaldson Adoption Institute, founded in 1996, is a national not-for-profit organization devoted to improving adoption policy and practice. They provide a wealth of research resources, from abstracts of published articles to survey data and reports on a variety of adoption topics. The "Newsroom" portion of their site provides up-to-date summaries of adoption-related stories from a variety of news sources, along with an archive of past stories. Readers can request an e-mail summary of news.

MEDLINEplus: Adoption

http://www.nlm.nih.gov/medlineplus/adoption.html

Research guide from the National Library of Medicine organizes sites into the following categories: general overviews, coping, specific conditions/aspects, law and policy, dictionaries, directories, organizations, and statistics. Also provides a link to retrieve current journal articles on the topic from the MEDLINE database.

National Adoption Information Clearinghouse (NAIC)

http://naic.acf.hhs.gov

This service of the U.S. Department of Health and Human Services is the key site for reliable information on adoption topics. Main site categories include databases, publications, laws, statistics, conferences, a searchable National Adoption Directory (use to locate people, groups, agencies, and services), and a bibliographic database with summaries of more than 4,500 publications. Other sections of the site provide resources of interest to adopted persons, birthparents, adoptive parents, and professionals.

U.S. Department of State: International Adoption

http://travel.state.gov/adopt.html

Provides legal information on international adoptions, a booklet that offers an overview of the process, updates and notices about problems with adoptions, and country-specific adoption flyers.

Law/Legislation

Adoption Legal Issues (NAIC)

http://naic.acf.hhs.gov/laws/

Good starting point for research on laws pertaining to adoption. Provides links to texts of important federal laws, such as the Adoption and Safe Families Act of 1997 (P.L. 105-89) and the Intercountry Adoption Act of 2000 (P.L. 106-279). Includes an executive summary that condenses all the pertinent federal laws into one document and other summaries of state legislation on various topics (putative fathers, consent to adoption, adoption expenses). Also includes a summary of laws regarding international adoptions finalized abroad.

National Center for Adoption Law and Policy

http://www.law.capital.edu/adoption/

The Center, located at Capital University Law School, provides a variety of research and educational services, including a weekly adoption news and case law summary service that users may subscribe to or view on the Web site. The Center's

Adoption LawSite project aims to provide a searchable database of the statutes, regulations, key cases, and leading explanatory law review and practice journal articles concerning child welfare and adoption laws of each U.S. state. Federal child welfare and adoption law materials are also provided. The site includes plain English summaries of most of the material contained within it. This is the premier research site for adoption law.

Data Sites

Adoption Statistics (NAIC)

http://www.calib.com/naic/stats/

This site notes that "There is no current public or private attempt to collect comprehensive national data on adoption." States are required to collect data on all adopted children who were placed by the state child welfare agency or by private agencies under contract with the public child welfare agency. States are encouraged to report other adoptions that are finalized in the state. Most new statistical information about adoption and related areas is being gathered and analyzed by private organizations, through private surveys and research. This site presents reports and data summaries from a variety of these sources on adoption-related topics.

AFCARS: Adoption and Foster Care Analysis and Reporting System

http://www.acf.hhs.gov/programs/cb/dis/afcars/

AFCARS (Adoption and Foster Care Analysis and Reporting System) is a system from the U.S. Department of Health and Human Services for collecting data on children in foster care and on children who have been adopted under the auspices of state child welfare agencies. Data lag (time of collection to time reported) is at least two years, so the latest report available in 2003 was for 2001.

Minnesota Texas Adoption Research Project

http://fsos.che.umn.edu/mtarp/

Some adoption professionals believe that open adoption (in which contact occurs between the adoptive family and birthparents) should be standard practice, while others argue that openness is harmful. This ongoing research project "focuses on the consequences of variations in openness in adoption for all members of the adoption triad: birthmothers, adoptive parents, and adopted children, and for the relationships within these family systems." The site presents a summary of findings to date.

Advocacy Sites

—*Promote Adoptee Rights*

American Adoption Congress

http://www.americanadoptioncongress.org

Bastard Nation

http://www.bastards.org

Voices of Adoption

http://www.ibar.com/voices/

—*Promote Adoption of Waiting Children*

National Adoption Center

http://www.adopt.org

North American Council on Adoptable Children (NACAC)

http://www.nacac.org

Animal Rights

Summary

Most people today believe that causing unnecessary harm to an animal is
wrong. Our laws reflect that sentiment.
Neglecting a pet is a misdemeanor crime,
and more severe forms of animal cruelty
are considered felonies. However, no
laws protecting animals existed until the
1800s.

Before that time, attitudes toward
animals were different. Animals were
seen as property rather than as creatures
capable of experiencing pain and suffering. It was not until after the Civil War
that animal rights became a major public
issue in the United States. The American
Society for the Prevention of Cruelty to Animals (ASPCA) was founded in
1866. By 1907 every state had an anticruelty law in place.

Keywords
Animal cruelty
Animal experimentation
Animal use in product testing
Animal welfare
Cruelty-free products
Humane slaughter
Hunting and trapping
Laboratory animals
Vegans
Vegetarianism
Vivisection

Related Topics
Genetic engineering

Important federal animal protection legislation includes the 1958 Humane
Slaughter Act, a law that requires meatpackers to provide animals with some
form of anesthetization prior to slaughter, and the Animal Welfare Act, passed in
1966 and broadened several times in later years. This law sets a minimum standard for the treatment of animals in laboratories and by handlers, and it imposes
penalties on violators.

During the twentieth century, use of animals in medical laboratories, on
factory farms, and for other business purposes increased. Animal experimentation, also referred to as vivisection, was accepted within the medical community,
but many ordinary people regarded the practice as barbaric, and an
antivivisection movement took shape. The National Research Council estimates
that 17 to 22 million animals are currently used in research each year in the
United States. Approximately 95 percent are rodents. The USDA Animal and
Plant Health Inspection Service (APHIS) inspects animal research facilities to
ensure compliance with current laws.

Opponents of animal experimentation believe that it is always wrong to inflict pain on an animal, even if it has the potential to save human lives. Others believe that some animal studies may be acceptable if the expected benefits are

great enough. They support careful review of all proposed experiments by committees of nonpartisan reviewers. A third contingent supports continued use of animals in laboratory experiments with no new restrictions. They believe that it is unethical not to employ all possible means to save human life. They also contend that the National Institutes of Health (NIH) guidelines for care of laboratory animals, which are used by many research facilities, and existing federal laws, such as the Health Research Extension Act of 1985 and the Animal Welfare Act, already protect animals against unnecessary cruelty and ensure that research animals are well cared for.

During the 1970s, animal advocates developed a broader agenda. Philosopher Peter Singer argued that animals, like humans, are capable of suffering. Just as it is immoral to inflict pain on humans, Singer claimed, it is wrong to inflict pain on animals. Singer's 1975 book *Animal Liberation* gave rise to a new activist movement. Proponents maintain that animals do not exist to satisfy human needs and should therefore never be killed, held captive, or made to suffer for the benefit of people. Those who avoid eating meat, dairy products, eggs, or other products made by taking advantage of animals are known as vegans. Vegans and other animal advocates also challenge the moral aspects of hunting, wearing fur or leather, buying products such as cosmetics that were tested on animals, and using animals for entertainment in circuses and zoos.

Web Sites

Reference Sites

Altweb: Alternatives to Animal Testing on the Web

http://altweb.jhsph.edu

This clearinghouse from the Johns Hopkins Center for Alternatives to Animal Testing provides news, publications, databases, calendars, and a wide variety of other information resources to assist scientists and others seeking alternative research methods or those who wish to learn more about this topic.

Animal Concerns Community

http://www.animalconcerns.org

This site, sponsored by the Envirolink Network, is a clearinghouse for information on the Internet related to animal rights and welfare. Links to articles, organizations, publications, e-mail lists, and other resources on animal health, animal rescue, breeding, companion animals, hunting and trapping, factory farms, laboratory animals, legislation, etc. Includes news, a discussion forum, and a list of recommended vegan products.

Animal Welfare Information Center

http://www.nal.usda.gov/awic/

This information gateway from the National Agricultural Library provides links to news, government and legal sources, databases, and publications. It includes topical sections on hot topics, lab animals, farm animals, companion animals, zoos, and circus animals.

Tom Regan Animal Rights Archive

http://www.lib.ncsu.edu/arights/

This site, from North Carolina State University Libraries, links to information resources in the following categories: animal experimentation, animal rights, animal rights law, animals in entertainment, clothing, diet ethics, exhibitions, farmed animals, organizations, and wildlife. Also provides a detailed description of the Tom Regan Collection held by the Libraries. The collection contains correspondence, research files, drafts, reprints, and audiovisual materials that span the professional career of one of the most widely known authorities on animal rights.

News Sites

Animal News Center

http://www.anc.org

Site features current information as well as editorials. Categories include pet news, farm news, lab news, wildlife news, and top stories.

Yahoo! News: Full Coverage: Animal Welfare

http://fullcoverage.yahoo.com/fc/

Search Full Coverage for the term "animal rights". Select the Full Coverage Category for "World: Animal Welfare" to view news stories, editorials, feature articles, audio/video resources, Web sites, and links to other specialized news sources on this topic.

Law/Legislation

Animal Rights Law Project

http://www.animal-law.org

This site from Rutgers University School of Law brings together relevant statutes and regulations, case law, handbooks (on civil disobedience for activists and on companion animals), commentary, and essays on animal rights law.

Health Research Extension Act of 1985

http://grants.nih.gov/grants/olaw/references/hrea1985.htm

Presents text of the law that applies to treatment of research animals.

Data Sites

Animal Care Publications and Policy

http://www.aphis.usda.gov/ac/publications.html

Site from the Animal and Plant Health Inspection Service (APHIS) of the USDA provides links to many legal and data sources, including fact sheets, animal care regulations, manuals, and reports of enforcement activities, violation summaries, industry reports, and facility lists.

Guide for the Care and Use of Laboratory Animals

http://www.nap.edu/readingroom/books/labrats/

This resource was first published in 1963 under the title *Guide for Laboratory Animal Facilities and Care* and has been revised many times. This publication is widely accepted as a primary reference on research animal care and use.

Advocacy Sites

—Support Use of Animals in Business and Research

Americans for Medical Progress

http://www.ampef.org

Animal Agriculture Alliance

http://www.animalagalliance.org

Foundation for Biomedical Research

http://www.fbresearch.org

National Animal Interest Alliance

http://www.naiaonline.org

—Support Animal Rights and Alternatives to Experimentation

Animal Welfare Institute

http://www.awionline.org/

National Anti-Vivisection Society

http://www.navs.org

People for the Ethical Treatment of Animals (PETA)

http://www.peta.org

Physicians Committee for Responsible Medicine

http://www.pcrm.org

Assisted Suicide

Summary

Suicide is the deliberate and intentional destruction of one's own life. At times, terminally ill patients may decide to forgo medical treatment to hasten their own deaths. Some individuals create "living wills," which define for medical personnel how the person wishes to be treated when life-threatening circumstances arise. Often a living will (also called an advanced care directive) includes a "do not resuscitate" order, requesting that no special actions be taken to prolong the person's life. Technically, this does not comprise suicide, since the person's death occurs as a result of illness or injury.

Keywords
Advanced care directives
Death with Dignity Act
Do not resuscitate request
Dr. Kevorkian
Euthanasia
Living will
Mercy killing
Palliative care
Physician-assisted suicide
Terminal sedation

Assisted suicide is a person's voluntary suicide with help from another individual. The term *assisted suicide* may also refer to the act of providing an individual with the means to commit suicide, knowing that he or she plans to end his or her own life. If a doctor provides medications or other means of committing suicide with the understanding that a patient may intentionally use them to end his or her own life, this action is referred to as physician-assisted suicide.

Euthanasia, sometimes called "mercy killing," is defined as the act or practice of ending the life of another person who is suffering from a terminal illness or an incurable condition, by lethal injection (active euthanasia) or the suspension of extraordinary medical treatment (passive euthanasia). Assisted suicide is different from euthanasia, in which a person other than the patient ends the patient's life as painlessly as possible for merciful reasons. Someone other than the patient is the final cause of the patient's death. Assisted suicide involves a more direct action by the person who dies than does euthanasia. For example, in a case of assisted suicide, although a physician may prescribe a lethal dose of medication, the patient administers the medication.

As technological advances in medicine have enabled doctors to keep patients alive for longer periods of time, legal rights to forgo medical intervention have developed. During the 1970s, the right of a patient to refuse treatment was established by various court cases. In the United States and Canada, a mentally competent patient has a legal right to refuse treatment. If a patient refuses treatment, the physician is obligated to forgo treatment, even if honoring the refusal will result in death. A physician's compliance with the refusal is not considered a crime. However, the law does distinguish between allowing a person to die and assisting a person to die.

Today the debate over the right to die extends to issues of active euthanasia and assisted suicide. People who believe that assisted suicide should be legalized maintain that individuals should have control over the timing and manner of their own deaths. Opponents contend that legalizing assisted suicide will cause many problems and that vulnerable individuals may be coerced into suicide as a result of financial pressure. Religious opposition to assisted suicide is often based on the belief that God is the giver of life and should determine when it ends.

The American Medical Association's Code of Ethics opposes physician participation in patient suicides, stating that: "Physician assisted suicide is fundamentally incompatible with the physician's role as healer, would be difficult or impossible to control, and would pose serious societal risks. Instead of participating in assisted suicide, physicians must aggressively respond to the needs of patients at the end of life." The AMA urges more attention to providing better palliative care, treatment aimed at relieving symptoms and pain, for incurably ill patients.

In the early 1990s, the actions of a retired Michigan pathologist, Dr. Jack Kevorkian, brought public attention to the issue of physician-assisted suicide. Dr. Kevorkian was openly helping individuals end their lives with a "suicide machine" he designed. The device administered an anesthetic and then a lethal injection through an intravenous line. In 1999 a jury found Kevorkian guilty of second-degree murder and sentenced him to prison because he directly administered lethal drugs to an incurably ill person who had asked to be put to death.

The majority of U.S. states have laws defining assisting in the suicide of another as a felony, punishable by imprisonment. Only one state, Oregon, has adopted a law specifically allowing physician-assisted suicide. In 1994 voters in Oregon approved the Death with Dignity Act, which authorized physicians to prescribe lethal doses of medication for terminally ill patients. Opponents challenged the constitutionality of the law and prevented its enforcement. In 1997 the U.S. Supreme Court ruled that state statutes prohibiting assisted suicide do not violate the Constitution. The Court's decision means that each state may determine whether to prohibit or permit (and otherwise regulate) assisted suicide. Oregon voters again approved the law after the Supreme Court ruling. According to the 2002 annual report of the Oregon Department of Human Services, 129 patients have died after ingesting a lethal dose of medication between 1998 and 2002.

Web Sites

Reference Sites

Doctor Assisted Suicide: A Guide to Web Sites and the Literature

http://www.longwood.edu/library/suic.htm

Covers legal issues related to this topic, with links to relevant statutes, as well as articles, books, Web sites, radio and television programs, and a chronology of events.

Euthanasia and Physician-Assisted Suicide: All Sides

http://www.religioustolerance.org/euthanas.htm

Provides an introduction and overview of the topic, describes the ethical controversy and the viewpoints of various religious organizations, summarizes legal issues in the United States and abroad, summarizes news, and organizes links to relevant sites.

Physician-Assisted Suicide: Ethical Topics in Medicine

http://eduserv.hscer.washington.edu/bioethics/topics/pas.html

Site from University of Washington School of Medicine provides background on the issue, outlines arguments in favor of and opposed to the practice, and provides two brief case studies along with discussion.

Voluntary Euthanasia

http://plato.stanford.edu/entries/euthanasia-voluntary/

Lengthy article in the *Stanford Encyclopedia of Philosophy* discusses morally necessary conditions for voluntary euthanasia, outlines the moral cases for and against the practice, and provides a useful bibliography of articles and sites for additional research.

News Sites

Yahoo! News: Full Coverage: Assisted Suicide Debate

http://fullcoverage.yahoo.com/fc/

Search Full Coverage for the term "suicide". Select the Full Coverage Category for "US: Assisted Suicide" to view news stories, editorials, feature articles, audio/video resources, Web sites, and links to other specialized news sources on this topic.

Law/Legislation

Death with Dignity: The Law

http://www.deathwithdignity.org/law/

This advocacy organization presents legal texts, court decisions, and proposed legislation related to assisted suicide.

Oregon Department of Human Services: Physician Assisted Suicide

http://www.dhs.state.or.us/publichealth/chs/pas/pas.cfm

Official site from the Oregon Department of Human Services, which administers the state's Death with Dignity law, provides text of law, administrative rules, and annual statistical report on how the law is being applied by physicians and patients in the state.

Physician Assisted Suicide

http://www.med.upenn.edu/bioethic/PAS/

Site provides texts of U.S. Supreme Court decisions and many amicus briefs filed in support of both sides of the case. Also links to texts of several proposed federal laws as well as state court decisions on the topic of physician-assisted suicide.

Data Sites

Assisted Suicide: A Disability Perspective

http://www.ncd.gov/newsroom/publications/suicide.html

This position paper from the National Council on Disability outlines the reasons that this organization opposes assisted suicide and provides insights from the perspective of disabled individuals. Report notes that "legalizing assisted suicide seems to risk its likely use, the ultimate manifestation of prejudice against people with disabilities in our society, as a means to unnecessarily end or to coerce the end of people with disabilities' lives."

Frontline: The Kevorkian Verdict

http://www.pbs.org/wgbh/pages/frontline/kevorkian/

Site provides background on Dr. Kevorkian, the "suicide doctor" convicted of murder for his actions. Includes information on relevant laws, views of physicians, and interviews (in both text and audio formats) with four of his patients who died.

Suicide Prevention Fact Sheet

http://www.cdc.gov/ncipc/factsheets/suifacts.htm

Site offers a general statistical overview of suicide in the United States along with links to a variety of reports and organizations that provide other data on the topic.

Advocacy Sites

—*Against Suicide*

American Foundation for Suicide Prevention

http://www.afsp.org

Euthanasia.com

http://www.euthanasia.com

Family Research Council: Human Life and Bioethics

http://www.frc.org/context.cfm?c=RESEARCH

Not Dead Yet

http://www.notdeadyet.org

—*Support the Right to Die*

Compassion in Dying Federation

http://www.compassionindying.org

Death with Dignity National Center

http://www.deathwithdignity.org

End of Life Choices

http://www.endoflifechoices.org

Censorship

Summary

Censorship is the act of repressing or deleting anything that might be objectionable. Censorship is usually practiced when material undermines the established government, morality, or religion. It is often viewed as an opposing force to democracy, which depends on an enlightened and informed society. In fact, the First Amendment to our Constitution was created to secure citizens' rights to express themselves freely. Censorship can occur in a variety of venues and for a variety of reasons. However, those who advocate selected censorship would argue that some speech is harmful to citizens and therefore can be destructive to a healthy society.

Keywords
Banned books
Child pornography
Community standards
First Amendment
Free speech
Freedom of the press
Hate speech
Intellectual freedom
Internet filtering
Obscenity
Parental Advisory Label (music)
Pornography
Rating systems

Related Topics
Civil liberties
Hate groups and crimes

Political censorship occurs when the government chooses to withhold information from its citizens or from the press or other industry that is trying to convey that information to citizens. This might occur because the government finds the information heretical, seditious, embarrassing, or harmful to national security.

Social censorship exists within the realm of cultural expression. Music, art, books, theater, software, and other cultural expressions may be censored for fear they will be offensive to the community for reasons such as sexuality, profanity, or violence. Controversies have arisen in the past when government grants have funded art that some view as objectionable.

Some people advocate forms of censorship to protect children. Television, the recording industry, and now various Internet, software, and gaming organizations have been the center of many such controversies. Rather than viewing themselves as censors, advocates of such campaigns see themselves as protectors. Many of these confrontations have resulted in rating systems for movies, television, software, and the recording industry. For instance, most computer games are now rated for violence or sexual content.

There is speech that does not enjoy protection from the freedom of speech law. The Supreme Court declared that obscenity is not protected by the Constitution. Child pornography has been outlawed by legislation in all states. Speech likely to incite "imminent lawless action," or where the speech presents a "clear and present danger" to the security of the nation is not protected. Libel or slander may be subject to prosecution when evidence of malice can be proven. These laws vary from state to state. Finally, the government can ban deceptive commercial speech.

"Community standards" are generally the tool courts use to determine when an expression is legally obscene and thus not protected by First Amendment rights. No state can legislate community standards; rather, judges and juries must make decisions when an issue makes its way to court.

New technologies often spark discussions of censorship and free speech until the technology has been around long enough for standard uses and practices to become agreed upon by society as a whole. The Internet is the center of many of the current debates about censorship. For instance, some communities require public libraries to use filtering software to protect children from pornography on the Web. Opponents of filtering software claim that it is not sophisticated enough to distinguish pornography from educational or medical material, thus potentially keeping the exact information users might need out of reach. The Supreme Court recently upheld the rights of communities to require such filters in public libraries.

Web Sites

Reference Sites

Censorship Pages

http://www.booksatoz.com/censorship/

A portal to Web sites on censorship and the Internet, banned books, online discussion groups, articles, and censorship quotations.

Frontline: American Porn

http://www.pbs.org/wgbh/pages/frontline/shows/porn/

A highly informative online documentary of the business, political, and legal aspects of pornography in the United States.

Public Agenda Online: Internet Speech and Privacy

http://www.publicagenda.org

Select "Internet Speech and Privacy" from the list of Issue Guides. Provides an overview, framing of the issues, facts, public opinion, and links to other sites on this topic.

Speech Issues

http://legacy.eos.ncsu.edu/eos/info/computer_ethics/speech/

Part of an "Ethics In Computing" site maintained by university professor Edward F. Gehringer. This site provides links to quality materials on topics related to speech in computing such as: pornography, hate speech, Internet filters, the Communications Decency Act, and more.

News Sites

Free Expression Network Clearinghouse

http://www.freeexpression.org

This site provides recent news articles of interest to the free expression debate. Recent articles are highlighted on the home page, and older articles are listed by broad topical area (censorship, free speech, Internet, in court, legislation, schools). The Resources page provides an excellent list of organizations involved in the protection of freedom of speech issues.

Free Speech Coalition

http://www.freespeechcoalition.com/home.htm

Useful for finding specific occurrences of censorship by state. Gives recent events or court cases that relate to free speech issues.

Law/Legislation

Findlaw: Cyberspace Law: Free Expression

http://www.findlaw.com/01topics/10cyberspace/freedom/sites.html

Provides links to law sites, statutes, organizations, newsletters, and more concerned with issues of the legal aspects of free expression online.

National Obscenity Law Center

http://www.moralityinmedia.org/nolc/

Although the purpose of this site is to advocate for morality, it fairly represents actual legislation related to issues of obscenity.

Data Sites

EPIC Archive—Free Speech

http://www.epic.org/free_speech/

Provides an overview of free speech protection, the First Amendment and technology, international developments, and a list of organizations involved in protecting free speech.

First Amendment Handbook

http://www.rcfp.org/handbook/

Published by the Reporters Committee for Freedom of the Press, this handbook gives journalists guidelines on what is legal to publish and how to handle issues of censorship in their reports.

Principal FOIA Contacts and Federal Agencies

http://www.usdoj.gov/foia/foiacontacts.htm

Each federal agency has a Freedom of Information Act (FOIA) office to contact when you desire information from that agency. This Department of Justice site lists all of the federal contacts for all agencies. There is also some basic information about how FOIA requests work.

Society of Professional Journalists: Freedom of Information Resources

http://www.spj.org/foia.asp

"Resources for journalists and the public on issues involving access to government records and activities and freedom of information education."

Advocacy Sites

—For Censorship

Citizens for Community Values

http://www.ccv.org

National Campaign to Stop Pornography

http://www.thencsp.com

National Coalition for the Protection of Children and Families

http://www.nationalcoalition.org

—Against Censorship

American Civil Liberties Union

http://www.aclu.org

Center for Democracy and Technology

http://www.cdt.org

Electronic Frontier Foundation

http://www.eff.org

Free Expression Policy Project

http://www.fepproject.org

National Coalition Against Censorship

http://www.ncac.org

Recording Industry Association of America

http://www.riaa.org

Reporters Committee for Freedom of the Press

http://www.rcfp.org

Church and State

Summary

Many of America's founders endured persecution under state-sponsored religions, provoking the call for the separation of church and state as established in the First Amendment to the Constitution. It declares that: *"Congress shall make no law respecting an establishment of religion, or prohibiting the free exercise thereof."* This is one of Americans' civil liberties. There is constant tension between what is referred to as the "establishment clause," which states that government shall not endorse religion, and the "free exercise clause," which allows citizens to practice their own religion freely.

A poll done by the Roper Center in 1999 (see the iPoll database mentioned in the "All Topics" chapter) shows that over 90 percent of Americans believe in God or a higher power, which seems to indicate that America is a religious and spiritual nation. However, of those believers, 63 percent are Protestant, 26 percent are Catholic, 2 percent are Jewish, 7 percent are none, and 2 percent are "something else". These disparities in affiliation are telling when seeking to understand the tension that exists over religious liberties.

Those who would expand the role of religion in society wish to do so to enhance the spiritual nature that seems to be inherent in Americans. Some feel that America has become overly secularized and does not adequately reflect the intentions of the founding fathers to allow its citizens free expression of their religious impulses or to use religion to affect society. They claim that secularization is removing the moral structure of the nation. For instance, there have been some communities fighting to keep a copy of the Ten Commandments on the walls of public high schools. Such activity has been declared unconstitutional. There is sentiment that the believers who represent over 90 percent of society are restricted by the views of the fewer than 10 percent who have no spiritual belief. In general, this side of the argument emphasizes the "free exercise clause".

Keywords
Conscientious objection to war
Creationism/evolution
Establishment clause
Faith-based initiatives/
    charitable choice
First Amendment
Free exercise clause
Pledge of Allegiance
Religious rights/liberty
Religious tolerance
School prayer
School vouchers/choice
Tax-exempt status

Related Topics
Civil liberties
School reform

Those who seek to keep a firm wall of separation, which restricts the role of religion in society, believe that too often it is the majority religion's point of view that is imposed on citizens. There are times when the belief system of the majority runs counter to the civil liberties of other citizens, causing oppression or persecution of individuals. An example might be a conservative Christian landlord who will not rent housing to gay couples. Another concern is the use of public dollars to support religious causes. For instance, a religious organization that assists the homeless might receive public money to house and feed these individuals and yet require recipients to participate in a strictly affiliated religious service that runs counter to the individuals' beliefs. In general, this side of the argument emphasizes the "establishment clause" of the First Amendment.

Recent events that have tugged at this argument include President Bush's creation of a Faith-based Initiatives program providing funding to religious organizations that provide social services such as helping the homeless, impoverished, and needy in society. Another issue has been the school voucher program providing public funds to disadvantaged families allowing them to send their children to private (often religious) schools and escape the low-achieving public schools in their neighborhoods. Perennial issues include the role of religion in public schools, including teaching creationism and evolution, school-supported prayer, freedom of religious organizations to meet on school grounds, and discussions involving religion in the classroom. There have been recent attempts to remove the phrase "under God" from the Pledge of Allegiance.

One other thread of the church and state debate is the issue of religious tolerance. The September 11, 2001, terrorist attacks raised the profile of the Muslim religion in America. The attacks have caused some Americans to feel threatened by Islam; they express sentiments that it is an anti-American and pro-terrorist religion. Others have called for religious tolerance, deeper understanding of the faith, and increased communication between religious groups. This tension has renewed interest in the potential and actual restrictions of religious liberties in the midst of national security concerns.

Web Sites

Reference Sites

First Amendment Center

http://www.firstamendmentcenter.org

Provides information on all aspects of the First Amendment (speech, assembly, and religion). Click on "Religious Liberty" for an overview, legislative histories, links to other sites, publications by this organization, and more.

J.M. Dawson Institute of Church-State Studies

http://www3.baylor.edu/Church_State

An academic institution concerned with research on this topic. Most useful are the links and publications options on the home page. The links list leads to primary and secondary source material, arranged in an historical outline of the issue. The publication link allows readings from selected articles in the "Journal of Church and State."

Religious Liberty: An Introduction to the Issues

http://www.iwgonline.org/liberty

Although this is presented by a group that advocates religious tolerance, their overview of the issues is succinct yet representative. A good place to put the issues into context.

News Sites

Press Release Archive—AU.org

http://www.au.org/press.htm

Although this is part of the pro-separation organization "Americans United," they maintain perhaps the best and most up-to-date service for news regarding church and state issues.

Yahoo! News Full Coverage: Religion

http://fullcoverage.yahoo.com/fc/

Search Full Coverage for the term "religion". Select the Full Coverage Category for "World: Religion" to view news stories, editorials, feature articles, audio/video resources, Web sites, and links to other specialized news sources on this topic. Although world religion is covered on this updated news page, American religious news is prominent.

Law/Legislation

FindLaw: U.S. Constitution: First Amendment

http://caselaw.lp.findlaw.com/data/constitution/amendment01/

Provides an annotated explanation of religion in America as noted in the First Amendment. This is a helpful overview of the law.

LLRX: The Establishment Cause: A Selective Guide to the Supreme Court's Christmas Cases

http://www.llrx.com/features/christmas.htm

A "lighthearted [yet well annotated] guide to the literature concerning the Supreme Court's analysis of the Establishment Clause as it relates to the Christmas holiday."

Religious Liberty Archive: Rothgerber Johnson & Lyons LLP, Colorado Springs, CO

http://www.churchstatelaw.com

Current developments, cases, statutes, federal law, state law, historical material, and links to related sites are all provided by this law firm, which represents many religious organizations facing legal challenges.

Data Sites

American Religion Data Archive

http://www.thearda.com

Maps and reports providing quantitative data on religion in America. The collection includes data on churches and church membership, religious professionals, and religious groups (individuals, congregations, and denominations).

Faith-Based and Community Initiatives

http://www.whitehouse.gov/government/fbci/

The official site for this White House office. Includes the administration's perspective on the overview of faith-based initiatives issues, current news related to this effort, an archive of President Bush's speeches related to the issue, and information for religious organizations to seek funding from this department.

Liberty Magazine

http://www.libertymagazine.org

An online journal devoted to the issue of religious liberty. Many scholarly articles are available for free.

Religion and Public Schools (U.S. Dept. of Education)

http://www.ed.gov/policy/gen/guid/religionandschools/

Includes current and archived guidelines for public schools to handle the issue of religion in school.

Religion and the Founding of the American Republic

http://lcweb.loc.gov/exhibits/religion/

Primary source materials and historical narratives provide insights into the historical meaning of religious freedom in the United States.

Advocacy Sites

—For Religious Tolerance/Protection

The Beckett Fund for Religious Liberty
http://www.becketfund.org

Center for Law and Religious Freedom (Christian Legal Society)
http://clsnet.org/clrfPages/aboutCenter.php

Promoting Religious Tolerance Understanding and Freedom
http://www.religioustolerance.org

—For Separation/Restriction of Religion

Americans United for Separation of Church and State
http://www.au.org

Freedom from Religion Foundation
http://www.ffrf.org

National Center for Science Education
http://www.natcenscied.org

People for the American Way
http://www.pfaw.org

—Against Separation/Expanded Role of Religion

American Center for Law and Justice
http://www.aclj.org

Explicitly Christian Politics—NRA
http://www.natreformassn.org

National Legal Foundation
http://www.nlf.net

Religious Freedom Amendment
http://religiousfreedom.house.gov

Civil Liberties

Summary

The first ten amendments to the constitution, known as the Bill of Rights, comprise what we call American civil liberties. Civil liberties, or individual freedoms, protected through the U.S. Bill of Rights, include freedom of speech, association, assembly, and religion (through the separation of church and state); equal protection under the law (regardless of race, sex, religion, or national origin); the right to due process; the right to privacy (as a citizen and employee); the right to bear arms; the freedom from undue search and seizure; and the freedom from cruel and unusual punishment. Another term often used in place of civil liberties is "civil rights". However, the term "civil rights" often conjures up very specific notions of rights for groups such as African Americans, the disabled, or women. (Consider the Civil Rights Movement of the 1960s, the Americans with Disabilities Act of 1990, etc.)

Globally, civil liberties are often expressed as "human rights". The United Nations Office of the High Commissioner of Human Rights outlines global human rights in its *Universal Declaration of Human Rights*. Some of the liberties addressed by this group are freedom from torture and inhuman treatment, involuntary disappearances, arbitrary executions, capital punishment; freedom of opinion and expression and assembly; and the right to a fair trial, religion, and adequate housing. While the United Nations documents do not govern our land, they do highlight the most agreed upon liberties of civilized society and often reflect what is found in our own constitution. However, considerations of these issues as national versus international concerns will affect the research process and the line of argument in deliberating issues of civil liberties.

Keywords
- Civil rights
- Disability rights
- Equal protection
- Equality
- Flag burning/flag desecration
- Human rights
- Indigent defense/rights of the poor
- Juvenile justice
- Police brutality
- Privacy
- Segregation
- U.S. Patriot Act
- Victim's rights
- Women's rights
- Workplace rights

Related Topics
- Censorship
- Church and state
- Gay rights
- Gun control
- Homeland security
- Terrorism

Civil liberties protect individuals from governing authorities and from majority opinions. Arguments against civil liberties rarely exist, especially in democratic societies. Therefore, in America the arguments will instead be about how far various liberties should extend, when the extension of one group or person's liberty impinges upon another, and when government is justified in limiting individual freedoms to ensure greater security. For instance, one person's desire for free and open information may infringe upon another person's right to privacy. Some Americans have burned the American flag in protest of national policies and as a right of free expression, while other denounce such action as treasonous. Police, who are protecting the interest of a municipality, have often been accused of going too far physically in handling the suspect of a crime, infringing on his or her right to due process. As is covered more completely in the "Censorship" chapter, freedom to express sexual or violent ideas in words or pictures may infringe upon parents' rights to protect their children from what might be harmful to them psychologically. And the freedom of one group to exercise their religion openly may cause them to act in ways that restrict or oppress individuals who are not a member of that religion. (See the "Church and State" chapter).

One major focus of civil liberties recently is the U.S. Patriot Act, which was passed in response to the September 11, 2001, terrorist attacks. It is meant to provide the American government with better information to find and arrest terrorists. However, opponents to this law claim that it too severely invades the privacy of Americans.

Another continuing issue of civil liberties is the maintenance of privacy in the age of the Internet. Employers can access e-mail and cached Web traffic information from employees' computers. With so much information about individuals online, and hackers always learning new ways to access that information, there have been many instances of "identity theft" or invasion of privacy. This extends to issues of access to medical records, telephone numbers, and credit card numbers.

Web Sites

Reference Sites

Electronic Privacy Information Center (EPIC)

http://www.epic.org

This is a public interest group located in Washington, D.C. Its Web site informs encyclopedically as well as with breaking news about emerging privacy and other civil liberty issues.

Human Rights Watch

http://www.hrw.org

Although Human Rights Watch is an advocacy group, the Web site is focused on reporting news and political hearings. Provides human rights information by country or by issue.

NPR Special Report: Liberty vs. Security

http://www.npr.org/programs/specials/liberties

Delves into the questions of how far government can go to curb civil liberties in the name of national security. NPR provides tapes, analysis, and a roundtable discussion of the Bush administration's appearance before the Senate Judiciary Committee to answer this question.

News Sites

Guardian Unlimited: Special Reports: Privacy on the Internet

http://www.guardian.co.uk/netprivacy/

Comprehensive news coverage about Internet privacy from a UK perspective.

Yahoo! News: Full Coverage: Civil Liberties

http://fullcoverage.yahoo.com/fc/

Search Full Coverage for the term "civil liberties". Select the Full Coverage Category for "US: Civil Liberties" to view news stories, editorials, feature articles, audio/video resources, Web sites, and links to other specialized news sources on this topic. Full coverage on privacy is also available. Search the term "privacy" for a list of related full coverage headings.

Law/Legislation

American Civil Liberties Union—Legislative Update

http://www.aclu.org/legislative/legislativemain.cfm

Organizes press releases, action items, and legislative documents by issue.

EPIC Bill Track

http://www.epic.org/privacy/bill_track.html

Tracks privacy, speech, and civil liberties bills in the current congress.

Data Sites

Attack on Civil Liberties: The Village Voice

http://www.villagevoice.com/specials/civil_liberties

This liberal publication offers an online archive of articles it has published regarding civil rights issues.

CATO Institute: Civil Liberties

http://www.cato.org/current/civil-liberties

This conservative organization presents articles, data, and analysis of civil liberties in the traditional sense as well as in light of terrorist activities.

Howstuffworks: Security Channel Homepage

http://computer.howstuffworks.com/channel.htm?ch=computer&sub=sub-security

Technical descriptions of how Internet monitoring is done. Also see the "wiretapping" resource on this site.

NARA | The National Archives Experience

http://www.archives.gov/national_archives_experience/charters.html

Read the primary source document establishing American civil liberties.

Office of the United Nations High Commissioner for Human Rights

http://www.unhchr.ch

Press releases and UN documents relating to international human rights. Also includes the *Universal Declaration of Human Rights* in 300 languages.

Privacy Rights Clearinghouse

http://www.privacyrights.org

Collection of fact sheets and reports published by the Utility Consumers' Action Network.

Privacy.org

http://www.privacy.org

"The site for news, information and action."

Advocacy Sites

—For Civil Rights

American Civil Liberties Union

http://www.aclu.org

Anti-Defamation League (ADL)

http://www.adl.org

Bill of Rights Defense Committee

http://www.bordc.org

CPSR Cyber-Rights

http://www.cpsr.org/cpsr/nii/cyber-rights/

EFF (Electronic Frontier Foundation)

http://www.eff.org

People for the American Way

http://www.pfaw.org

—Checks on Civil Rights

American Civil Rights Union

http://www.civilrightsunion.org

Center for Individual Rights

http://www.cir-usa.org

—Human Rights

Amnesty International

http://www.amnesty.org

Lawyers Committee for Human Rights

http://www.lchr.org

Corporate Responsibility

Summary

In 2000, business news was dominated by allegations of corporate corruption against top executives accused of fraud, outside auditors who failed to monitor company financial dealings, and Wall Street analysts who recommended the stock of companies that were actually in economic distress. The Enron scandal was the first of several, revealing flaws in corporate behavior that eventually resulted in new government intervention and regulation of business.

Enron Corporation, an energy trading company based in Houston, was the seventh-largest company in the United States in 2000. By the end of 2001, Enron had filed for what was then the largest bankruptcy in U.S. history. As subsequent investigations revealed, the company managed for many years to inflate its success through an elaborate series of accounting maneuvers. Enron was able to conceal the fact that it was losing massive amounts of money by setting up and shifting money into a complicated network of phony partnerships. That allowed the company to present itself as highly profitable, when in reality it was hiding losses inside a web of obscure accounting.

In October 2001, when the company reported a large loss, the Securities and Exchange Commission (SEC) began a formal investigation of the partnerships. Reports emerged that Enron executives had sold millions of shares in the company before the company's precarious finances were made public, while at the same time trying to talk investors and employees into holding onto their shares. Enron employees who owned company stock through their 401(k) retirement plans were actually prevented from selling their shares. Employees lost more than $1 billion overall from their retirement funds.

The Justice Department opened a criminal probe of Enron. Enron's accounting firm, Arthur Andersen LLP, under scrutiny for certifying inaccurate Enron financial statements, admitted that it had shredded documents related to the energy company audit. The ability of the accounting industry to function properly has profound implications for the decisions of investors and the health of the economy. All publicly traded companies are subject to periodic auditing

Keywords
Accounting Oversight Board
Big Five accounting firms
CEO salaries
Corporate bankruptcy
Corporate greed
Enron scandal
Sarbanes-Oxley Act of 2002
Shareholder activism
Socially responsible investing

Related Topics
Fair wages

by outside accountants, to verify that the companies accurately represent themselves to the investing public. Investors rely on the honesty of these audits to measure a company's health and decide whether to invest in it.

The shredding revelation caused investigators to look at the practices of not only Andersen but also other U.S. accounting firms. Many people called for stricter regulation of the accounting industry. Arthur Andersen was eventually indicted for destroying documents. In June 2002, a federal jury convicted Arthur Andersen of obstruction of justice.

The Enron episode came as a considerable shock to the U.S. financial system. As it turned out, Enron was not the only company that was failing due to questionable, if not criminal, activity. The period after Enron's failure saw collapses or investigations at Global Crossing Ltd., Adelphia Communications Corp., ImClone Systems Inc., Tyco International Ltd., Dynegy, and WorldCom Inc. In July 2002, WorldCom took from Enron the dubious distinction of declaring the largest bankruptcy in U.S. history.

Some saw tighter regulations as a way to help restore confidence in U.S. businesses and those who monitor them. To that end, in July 2002 President Bush signed the Sarbanes-Oxley Act, billed as the most extensive overhaul of laws regarding corporate governance, accounting, and securities fraud to be passed since the 1930s. The law called for the establishment of a Public Company Accounting Oversight Board, which could levy steep fines on individuals or companies.

The continuing disclosures of financial misdoing also shattered investors' confidence. The U.S. Securities and Exchange Commission (SEC) also ordered chief executive officers and financial officers of the largest U.S. companies to personally certify that their customary reports to the SEC were complete and accurate. The new SEC rule made executives personally liable for errors.

These government responses to corporate scandals have helped to restore some public confidence and encourage businesses to act ethically. Others have taken a different route in an attempt to make large corporations behave in a socially responsible manner. Many individuals, social advocacy groups, and others, such as public employee pension funds, use shareholder power to make their investments work toward achieving social goals through Socially Responsible Investing (SRI). SRI considers both the investor's financial needs and an investment's impact on society. This involves screening companies based on social or environmental criteria before investing in them.

Some shareholders have also become involved in actively advocating for change within companies, using proxy-voting campaigns to make an impact on corporate policies. Every shareholder in a company receives proxy resolution and voting materials to inform investors of issues for consideration at the company's annual general meeting each year. Shareholders can also submit proposals or resolutions to be included on the company proxy statements. Some issues that investors have taken proxy action on include pay disparity, sexual orientation policies, excessive CEO compensation, human rights violations, and environmental practices of companies.

Web Sites

Reference Sites

Business Ethics

http://www.web-miner.com/busethics.htm

This guide, prepared by a librarian, provides an annotated list of resources in these categories: articles and publications, case studies, corporate codes of ethics, professional organizations, resources, and centers.

Corporate Library

http://www.thecorporatelibrary.com

Corporate Library is an independent investment research firm specializing in corporate governance and the relationship between company management, boards, and shareholders. Most general content on the site is available at no cost. The site includes news briefs; a searchable company database (S&P 500) that provides general information about the CEO and the company's board, with links to CEO contracts when available; investor relations pages; and proxy information. Browse the Shareholder Action section of the site by company to view shareholder proposals on a variety of topics. The Study Center provides background on topics such as accounting, compensation, global governance, scandals, and shareholder rights.

Hoover's Online

http://www.hoovers.com

Hoover's is a great starting point for research on publicly held companies (those that issue stocks). Entries provide a capsule company overview, financial data, news, and industry categories, for comparisons with similar companies.

News Sites

CNN Money: Special Report: Corporate Corruption

http://money.cnn.com/news/specials/corruption/

Links to current news stories related to corporate corruption and scandals; includes a sidebar that provides brief summaries of recent events for various companies and individuals, listed under categories such as "busted," settled, under investigation, and CEOs in trouble.

Washingtonpost.com: Corporate Ethics

http://www.washingtonpost.com/wp-dyn/business/specials/corporateethics/

This special report provides current news stories as well as some useful features: primers on corporate crimes in America, Martha Stewart, Enron, corporate governance, regulatory agencies, and timelines for the major corporate scandals.

Yahoo! News: Full Coverage: Corporate Reform

http://fullcoverage.yahoo.com/fc/

Search Full Coverage for the term "corporate reform". Select the Full Coverage Category for "US: Corporate Reform" to view news stories, editorials, feature articles, audio/video resources, Web sites, and links to other specialized news sources on this topic.

Law/Legislation

Findlaw: Special Coverage: Enron

http://news.findlaw.com/legalnews/lit/enron/

Provides current news along with an extensive collection of legal and congressional documents related to the investigation and prosecution of Enron officials. Findlaw maintains similar sites related to the Tyco and Worldcom corporate scandals.

Sarbanes-Oxley Act of 2002

http://news.findlaw.com/hdocs/docs/gwbush/sarbanesoxley072302.pdf

Full text (in pdf format) of this law, passed in the wake of the Enron scandal, which established a public company accounting oversight board and made other changes to regulations regarding disclosure and penalties for fraud.

Data Sites

Executive PayWatch

http://www.aflcio.org/corporateamerica/paywatch/

Site from the AFL-CIO union provides the PayWatch Database for companies listed in the Standard and Poor's Super 1500 Index. Browse by company name or search using various criteria to find a CEO's total compensation (salary, bonus, stock awards, options, etc.) and to see how it compares to other workers' earnings. Also includes analysis of trends, information on executive retirement plans, and case studies.

U.S. Securities and Exchange Commission: Search EDGAR

http://www.sec.gov/edgar/searchedgar/webusers.htm

Search corporate SEC filings to locate company quarterly and annual reports, proxy filings, prospectuses, etc.

Advocacy Sites

—*Promote Citizen Activism Against Corporations*

Citizen Works

http://www.citizenworks.org

Corporate Accountability Project

http://www.corporations.org

CorpWatch

http://www.corpwatch.org/home/PHH.jsp

—*Promote Corporate Social Responsibility*

Business for Social Responsibility

http://www.bsr.org

Interfaith Center on Corporate Responsibility

http://www.iccr.org

Shareholder Action Network

http://shareholderaction.org

Death Penalty

Summary

Controversy over the death penalty has existed in this country since the beginning of the twentieth century. Public opinion has historically favored use of the death penalty as punishment for murder but is subsiding over time. In the world community, the United States is criticized for use of the death penalty and is in the minority of democratic countries that legalize or employ it.

As of July 2000, there were 3,682 inmates on death rows throughout the United States. Thirty-eight states allow the death penalty, in all cases for murder only.

Keywords
Capital punishment
Commuted sentences
Cruel and unusual punishment
DNA evidence
Electric chair (electrocution)
Habeas corpus petition
Juvenile executions
Lethal injection
Stay of execution
Televised executions

Related Topics
Prisons

Since the 1930s the largest number of inmates executed in one year has been 200 (during the 1930s). In the most recent decade, the largest number of executions in a year was 98. The federal government is allowed to seek the death penalty for murder, treason, espionage, and high-level drug trafficking. Timothy McVeigh, convicted of the Oklahoma City bombings, is the only federal prisoner executed since 1963. There were no executions between the years 1972 and 1976 because the "Furman Decision" declared the death penalty to be unconstitutional for reasons of a "wanton and freakish pattern of use." In 1976 states began to revise their statutes to answer this charge, and use of the death penalty again became legal.

Those who favor use of the death penalty see it as just punishment for those who themselves have killed. It is seen as a means of ensuring that such violent criminals are completely removed from society to never harm again. Some believe that it is not fair for society to support such criminals for the rest of their lives in prisons at the expense of taxpayers. Others claim that it is not fair that relatives of the victims no longer have their loved one in their midst, while the person responsible for the victim's death is allowed to continue with his or her life. Finally, supporters of the death penalty see it as a punishment that will help to deter others from committing murders because of this horrible consequence.

Opponents of the death penalty argue that it is wrong to kill people, whether it is state-sanctioned punishment or outright murder. Some will claim that killing is an immoral way for the state to send the message that killing is wrong. Other opponents argue that it is an unfair system punishing the poor, mentally ill, and minorities more than the rest of society. Another reason for opposing the death penalty is fear that the legal process is flawed and that innocent persons are sometimes executed. Opponents also say that a life sentence is an equally effective way to remove a criminal from the rest of society.

Some interesting issues have arisen that strengthen public support for the death penalty. For instance, some prisoners serving life sentences have needed extensive and expensive medical care. Is it right to give an organ transplant to a death row inmate before a law-abiding citizen? How will society pay for the increased medical expenses of an aging prison population?

Other cases have arisen that seem to cause citizens to question support of the death penalty. The high profile case of Karla Faye Tucker in Texas caused people to question the value of executing a prisoner who seems truly reformed. New DNA technology that can provide concrete evidence of innocence or guilt has been used to set several death row inmates free who were wrongly convicted. Statistics showing the large number of mentally ill and minority death row inmates even caused one governor (George Ryan of Illinois) to commute the death penalty sentence of every death row inmate in his state. In some states, juvenile criminals convicted of violent crimes have been sentenced to death, causing many to question the sanity of the punishment and wondering what society should instead be doing to keep such young people from reaching this point.

Web Sites

Reference Sites

Death Penalty for Teachers

http://teacher.deathpenaltyinfo.msu.edu

A curriculum guide for teachers to teach about the death penalty in high schools. It provides the pro and con arguments, state data, courtroom cases, and links to other online resources.

Focus on the Death Penalty/University of Alaska Anchorage Justice Center

http://www.uaa.alaska.edu/just/death/

Full coverage of this topic, including the history, statistics, death row, the issues, links to organizations concerned with the topic, and international aspects of the debate.

Frontline: The Execution

http://www.pbs.org/wgbh/pages/frontline/shows/execution/

Investigative report on the inner workings of the death penalty. Provides an outline of the pro and con arguments, readings on the topic, and a microscopic look at the issues behind one death row inmate. Also addressed is an in-depth answer to why Texas puts more inmates to death than any other state. On the Frontline home page, you can also find "Angel on Death Row", a documentary following one inmate's execution.

News Sites

Death Penalty News and Updates

http://people.smu.edu/rhalperi

Although this site is provided by anti-death penalty advocate Rick Halperin, it is very up-to-date, taking news from a variety of national sources.

Yahoo! News: Full Coverage: Death Penalty

http://fullcoverage.yahoo.com/fc/

Search Full Coverage for the term "death penalty". Select the Full Coverage Category for "US: Death Penalty" to view news stories, editorials, feature articles, audio/video resources, Web sites, and links to other specialized news sources on this topic.

Law/Legislation

LII: Law about. . . the Death Penalty

http://www.law.cornell.edu/topics/death_penalty.html

Provides an overview of legislation regarding the death penalty, with links to federal and New York state statutes, links to other states' laws, and additional key legal resources.

Data Sites

Bureau of Justice Statistics/Death Penalty Statistics

http://www.ojp.usdoj.gov/bjs/cp.htm

Provides summary findings, links to detailed reports by year, and demographics of death row inmates.

Death Penalty Information Center

http://www.deathpenaltyinfo.org

Although this group is opposed to the death penalty, there are volumes of data on the death penalty here, including statistics, names, articles, and more.

Execution Tapes

http://www.soundportraits.org/on-air/execution_tapes/

A collection of sound recordings and transcripts of execution proceedings in Georgia. Although recordings are generally not allowed during executions, these twenty-two recordings were made by the Georgia Department of Corrections for its own records and made available to the public through the efforts of an attorney.

Sourcebook of Criminal Justice Statistics

http://www.albany.edu/sourcebook/

Among other crime data, there is much about the death penalty, including public opinion statistics, demographics of death row inmates, and trends regarding murders and death sentences.

Advocacy Sites

—For the Death Penalty

Criminal Justice Legal Foundation

http://www.cjlf.org

Death Penalty Information@DPInfo.com

http://www.dpinfo.com

The New American: Issues in Focus: Death Penalty

http://www.thenewamerican.com/focus/cap_punishment

Pro-Death Penalty.com

http://www.prodeathpenalty.com

—Against the Death Penalty

Death Penalty—Amnesty International

http://www.amnestyusa.org/abolish/

Death Penalty Religious

http://www.deathpenaltyreligious.org

HRW: The Death Penalty in the U.S.A.

http://www.hrw.org/campaigns/deathpenalty/

Juvenile Death Penalty

http://www.abanet.org/crimjust/juvjus/juvdp.html

Prison Activists Resource Center—Death Penalty

http://www.prisonactivist.org/death-penalty

Diversity

Summary

The term *diversity* encompasses the consideration of peoples from all genders, religions, races, ethnicities, and sexual orientations. At its most comprehensive level, a discussion about diversity will include an examination of the roles of all these groups in society. In reality, many who claim an interest in diversity may only be concerned with one or two subgroups. In fact, sometimes one group's culture or religious affiliation may prevent it from being open and welcoming to another group.

Various civil rights movements in American history have arisen to address the oppression felt by minority groups and have culminated in the current notion of diversity. In the 1950s and 1960s the Civil Rights Movement advanced the cause of African Americans. The 1970s was a decade of the "Women's Liberation" movement. The early 1990s saw the enactment of the Americans with Disabilities Act. Throughout the 1990s political activism of gay rights groups increased, but gay rights remains a largely unresolved issue. A recent Supreme Court decision striking down sodomy laws may pave the way for increased rights of gays. Most of these movements not only seek to increase the political voice of constituents but intend to increase individuals' economic, political, and educational standings.

Those who promote diversity claim a richness of the American experience that comes from including people of all kinds. Proponents of diversity seek to "increase the volume" of the voices of minority groups in relation to majority groups. There is sentiment that each group is enriched through an understanding of the mores, values, history, and culture of another group. Promotion of diversity allows people to meet each other on a personal level and relate with greater tolerance and understanding. Some proponents of diversity are more open to increased immigration and globalism. Some are advocates of diversity because they belong to one of the minority groups and want an equal share in society. Some perceive the most basic necessity to ensure that all citizens have equal rights and opportunities.

Keywords
Affirmative action
Equal opportunity
Equal protection
Ethnicity
Multiculturalism
Pluralism
Racial gerrymandering
Reverse discrimination
University of Michigan
    Supreme Court cases

Related Topics
Gay rights
Hate groups and crimes
Immigration
Race Relations

Opponents of diversity are not monolithic. Reasons for opposition might be religious, prejudicial, or a simple preference for the majority voice. Those who oppose increased diversity may do so because they feel that too much tolerance undermines their core values. There is sentiment that only so many differences can coexist before an implosion of values or relationships occurs. Some believe that more minorities must adjust to the values of the majority for societal harmony to exist. Some extreme factions argue for complete separation or even condemnation of various groups.

Affirmative action has been one political tool used to increase the role and profile of women and minorities in the workplace and in schools. Affirmative action is the program of increasing female and minority representation in workplaces and colleges and universities. The role of affirmative action in higher education has been seen as necessary to increase diversity in the hiring pools of professional and technical positions, as well as to create a richer learning environment. Diversity in the workplace has been welcomed by many businesses that feel the human face of diversity increases public opinion of and identification with their company or product. Proponents claim that it is the only way to repair historical discriminations that have locked some parts of society out of economic advantage.

Affirmative action critics claim that it is a form of "reverse discrimination" that only perpetuates the notion of discrimination. There has been increased criticism of this program in recent years, with many claiming that it has served its time and is now outdated and harmful to society. They claim that it undermines the true abilities of minorities and increases prejudice. Some states have outlawed state-level use of affirmative action, and the current presidential administration sought to do the same federally through the University of Michigan cases recently heard by the Supreme Court. The court's split decision on these cases upheld universities' rights to create a diverse student body while restricting their use of a point system to do so.

Racial gerrymandering has been used to create "majority-minority" voting districts to increase the numbers of minority lawmakers in office, giving them a stronger voice in public policy. Such programs receive much of the same kinds of support and criticism as does affirmative action.

Web Sites

Reference Sites

Affirmative Action and Diversity Project

http://aad.english.ucsb.edu

Contains pro and con points of view, definitions, recent news, state initiatives, economic reports and data, legal approaches, and pending state and federal legislation. A great starting point!

Diversity Resources

http://www.inform.umd.edu/EdRes/Topic/Diversity/

A comprehensive portal to online diversity resources.

News Sites

DiversityInc.com

http://www.diversityinc.com

Online magazine that keeps up with the latest happenings of a diverse workforce. Includes up-to-date legislative news as well as news about companies. For fuller access to the site, a free or paid registration is required.

Yahoo! News: Full Coverage: U.S. Affirmative Action

http://fullcoverage.yahoo.com/fc/

Search Full Coverage for the term "affirmative action". Select the Full Coverage Category for "US: Affirmative Action" to view news stories, editorials, feature articles, audio/video resources, Web sites, and links to other specialized news sources on this topic.

Law/Legislation

LII Law about: Equal Protection

http://www.law.cornell.edu/topics/equal_protection.html

Provides an overview of laws establishing equal protection rights and links to federal laws, state laws, and links to other sources.

U.S. Department of Labor: Equal Employment Opportunity

http://www.dol.gov/dol/topic/discrimination/

Federal regulations and laws on workplace diversity issues.

Data Sites

Digital Divide

http://www.pbs.org/digitaldivide/race-main.html

Examines issues of growing inequalities in cyberspace, which threaten to limit diversity online.

Diversity in the United States: U.S, Department of State

http://usinfo.state.gov/usa/diversity/

Governmental news, reports, official texts, and key documents relating to diversity in America. Also provides links to other online resources and print documents of interest.

Mapping Census 2000: The Geography of U.S. Diversity

http://www.census.gov/population/www/cen2000/atlas.html

From the U.S. Census Bureau, graphic representation of where various age and race groups live and are growing or declining in the United States.

Pluralism Project

http://www.pluralism.org

Concerned specifically with religious diversity in the United States. This site contains research reports, articles, a directory, images, and links to sites concerning religious diversity and pluralism.

Test of Courage

http://www.pbs.org/testofcourage/

A documentary about diversity told through the story of various individuals becoming firefighters.

U.S. Commission on Civil Rights

http://www.usccr.gov

News, reports, and briefings from this branch of federal government that monitors equality and rights issues of citizens because of their race, color, religion, sex, age, disability, or national origin.

Advocacy Sites

—*Supporting Diversity or Affirmative Action*

American Association for Affirmative Action

http://www.affirmativeaction.org

Benton Foundation (specifically digital divide)

http://www.benton.org

Civil Rights.org

http://www.civilrights.org

Tolerance.org

http://www.tolerance.org

—*Against Diversity or Affirmative Action*

Affirmative Action for Immigrants

http://pweb.netcom.com/ percent7Ejimrobb/affirmative.html

American Civil Rights Institute

http://www.acri.org

Multiculturalism and Diversity: The New Racism

http://multiculturalism.aynrand.org

VDARE.com

http://vdare.com

Drug Policy

Summary

Whatever position an individual or group takes on a national drug policy, facts show that drug abuse is the leading cause of a high crime rate, the breakup of two-parent families, and homelessness. Drug abuse causes 14,000 deaths per year related to drug crime and illness. There are between100,000 and 300,000 births each year of babies exposed in the womb to illegal drugs. Medical costs of all kinds related to drug abuse were over $150 billion in this country in 1997. Government officials see an official policy on drugs as a matter of public health concern.

The most common debate regarding the nation's drug policy is whether to view drug abuse as a criminal activity requiring tough action or a medical problem requiring education and treatment. Tough action has been the most common approach taken by the federal government since the mid-1970s. The phrase "war on drugs" encapsulates the mission of those who seek answers through larger police forces, better import controls, tough sentencing laws, and proactive movements against trafficking even where activities take place in other countries.

While not signaling a change in official government policy, some independent groups and governmental departments have undertaken a concurrent proactive educational and therapeutic approach. Many businesses create environments where employees who have drug problems can receive treatment for their addictions before punitive action is taken. Media campaigns have been launched by governmental and independent organizations to dissuade, mostly the young in society, against drug abuse. These campaigns are sometimes criticized for draining dollars that could otherwise be used for enforcing the law or for being too manipulative of youth's ideologies. Others hail them as an effective means of keeping teenagers off drugs.

A fairly recent (mid-1990s) experiment by the government has been to introduce "drug courts" into communities by offering grants for those communities who wish to try them. Drug courts are mostly used for first- or second-time

Keywords
- Anti-drug campaigns/Just Say No/D.A.R.E.
- "Crack" cocaine
- Criminalization of drug abuse
- Drug courts
- Drug czar
- Drug testing
- Legalization of illicit drugs
- Narcotics
- Substance abuse treatment
- War on drugs

Related Topics
- Prisons
- Substance abuse

drug offenders who are not violent. These courts maintain the discretion of issuing prison sentences or requiring abuse treatment programs. There has been some indication that the recidivism rate for those who have passed through drug courts is far lower than for those who have gone through the regular criminal justice system. However, critics contend that there is a problem with proper due process for such individuals and that their privacy rights are infringed. Treatment programs make use of drug testing.

The notion of drug testing is also a contested issue. Legally it is required for certain jobs where public safety is at stake (especially in transportation industries). When used in a workplace setting, drug testing is most often used to identify individuals who need therapy but is also used to screen who is hired. Critics of drug testing contend that it invades citizen privacy and is akin to "undue search and seizure" when it is done without a cause for suspicion. Testing teenagers is also a sharply divided issue, applauded by some as a protection of our young people and denounced by others as sending the wrong message and depriving them of their right to privacy.

One of the most common reasons for denouncing a "tough" drug policy is the reality that race plays in the criminalization of drug abuse. In the specific case of cocaine, laws punish buying and selling of "crack" more severely than powdered cocaine. Crack is a more addictive and violence-inducing form of cocaine. Some 88 percent of Americans charged with crack offenses are black. By comparison, only 38 percent of those charged with powder cocaine are black. There are much more complex roles that race plays in drug abuse and criminal activity, including disparate poverty rates.

The most polarizing debate regarding drug policy is whether to legalize illicit drugs. Proponents of legalization contend that the "war on drugs" has been lost. This effort has expended inordinate sums of money and effort, yet drug abuse has never fallen significantly. Backers say legalization would save billions of law enforcement, legal, and prison dollars. It would allow the nation to begin treating drug use as a medical problem and providing treatment. Natural competition would remove profit margin, providing less incentive to sell these drugs, and the drugs could be taxed like cigarettes and alcohol are now.

Opponents claim legalization would be a threat to public safety and would create a pandemic problem of abuse, largely affecting young people. Legalization would legitimize the use of these drugs. Crime rates would not be reduced because people on drugs commit so many crimes. Critics contend that large healthcare costs would overtake whatever revenues are collected in taxes, which can be proven by statistics on cigarettes and alcohol abuse. Society would experience a loss of economic productivity.

Web Sites

Reference Sites

Frontline: Drug Wars

http://www.pbs.org/wgbh/pages/frontline/shows/drugs/

A documentary of the drug problem and policies in the United States. Looks at the business of trafficking drugs, the buyers, and the enforcers, and has links to several research reports on the issue. Also see "Snitch," a Frontline report on the issue of how informants have become a key piece in prosecuting drug crimes. Exposes the problems of dealers and traffickers receiving reduced sentences while users and petty thieves receive maximum sentences.

NCJRS In the Spotlight: Drug Courts

http://www.ncjrs.org/drug_courts/summary.html

Provides an overview of what drug courts are and how they function. Includes data, legislation, and grants regarding drug courts.

Public Agenda Online: Illegal Drugs

http://publicagenda.org

Click on the Issue Guides link and select "Illegal Drugs." Provides an overview, outline of the debate, facts, public opinion, recent news, and links to other resources to consult. An excellent starting point.

News Sites

National Drug Strategy Network

http://www.ndsn.org

See "NewsBriefs" for up-to-date links to news stories regarding drugs and drug policy.

Yahoo! News: Full Coverage: Drug Trade

http://fullcoverage.yahoo.com/fc/

Search Full Coverage for the term "drug trade". Select the Full Coverage Category for "World: Drug Trade" to view news stories, editorials, feature articles, audio/video resources, Web sites, and links to other specialized news sources on this topic.

Law/Legislation

LII: Law about . . . Alcohol, Tobacco, and Controlled Substances

http://www.law.cornell.edu/topics/alcohol_tobacco.html

Provides an overview of laws that govern these topics as well as recent court cases, federal law, and state law.

Data Sites

Bureau of Justice's Drugs and Crime Page

http://www.ojp.usdoj.gov/bjs/drugs.htm

A collection of BJS reports and publications detailing drug crime statistics and trends.

Drug Policy Research Center (RAND)

http://www.rand.org/multi/dprc/

This RAND organization works to collect data and research that enlightens issues of drug policy. Many research reports and summaries are available on the Web site.

Informing America's Policy on Illegal Drugs:
What we don't know keeps hurting us

http://www.nap.edu/books/0309072735/html

A more than 400-page report by the National Research Council that examines the determinants, consequences, prevention, and treatment of drug use. Includes data on various aspects of drug use.

Office of National Drug Control Policy

http://www.whitehousedrugpolicy.gov

The official Web site for the current administration's drug policy and programs. Includes access to trend data as well.

Substance Abuse Policy Research Program

http://www.saprp.org

See the "Policy Maker Resources" section for access to key findings produced from grants this organization has funded.

TRAC DEA

http://www.trac.syr.edu/tracdea/

Data gathered by the government watchdog research center, TRAC, based at Syracuse University. Provides trends in legislation, arrests, and sentencing nationally and by district.

Advocacy Sites

—Pro-Treatment/Education

The Anti-Drug

http://www.theantidrug.com

Drug Policy Alliance

http://www.drugpolicy.org

Drug Strategies

http://www.drugstrategies.org

Institute for a Drug-Free Workplace

http://www.drugfreeworkplace.org

Partnership for a Drug Free America

http://www.drugfreeamerica.org

Stop the Drug War: The Drug Reform Coordination Network

http://www.drcnet.org

—Pro-Punishment/Sentencing

Drug Enforcement Administration

http://www.usdoj.gov/dea/

Drug Watch International

http://www.drugwatch.org

National District Attorneys Association

http://www.ndaa-apri.org

National Families in Action

http://www.nationalfamilies.org

—*For Legalizing Drugs*

ACLU: Drug Policy

http://www.aclu.org/DrugPolicy/

NORML

http://www.norml.org

Election Reform

Summary

The perennial issue in the realm of election reform is campaign finance reform. Reports of corruption in raising funds and garnering votes are as old as the election of our first president, George Washington. Modern laws regulating how funds are raised for political campaigns largely sprang from the expensive use of television advertising during the 1950s and 1960s. The Watergate scandal in the 1970s also prompted a variety of reform laws, including the creation of the Federal Elections Commission to oversee the voting process. The *Buckley v. Valeo* case, decided by the Supreme Court in 1976 overturned some of this legislation, upholding limits on individual giving to a campaign but declaring limits on campaign spending unconstitutional. Most recently, the Internet has prompted new ideas for grassroots campaigning that will either sidestep many of the issues or create new opportunities for corruption and need for oversight. Issues of election reform are being grappled with at the federal as well as state levels.

Keywords
- Bipartisan Campaign Reform Act of 2002
- *Buckley v. Valeo*
- Campaign finance reform
- Clean money/public funding of elections
- Federal Election Commission
- Federal Elections Campaign Act
- Hard money
- Help America Vote Act (HAVA)
- Internet campaigning
- Internet voting
- Issue ads
- Lobbying
- Soft money
- Special interests
- Spending limits
- Term limits
- 2000 presidential election
- Voting machines
- Voting reform

In the last twenty years or so, the biggest debates over campaign finance reform have centered around how to manage the vast amounts of dollars contributed to campaigns that give an edge to "special interests." Special interests can be any group with a shared interest in a public policy issue. Often the special interests are backed by large corporate dollars with a financial stake in how an issue is decided. There is concern that corporate dollars (or dollars of wealthy people) drive much of the campaigning, and that "normal folks" are left out of the process. Special interests are involved in lobbying, also controversial in the political process.

Another problem with campaign laws has been that while there were limits to how much an individual or corporation could give to a candidate's campaign, there were no limits to what contributions could be made to political parties, which they in turn use on behalf of their candidates. This is referred to as "soft money." The most effective result of a push for limits on soft money has been accomplished through the Bipartisan Reform Campaign Act of 2002 (known in the Senate as the McCain-Feingold bill and in the House as Shays-Meehan), which bans soft money contributions while doubling the amount of hard money direct contributions allowed by individuals to candidates. It also puts more limits on the use of issue ads. That law met with immediate legal challenges but was upheld by the Supreme Court in December 2003. (Some say these limits on spending are a limit to First Amendment rights.)

Some groups advocate reform based on public financing of campaigns, or "clean money." Advocates of this type of reform consider that providing candidates with public funds will leave them beholden to no interest group and will allow greater input from the grassroots. Current funding laws allow candidates to receive matching public funds after meeting specified fundraising levels, but advocates of clean money reform would increase the role that public financing plays in elections. Such legislation has been largely unsuccessful.

Another type of election reform resulted from the 2000 presidential election. This highly contested election, in which there were scenes of election officials in Florida reviewing ballots by hand and unexpected results in precincts blamed on poorly designed ballots, has caused some to call for tighter requirements for state election boards. The Help America Vote Act (HAVA) is one effort to modernize election procedures and provide for replacement of antiquated voting booths and training of poll workers, among other things.

As mentioned previously, the Internet is also causing changes in elections. Some perceive that elections will soon be held online, removing the need for the elaborate physical voting protocols currently in use nationwide. However, others believe that the technology requires much more development before integrity in the process can be ensured. In addition, candidate Web sites are moving beyond the static role of listing a candidate's views and soliciting contributions. New registration and communication tools available via the Web are having a big effect on how grassroots efforts can be strengthened by this tool. Some wonder if the Internet can solve many of the problems related to grassroots involvement that legislation has been attempting to solve for years.

Web Sites

Reference Sites

Campaign Finance Reform: A Sourcebook

http://www.brook.edu/gs/cf/sourcebk/default.htm

An online and abridged copy of an in-depth study done by the Brookings Institute to "help reformers and interested citizens understand how current campaign finance practices have evolved from previous decisions made by legislative, judicial, and executive bodies and what might be entailed in moving the system in a desired direction."

Campaign Finance Reform: The Issue

http://www.opensecrets.org/news/campaignfinance/

Provides an issue profile, updates on key legislation, information on congressional committees involved in the issue, and tracking of special interests.

Campaign Finance Reform: University of Michigan Documents Center

http://www.lib.umich.edu/govdocs/campfin.html

A resource guide for finding online material, groups, and guides to issues of campaign finance reform.

Public Agenda Online: Campaign Finance

http://www.publicagenda.org

Select "Campaign Finance" from the Issue Guides link. This site provides an overview of the topic; frames the debate; gives position outlines; and provides public opinion data, statistical information, and links to useful resources for this controversial topic.

News Sites

Reform Institute

http://www.reforminstitute.org

Headed by John McCain, a champion of campaign finance reform, this institute provides a great way to keep up with news and issues related to reform. Users can sign up to receive e-mail updates on reform news.

Yahoo! News: Full Coverage: Campaign Finance

http://fullcoverage.yahoo.com/fc/

Search Full Coverage for the term "campaign finance". Select the Full Coverage Category for "US: Campaign Finance" (or "US Campaign Finance Archive" for older material) to view news stories, editorials, feature articles, audio/video resources, Web sites, and links to other specialized news sources on this topic.

Law/Legislation

Findlaw Legal News: Election 2000 Special Coverage

http://news.findlaw.com/legalnews/us/election/election2000.html

Includes the lawsuits, timeline, audio files, and other documents related to the disputed presidential election of 2000.

Presidential Election Law (JURIST)

http://jurist.law.pitt.edu/election/election2000-1.htm

A resource guide to broadcasting and financing laws. Provides summaries, links to articles, Supreme Court cases, and a variety of legal materials.

Data Sites

Brennan Center for Democracy Reform: Campaign Finance Reform

http://www.brennancenter.org/programs/programs_dem_cfr.html

Provides research reports on impending legislation and on various issues of campaign finance, such as soft money and issue ads.

Campaign Finance Institute

http://www.cfinst.org

An "institute that conducts objective research and education, impanels task forces and makes recommendations for policy change in the field of campaign finance."

Center for Public Integrity

http://www.publicintegrity.org

Special investigative reports of money and politics as they affect campaigns as well as lobbying. Some reports are aimed at the federal level and some investigate specific state issues.

Common Cause

http://www.commoncause.org

Click on "state organizations" to read about many reform efforts and debates taking place at the state level, or click on "campaign finance studies" for an archive of reports on campaign finance created by this organization.

Federal Election Commission (FEC)

http://www.fec.gov

Find legislation, news, current candidacy information, contributions by giver and candidate, previous election information, and more. This is the official government site for campaign financing issues.

Issue Ads @ APPC

http://www.appcpenn.org/issueads/

Reports on issue ads, profiles of the organizations funding them, and estimates of the amount of money they spent. The top five issues that were the target of issue ads are outlined, with the nature of the issue, amount of money spent, and list of who spent money on the issue.

National Institute on Money in State Politics

http://www.followthemoney.org

Database of campaign contributions in state government. Search by candidate, by PAC, or by ballot measures to find who is giving money to whom and who is getting money from whom.

Online News Hour: Congress and the Campaign Reform Fight

http://www.pbs.org/newshour/@thecapitol/cfr/

Video from episodes of the *NewsHour* regarding the debate in Congress over this issue in 2002.

Political Money Line

http://www.tray.com/fecinfo/

Provides searchable access to data from the FEC regarding contributions to federal campaigns.

Project Vote Smart

http://www.vote-smart.org

Tracks voting records, evaluations by special interest groups, and campaign contributions for more than 13,000 candidates and elected officials nationwide.

Advocacy Sites

—*For Reform/Limits to Soft Money*

DEMOS: A Network for Ideas and Action

http://www.demos-usa.org/demos

League of Women Voters

http://www.lwv.org

National Voting Rights Institute

http://www.nvri.org

—For "Clean Money" Reform

Center for Governmental Studies
http://www.cgs.org/projects/

Public Campaign
http://www.publicampaign.org

Public Citizen: Campaign Finance Reform
http://www.citizen.org/congress/campaign/

—Against Reform/Limits

Money and Politics—CATO Institute
http://www.cato.org/campaignfinance/

Energy Supply and Policy

Summary

Since 1958 the United States has consumed more energy than it has produced and has made up the difference by importing energy, primarily oil. During the 1970s and the early 1980s, energy prices soared and people worried about shortages. This concern led to the development of a renewable energy industry. Renewable energy is power produced from inexhaustible sources, such as the sun and wind. Unlike reserves of coal or oil, which will eventually be used up completely, the supply of renewable energy is unlimited. The federal government provided substantial support for development of alternative energy technologies.

Keywords
Arctic National Wildlife Refuge (ANWR)
Clean coal
Electric power deregulation
Energy conservation
Energy efficiency
Energy policy
Fossil fuels
Renewable energy sources
Utility companies

Related Topics
Global warming
Water resources

By the mid-1980s, there was a surplus of oil, and consequently oil prices dropped. Because of lower prices, production declined, and as consumption grew, foreign imports once again increased. During the 1980s, President Ronald Reagan sharply cut federal programs for energy and opposed government intervention in energy markets. He believed that the expansion of the federal government's role in energy policy was misguided and pursued a course of transferring the center of the decision-making process to the states, the private sector, and individuals.

During this period, a new type of energy company, known as an independent generator, emerged. Under the state laws that established utilities as monopolies, however, independent generators could not sell electricity directly to consumers. Instead, they sold wholesale amounts of power to utilities and other power producers. Many utilities found it cheaper to buy wholesale power from independent generators than to build new power plants or to update their old ones.

In 1992, Congress passed the Energy Policy Act, deregulating the wholesale power market by exempting independent generators from provisions that restricted interstate competition. Since the wholesale market for electricity has been deregulated, a number of states have passed laws to deregulate their retail electricity markets. Such laws allow independent energy producers to sell energy directly to consumers, not just to utilities. The laws also allow utilities to offer electricity to consumers outside of their regions. Deregulation advocates believe that this measure will result in great cost savings for energy consumers. Others are concerned that deregulation will result in the consolidation of the power industry into a few large energy conglomerates that could dominate the market and set prices.

An emerging factor in energy policy has been the environment. Concerns about pollution, ozone depletion, and global warming have led to regulation of emissions from automobiles, power plants, and other industrial users of fossil fuels. About 84 percent of U.S. energy comes from fossil fuels; nuclear power provides 8 percent. Approximately 8 percent of the energy consumed in the United States comes from renewable sources. Of the 8 percent, hydroelectric accounts for 4 percent, biomass 3 percent, and wind, solar, and geothermal energy for the remaining 1 percent.

Debate over the wisdom of government support for renewable energy continues today. Proponents of subsidies point toward the environmental advantages. Renewable forms of energy generally produce less pollution than fossil fuels. Opponents point to the cost, since most sources of renewable energy are currently more expensive than fossil fuels.

In 1991, President George H.W. Bush proposed an energy policy that promised to reduce U.S. dependence on foreign oil by increasing domestic oil production and nuclear power. He planned to achieve this by producing additional oil from environmentally sensitive areas, encouraging pipeline construction, simplifying the construction permit process of nuclear power plants, and increasing competition in the production of electricity. His proposals did not include government-directed conservation efforts or tax incentives.

Conservationists objected to increased offshore drilling, especially in the coastal plain of the Arctic National Wildlife Refuge (ANWR) in Alaska. They also wanted to see automobile fuel mileage increased and conservation methods stressed, rather than increasing the use of nuclear power. Now, more than ten years later, a different President Bush has reinvigorated efforts to search for oil in the Arctic and has developed a controversial energy plan that once again emphasizes free market strategies.

Web Sites

Reference Sites

EnergyIdeas Clearinghouse

http://www.energyideas.org

Describes itself as an objective and comprehensive resource for technical and practical information on efficient buildings, processes, practices, and programs, including online case studies, fact sheets, and reports. Information organized by topics (appliances, lighting, renewable resources) and business types (agricultural, commercial, etc.).

Fossil.energy.gov

http://www.fe.doe.gov

Site maintained by the U.S. Department of Energy provides background information, news, quick facts, more detailed data, and reports on fossil energy–related topics, such as the national energy policy, clean coal, electric power deregulation, oil and gas reserves, and regulation. Includes a search engine for a technical publications library.

Privatization.org

http://www.privatization.org

Site produced by the Reason Public Policy Institute provides background on this movement, statistics and trends, an overview of the pro and con arguments with links to readings for each position, and a number of publications.

U.S. Department of Energy, Energy Efficiency and Renewable Energy

http://www.eere.energy.gov

A gateway to hundreds of Web sites and thousands of online documents on energy efficiency and renewable energy topics, such as bioenergy, geothermal, hydrogen, ocean, solar, and wind power. Each topic's page provides an overview, links to related organizations and resources, and news stories.

News Sites

Planet Ark: Reuters World Environment News

http://www.planetark.com/dailynewshome.cfm

Browse daily environmental news stories from around the world; search the news archive by keyword or topic.

Washingtonpost.com: Energy Special Report

http://www.washingtonpost.com/wp-dyn/business/specials/energy/

This special section provides current energy-related news stories as well as a series of special reports published in 2001 on electricity deregulation, entitled "Power Shift."

Yahoo! News: Full Coverage: Energy Policy

http://fullcoverage.yahoo.com/fc/

Search Full Coverage for the term "energy." Select the Full Coverage Category for "US: Energy Policy" to view news stories, editorials, feature articles, audio/video resources, Web sites, and links to other specialized news sources on this topic .

Law/Legislation

National Energy Policy

http://www.whitehouse.gov/energy/

The National Energy Policy Plan (NEPP) of the Department of Energy Organization Act of 1977 (PL 95-91) requires the president to submit to Congress every two years a national energy policy plan. This plan includes energy objectives and strategies as well as projections of energy supply, demand, and prices.

NRDC: Environmental Legislation

http://www.nrdc.org/legislation/legwatch.asp

The National Resources Defense Council (NRDC) is an advocacy organization that provides reports, unpublished research, policy and technical analyses, congressional testimony, and other materials by NRDC's lawyers, scientists, and analysts. Their weekly *Legislative Watch* bulletin tracks movement of environmental bills in Congress.

Sierra Club: Votewatch

http://www.sierraclub.org/votewatch/

The Sierra Club has been monitoriing congressional activity on environmental issues since the 106th Congress (1999). It summarizes all of the proposed legislation on this site and provides a complete roster of votes for each bill or amendment.

Data Sites

Energy Information Administration

http://eia.doe.gov

This U.S. government site provides current and historical data for various types of fuels (petroleum, natural gas, electricity, coal, nuclear, renewable, and alternative), by geographic area or sector, and by topics (imports/exports, climate change, etc.). Includes background briefs, analyses, and forecasts for many countries as well.

International Energy Agency

http://www.iea.org

The IEA is an autonomous agency linked with the Organisation for Economic Co-operation and Development (OECD). The twenty-six member countries share energy information and coordinate their energy policies. The site provides a variety of statistical publications, country studies, and reports.

Advocacy Sites

—*Promote Interests of Utility Companies*

American Public Power Association

http://www.appanet.org

Edison Electric Institute

http://www.eei.org

—*Promote Privatization*

Electric Power Supply Association

http://www.epsa.org

National Center for Policy Analysis: Energy Issues

http://www.ncpa.org/iss/ene/

—*Promote Renewable Energy Sources*

Renewable Energy Policy Project

http://www.repp.org

Union of Concerned Scientists: Clean Energy

http://www.ucsusa.org/clean_energy/

Fair Wages

Summary

The minimum wage is the minimum amount employers are required to pay most workers. In the United States, Congress has raised the wage eighteen times since the Fair Labor Standards Act mandated the first federal minimum wage of 25 cents per hour in 1938. In 1997, the minimum wage was increased to its current level, $5.15 per hour. Many states also have minimum wage laws, and in some cases the state minimum wage is higher than the federal level. In states where the minimum wage is lower, most employers must pay workers at the federal level.

Keywords
Child labor
Earned income tax credit
Income gap
Labor unions
Living wage
Minimum wage
Poverty level
Sweatshops

Related Topics
Corporate responsibility
Welfare reform
World trade

A full-time minimum-wage earner currently earns $10,300 annually, slightly above the 2002 federal poverty level of $ 8,860 for individuals. About 2 million Americans earn the federal minimum wage, working in fast food restaurants, doing janitorial work, or other entry-level jobs, according to the Bureau of Labor Statistics (BLS). An estimated 1.7 million workers earn less than the minimum wage, usually in jobs where their wages are enhanced by tips or sales commissions. Most of them work in retail, agriculture, or food service industries.

When an increase in the minimum wage is proposed, most Republicans and business interests voice opposition. They claim that forcing employers to pay more for labor will cause them to lay off workers or eliminate jobs. Critics also contend that this will cause some small businesses to fail. The U.S. Chamber of Commerce, the National Restaurant Association, and the National Federation of Independent Businesses have all lobbied against minimum-wage increases. Republicans typically propose an alternative package of tax breaks and credits, intended to increase take-home pay for workers without increasing the minimum wage.

Others believe that raising the minimum wage is a moral issue, a matter of doing the right thing for people who work hard and want to get out of poverty. A higher minimum could enable businesses to attract and keep high-quality workers, thus cutting down on the problems created by high job turnover. They say that higher wages could also boost morale and productivity.

The income gap between rich and poor in the United States has grown during the past two decades. According to an analysis of U.S. Census data by the Center on Budget and Policy Priorities, "the number of people living in poverty rose by 1.3 million in 2001, to 32.9 million. Median household income—the income of the household in the middle of the income spectrum—fell by $900 to $42,200. In addition, the share of the national household income going to the top five percent of the population reached an all-time high, while the shares going to the bottom, the next-to-bottom, and the middle fifths of the population fell to all-time lows."

Some reasons for the increasing wage gap are a decline in low-skill jobs based in the United States, as manufacturers move their operations to countries where labor is cheaper; fewer workers belonging to labor unions; and a decrease in the real value of the minimum wage. The Census Bureau also notes that the increase in single parent and small households, which generally have lower incomes, has increased the wage gap. Over time, tax policies also have changed in ways that require the richest Americans to pay an ever-smaller proportion of their income in taxes.

Some analysts fear that the income gap is trapping the lowest-paid workers in poverty. Many people with full-time jobs are classified as "working poor," unable to satisfy their basic needs. Conservatives downplay the importance of the gap in wages, noting that a substantial difference in incomes is a natural part of a capitalist economy. Republicans argue that reducing taxes, thus increasing take-home pay, is an effective way to encourage prosperity in the United States.

"Living wage" laws are a popular yet controversial tactic for reducing the income gap. Supporters argue that the federally mandated minimum wage is not high enough to guarantee workers a salary that can support them. These laws, generally approved on the city or county level, require certain employers to pay their workers a living wage. Some also mandate that the employees receive benefits such as health insurance. The laws are generally targeted at businesses that either receive government contracts or have received special tax breaks or other financial benefits from the government. Since the mid-1990s, forty cities and counties in seventeen states have established living wage laws.

Americans have also become concerned with fair wages for foreign workers, especially since many of the products we purchase are manufactured abroad. In some countries, sweatshop labor is common. A sweatshop is defined as a workplace where workers are subjected to extreme exploitation. Often sweatshop workers endure long hours and hazardous working conditions; many workers are children or women. Sweatshops, especially in the garment industry, exist in the United States as well. There is a growing movement to boycott products made in this manner. In 2001, New York City passed an anti-sweatshop procurement bill, making it illegal for city tax dollars to be used for apparel (e.g., police uniforms) and textiles made in sweatshops. New York is the ninth city to pass an anti-sweatshop ordinance.

Web Sites

Reference Sites

AFSCME Laborlinks

http://www.afscme.org/otherlnk/

This guide, produced by a labor union, includes links to AFSCME publications as well as external Web sites, organized into categories such as bargaining, employee benefits, labor studies, legal, news, reference, occupational safety, women's' resources, workers' compensation, and privatization.

Labor Research Portal

http://www.iir.berkeley.edu/library/laborportal/

This research guide from the University of California's Institute of Industrial Relations Library is organized along topical lines, covering employee rights, labor culture, temporary workers, labor unions, organizing, labor news sources, and government sources. Includes a Labor Contracts Database, with full text of union contracts organized by state, union name, and occupation.

News Sites

Yahoo! News: Full Coverage: Labor and Workplace

http://fullcoverage.yahoo.com/fc/

Search Full Coverage for the term "labor". Select the Full Coverage Category for "Business: Labor and Workplace" to view news stories, editorials, feature articles, audio/video resources, Web sites, and links to other specialized news sources on this topic.

Law/Legislation

Employment Law Guide

http://www.dol.gov/asp/programs/guide.htm

The Guide describes the statutes and regulations administered by the Department of Labor (DOL) that affect businesses and workers, including the Fair Labor Standards Act, the Occupational Safety and Health Act, migrant and agricultural worker legislation, and laws pertaining to noncitizens.

Minimum Wage

http://www.dol.gov/dol/topic/wages/minimumwage.htm

This overview from the U.S. Department of Labor provides information on the minimum wage and links to a clickable map that shows state minimum wage data, laws and regulations on this topic, and similar overview pages on a variety of other wage-related topics, such as back pay, overtime pay, holiday pay, severance pay, merit pay, and tips.

Data Sites

Bureau of Labor Statistics

http://www.bls.gov

Provides a wide range of current and historical data on wages, earnings, benefits, safety, and health issues.

National Compensation Survey

http://www.bls.gov/ncs/

This study presents comprehensive measures of occupational earnings, cost trends, benefit availability, and detailed plan provisions. Data are available for metropolitan and non-metropolitan areas, broad geographic regions, and on a national basis. Wage data include average hourly wages for up to 480 occupations and are shown by industry, occupational group, full-time and part-time status, union and nonunion status, establishment size, time and incentive status, and job level.

PERI: Labor Markets and Living Wages

http://www.umass.edu/peri/lw.html

This site from the Political Economy Research Institute at University of Massachusetts, Amherst, is a rich data source, providing working papers on this topic as well as links to other research reports on living wages and sweatshop labor.

Advocacy Sites

—Support Business Interests

Employment Policies Institute

http://www.epionline.org

HR Policy Association

http://www.hrpolicy.org

National Right to Work Committee

http://www.right-to-work.org

U.S. Chamber of Commerce

http://www.uschamber.com

—Support Labor Justice Issues

ACORN Living Wage Resource Center

http://www.livingwagecampaign.org

AFL-CIO: Your Job and the Economy

http://www.aflcio.org/yourjobeconomy/

Coop America's Guide to Ending Sweatshops

http://www.sweatshops.org

Fairjobs.org

http://www.fairjobs.org

National Campaign for Jobs and Income Support

http://www.nationalcampaign.org

Farmland

Summary

Agriculture is the dominant land use in the United States. More than 945 million acres are involved in agricultural production. The U.S. Department of Agriculture estimates that between 1992 and 1997, 11.2 million acres of farmland and other open spaces were lost to suburban development. The tendency of cities and suburbs ringing the urban cores of cities to sprawl outward is a serious problem, as reflected by the Sierra Club report that total land lost to sprawl in the United States is about 100 million acres.

Farmland is threatened by sprawl in every state. Although the amount of land lost varies, university extension agencies estimate that the rate of agricultural land conversion is higher than the rate of population growth. In addition to loss of farmland, unregulated growth results in loss of open space, wildlife habitat, and groundwater recharge areas, thus affecting our water supply as well.

In addition to residential tract development, another phenomenon is large-lot rural development, where single homes with large amounts of surrounding land are sprinkled throughout rural areas. Researchers note that there is a critical mass for this type of development and that when enough large residential lots are sold in rural areas, it drives agriculture into decline. Farmland is also lost to industrial use and to commercial campus-style "office parks."

Some methods for preserving farmland include state laws that create agricultural districts as well as laws that regulate urban zoning practices. Some local governments also impose lower property taxes on agricultural land, to encourage and assist farm owners to maintain their land in production. Conservation easements and purchase of development rights are other techniques used to protect farmland. A conservation easement (or conservation restriction) is a legal agreement between a landowner and a land trust or government agency that permanently limits uses of the land to protect its conservation values.

Supporters of farmland conservation believe that loss of farmland, especially in rapidly growing states like California, Texas, and Florida, may ultimately result in agricultural activity being concentrated in just a few states,

Keywords
Conservation easement
Factory farms
Farmland conservation
Farmland protection
Land use
Land trust
Sustainable agriculture
Urban fringe development
Urban sprawl

Related Topics
Food safety
Water resources

making our food supply more vulnerable to natural disasters and perhaps shortages. On the other side of the debate, home builders' associations believe that restricting growth in rural areas will sharply increase the cost of housing, pricing moderate and low-income families out of the housing market.

Factory farming is also seen as a threat to preservation of the small family farm. Factory farms are owned by corporations. Other common terms used are *corporate agriculture* or *agribusiness*. Some groups believe that factory farming emphasizes only high volume and profit, with little or no regard for environmental quality, human health, safe food, humane treatment of animals, and the rural economy.

The sustainable agriculture movement is a reaction to corporate or factory farming. It promotes agricultural production practices that protect soil fertility, wildlife, water quality, the environment, and family farming and farm communities. A related movement, community supported agriculture, aims to connect local farmers with local consumers, develop a regional food supply, maintain a sense of community, and encourage land stewardship.

Web Sites

Reference Sites

Agriculture Network Information Center (AgNIC)

http://www.agnic.org

Browse by subject or search this portal site to locate useful Web sites related to agricultural topics such as farms, animal science, plant science, food and nutrition, and insects. The site is managed by a voluntary alliance of the National Agricultural Library (NAL), land-grant universities, and other agricultural organizations, in cooperation with citizen groups and government agencies. Participants develop Web sites and reference services in specific subject areas.

Alternative Farming Systems Information Center

http://www.nal.usda.gov/afsic/

This site from the National Agricultural Library provides descriptions of information sources on alternative agricultural systems and crops. Sections include organic farming, sustainable agriculture, community supported agriculture, aquaculture, soil management, and weed control.

Farmland Information Library

http://www.farmlandinfo.org

Site from the American Farmland Trust provides articles, statutes, legislative information, news, and data related to farmland protection, urban fringe development, and urban sprawl.

National Sustainable Agriculture Information Service

http://attra.ncat.org

This site, funded by the U.S. Department of Agriculture and managed by the National Center for Appropriate Technology, provides information and other technical assistance to farmers, ranchers, extension agents, educators, and others involved in sustainable agriculture in the United States. Sustainable agriculture, over the long term, enhances environmental quality and the resource base on which agriculture depends. Sections of the site provide an overview of sustainable agriculture and information on horticultural crops, field crops, soils, pest management, organic farming, and livestock.

News Sites

Stateline.org

http://www.stateline.org/index.do

Managed by the Pew Center on the States, the site was "founded in order to help journalists, policy makers and engaged citizens become better informed about innovative public policies." This is an excellent resource for news on issues of importance to states, such as welfare and social policy, land use and growth, environment, energy, and healthcare. Browse by topic or by state; search for keywords.

Yahoo! News: Full Coverage: Farming and Agriculture

http://fullcoverage.yahoo.com/fc/

Search Full Coverage for the term "farming". Select the Full Coverage Category for "US: Farming and Agriculture" to view news stories, editorials, feature articles, audio/video resources, Web sites, and links to other specialized news sources on this topic.

Law/Legislation

Farm Bill 2002

http://www.usda.gov/farmbill/

Provides full text of the latest bill along with summary information. The section on conservation outlines a new Farmland Protection Program (FPP), which provides matching funds to help purchase development rights to keep productive farm and ranchland in agricultural uses.

Data Sites

ERS/USDA Key Topics

http://www.ers.usda.gov/Topics/

The Economic Research Service offers a significant body of research and analysis on key topics, including agribusiness, biotechnology and genetically modified foods, crops, farm structure and performance, food market structures, food prices, food safety and consumer behavior, rural America, and U.S./state facts. Each provides a collection of data, publications, and other products and services.

National Agricultural Statistics Service

http://www.usda.gov/nass/

Includes data from the Census of Agriculture, conducted every five years, as well as historical and current data, charts, and maps on various topics such as farms, acreage, sales, production expenditures, crop prices, and livestock.

National Resources Inventory (NRI)

http://www.nrcs.usda.gov/technical/NRI/

This is a compilation of natural resource information on non-federal land in the United States that is conducted by the U.S. Department of Agriculture's Natural Resources Conservation Service in cooperation with the Iowa State University Statistical Laboratory. The inventory captures data on land cover and use, soil erosion, prime farmland soils, wetlands, habitat diversity, selected conservation practices, and related resource attributes. Data are collected every five years from sample sites in all fifty states, Puerto Rico, the U.S. Virgin Islands, and some Pacific Basin locations.

NRCS: State of the Land

http://www.nrcs.usda.gov/technical/land/

This site from USDA's Natural Resources Conservation Service provides data and analysis on land use, soil erosion, water quality, water supply, wetlands, and other issues regarding the conservation and use of natural resources.

USDA Agriculture Factbook

http://www.usda.gov/factbook/

Provides some data on farm types, acreage in use, and sales.

Advocacy Sites

—*Promote Sustainable Agriculture Methods*

Food First: Institute for Food and Development Policy

http://www.foodfirst.org

GRACE Factory Farm Project

http://www.factoryfarm.org

World Resources Institute: Agriculture and Food

http://www.wri.org/sustag/

—*Promote Farmland Preservation*

American Farmland Trust

http://www.farmland.org

Family Farmer.org

http://www.familyfarmer.org

Land Stewardship Project

http://www.landstewardshipproject.org

Sierra Club: Stop Sprawl

http://www.sierraclub.org/sprawl/

Food Safety

Summary

Conditions in the U.S. food and drug industries a century ago were very different than they are today. Use of chemical preservatives and toxic colors was not regulated, and sanitation was primitive. A "pure foods" movement, which began in the 1870s, along with the public outcry generated by *The Jungle*, Upton Sinclair's 1906 book exposing the horrendous conditions of the Chicago meat packing industry, ultimately resulted in changes to U.S. food laws. The Food and Drugs Act and the Meat Inspection Act, which established sanitary standards for the meat industry and required the inspection of animals before and after slaughter, were both passed in 1906.

The Food and Drugs Act was updated in 1938. The new Act required that safe tolerances for residues, such as pesticides, be established. It also authorized factory inspections and required food standards to be set up. In the United States, where food has government seals of inspection, consumers expect food to be safe. However, outbreaks of food-borne illness do occur and have caused public concern about food safety. The U.S. Department of Agriculture (USDA) estimates that 76 million illnesses, including 5,200 deaths, occur from food poisoning each year. At least thirty pathogens (harmful bacteria, viruses, chemicals, and parasites) are associated with food-borne illness. Bacteria such as E. coli, listeria, and salmonella are the most common causes of food-borne illnesses.

Irradiation of food is a measure used to eliminate bacteria. Scientists claim the process is safe and does not remove nutrients from the food or make it radioactive. Those who oppose irradiation believe that it may result in carcinogenic (cancer-causing) food. The U. S. Food and Drug Administration (FDA) has approved irradiation for spices and seasonings, enzymes, fruits, vegetables, grain products, and poultry.

Keywords
Biotech crops
Bovine growth hormone
Food additives
Food contamination
Food handling
Food processing plants
Food-borne pathogens
Genetically modified foods
Irradiation
Listeria
Mad cow disease
Organic foods
Pesticide residues
Salmonella

Related Topics
Animal rights
Farmland
Genetic engineering
Terrorism
World trade

Organic food is produced without using most pesticides, synthetic fertilizers, or bioengineering. Organic meat, poultry, eggs, and dairy products come from animals that are given no antibiotics or growth hormones. Before a product can be labeled "organic," a government-approved certifier inspects the farm where the food is grown to make sure the farmer meets USDA organic standards. Companies that handle or process organic food must also be certified.

Genetically modified foods are crop plants that have been modified in the laboratory to enhance desired traits, such as disease or herbicide resistance or improved nutritional content. Concerns about these foods fall into three categories: environmental hazards (unintended harm to other organisms), human health risks (creation of new allergens), and economic concerns (raising the cost of seeds, thus harming small growers). In the United States, genetically modified foods are regulated by three different government agencies. The Environmental Protection Agency (EPA) evaluates plants for environmental safety, the USDA evaluates whether the plant is safe to grow, and the FDA evaluates whether the plant is safe to eat.

In recent years, mad cow disease has raised new concerns about meat safety. Mad cow disease, formally known as bovine spongiform encephalopathy (BSE), gradually destroys the brain and central nervous system of infected animals. In the 1990s, some Britons died from a new strain of Creutzfeldt-Jakob disease (CJD), a human disease similar to mad cow. The following year, the British government announced that the new strain of CJD might be caused by the consumption of BSE-infected meat. For some time, British beef imports were prohibited in the United States. No known cases of the new strain of CJD have occurred in the United States.

Web Sites

Reference Sites

PBS: Harvest of Fear

http://www.pbs.org/wgbh/harvest/

This is the companion site to the Nova and Frontline television program that presents the debate over genetically modified food crops. Includes interviews with scientists, farmers, biotech and food industry representatives, government regulators, and critics of biotechnology; presents both sides of the debate, exploring both the risks and the benefits.

Pew Initiative on Food and Biotechnology

http://pewagbiotech.org

Aims to provide "news and information on agricultural biotechnology and genetically modified food from an independent and objective source for the public, media and policymakers." Site includes news releases, summaries, editorials and opinion, research reports, issue briefs, fact sheets, a glossary, data from polls, and links to a variety of other sites.

U.S. FDA Center for Food Safety and Applied Nutrition (CFSAN)

http://www.cfsan.fda.gov

This site provides recent food safety news and links to information sources on a wide variety of food safety topics, such as additives, dietary supplements, packaging, labeling, food-borne illness, pesticides, imports, and exports. Click on "Laws Enforced by the FDA" for links to Title 21 of the Code of Federal Regulations (CFR) and to texts of the Federal Food, Drug and Cosmetic Act, the FDA Modernization Act of 1997, and the Bioterrorism Act of 2002.

www.FoodSafety.gov

http://www.foodsafety.gov

This government portal site includes sections on consumer advice, food-borne pathogens, reporting problems, national food safety programs, federal and state government agencies, news and food safety alerts from the federal and state governments, and other topics, such as food law and regulations. Also includes a video library, with streaming videos that can be viewed online.

News Sites

Genomics: A Global Resource

http://www.biopad.org

Provides links to news stories on genomics, vaccines, emerging diseases, bioterrorism, and BSE/mad cow disease. Stories are from major news sources (UPI, Reuters, *New York Times*, *Science*, etc.) and university Web sites. Although sponsored by the Pharmaceutical Research and Manufacturers of America (PhRMA) trade group, it provides fair and thorough coverage.

Yahoo! News: Full Coverage: Food Safety

http://fullcoverage.yahoo.com/fc/

Search Full Coverage for the term "food safety". Select the Full Coverage Category for either "Health: Food Safety" or "Science: Genetically Modified Food" to view news stories, editorials, feature articles, audio/video resources, Web sites, and links to other specialized news sources on these topics.

Law/Legislation

FAOLEX

http://faolex.fao.org/faolex/

Describes itself as "the world's largest electronic collection of national laws and regulations, as well as treaties, on food, agriculture and renewable natural resources." Topics include agriculture, animals, environment, fisheries, food, forestry, land, plants, water, and wildlife. Legal texts are summarized and indexed in English, French, or Spanish. Useful for international or comparative perspective on these topics.

Milestones in U.S. Food and Drug Law History

http://www.fda.gov/opacom/backgrounders/miles.html

This site provides a chronology and brief descriptions of major events in the history of food and drug regulation in the United States since 1820.

Data Sites

Bad Bug Book

http://www.cfsan.fda.gov/~mow/intro.html

This handbook provides good background information on food-borne pathogenic microorganisms and natural toxins. It brings together in one place information from the Food and Drug Administration, the Centers for Disease Control and Prevention, the USDA Food Safety Inspection Service, and the National Institutes of Health. Each entry includes links to recent statistical information from the Centers for Disease Control and journal article citations from the MEDLINE database.

ERS/USDA Key Topics

http://www.ers.usda.gov/Topics/

The Economic Research Service offers a significant body of research and analysis on key topics, including agribusiness, biotechnology and genetically modified foods, crops, farm structure and performance, food market structures, food prices, food safety and consumer behavior, rural America, and U.S./state facts. Each provides a collection of data, publications, and other products and services.

USDA Food Safety and Inspection Service

http://www.fsis.usda.gov/OPHS/ophshome.htm

This site from the Office of Public Health and Science (OPHS) provides expert scientific analysis and data related to food safety. See the latest National Residue

Program Data for tables on veterinary drugs and pesticides in the egg product, meat, and poultry classes regulated by the FDA. Also provides current results of E. coli and salmonella testing programs.

Advocacy Sites

—Support Bioengineered Crops and Agribusiness Interests

Alliance for Better Foods

http://www.betterfoods.org

Biotechnology Industry Organization

http://www.bio.org

Council for Biotechnology Information

http://www.whybiotech.com

National Pork Producers Council

http://www.nppc.org

—Support Safe, Environmentally Sound Food Supply

Center for Food Safety

http://www.centerforfoodsafety.org

Organic Consumers Association

http://www.organicconsumers.org

Public Citizen: Critical Mass Energy and Environment Program

http://www.citizen.org/cmep/

Union of Concerned Scientists: Food and Environment

http://www.ucsusa.org/food_and_environment/

Gay Rights

Summary

The gay rights movement is a civil rights movement that seeks to eliminate "laws barring homosexual acts between consenting adults and that calls for an end to discrimination against homosexuals in employment, credit, housing, public accommodations, and other areas of life. Its ultimate aim is to encourage society's tolerance or acceptance of homosexuality" (*Britannica Online*).

Opponents have argued, from personal or religious belief, that homosexuality is immoral and thus does not deserve legal protection or societal approval. Some disagreement centers on whether homosexuality is an innate, biological predisposition. Gay rights opponents often believe that homosexual behavior stems from conscious lifestyle choice. Gay rights supporters argue that if homosexuality is biologically determined, then gays should be entitled to protection from discrimination, like ethnic minorities and women.

Gay rights issues that have gained recent prominence are

- Family issues (adoption, custody, guardianship, and inheritance);
- Military service ("don't ask, don't tell" policy);
- Marriage, civil unions, and domestic partnership; and
- Safety (hate crimes, assaults, and protection of gay youth from harassment).

A key U.S. Supreme Court decision in 2003, *Lawrence and Garner v. Texas*, struck down a Texas law against sodomy. This decision reverses an older ruling that states could punish homosexuals for what such laws historically called deviant sex acts. In the new decision, Justice Kennedy wrote for the court's majority: "The state cannot demean their existence or control their destiny by making their private sexual conduct a crime." Currently thirteen states have anti-sodomy laws on the books, and the court's ruling apparently invalidates those as well.

Keywords
Civil unions
Defense of Marriage Act (DOMA)
Domestic partnership
"Don't ask, don't tell"
Gay marriage
Hate crimes
Homophobia

Related Topics
Adoption
Civil liberties
Diversity
Hate groups and crimes

This decision alarmed those who oppose gay rights. They view it as a first step in granting equal protection under the law to homosexuals and ultimately leading to the legitimization of gay marriage. Congressional conservatives have responded with a proposal for a constitutional amendment to ban gay marriage. An amendment must be approved by two-thirds of Congress and then ratified by voters in three-fourths of the states to be added to the Constitution.

In 2000, Vermont became the first state to permit "civil unions" for gay couples. According to this law, parties to a civil union have all of the same benefits, protections, and responsibilities as are granted to spouses in marriage. The civil union must be dissolved by the state using the same laws as in divorce proceedings. However, many homosexuals believe that a "separate but equal" approach to solving this dilemma is inherently unfair, and continue to lobby for the right to marry. In June 2003, the high court of Ontario, Canada, ruled that the exclusion of same-sex couples from civil marriage violates the Canadian constitution and ordered an end to this practice. In November 2003, the Massachusetts Supreme Court ruled that same-sex couples are legally entitled to marry under the state constitution.

In the United States, many states, and the federal government, have enacted laws against gay marriage. The federal Defense of Marriage Act (DOMA) was signed in 1996. It does not bar marriage of same-sex couples, but it does prevent federal recognition of those marriages once they become legal in any state. It also gives states the option of not recognizing lawful marriages of same-sex couples licensed by other states. Opponents of DOMA laws as well as some legal scholars note that they violate the "Full Faith and Credit" clause (Article IV) of the Constitution and will eventually be overturned.

Web Sites

Reference Sites

Gay/Lesbian Politics and Law: WWW and Internet Resources

http://www.gaypoliticsandlaw.com

Describes itself as a "selected, annotated guide to the best and most authoritative resources on politics, law, and policy. Designed for students, scholars, teachers, journalists, activists, and citizens and maintained by Steve Sanders at Indiana University."

Homosexuality and Bisexuality

http://religioustolerance.org/homosexu.htm

Impartial consideration of topics such as religion and sexual orientation; gay rights; "healing" of gays and lesbians; and related essays, sermons, and testimonies.

Public Agenda Online: Gay Rights

http://www.publicagenda.org

Select "Gay Rights" from the list of Issue Guides. The site includes sections that provide an overview of issues, alternative viewpoints, data, recent news, public opinion surveys, etc.

News Sites

Yahoo! News: Full Coverage: Gay and Lesbian News

http://fullcoverage.yahoo.com/fc/

Search Full Coverage for the term "gay rights". Select the Full Coverage Category for "World: Gay and Lesbian News" to view news stories, editorials, feature articles, audio/video resources, Web sites, and links to other specialized news sources on this topic, such as PlanetOut and the Daily Advocate.

Law/Legislation

Don't Ask, Don't Tell, Don't Pursue

http://dont.stanford.edu

This database is produced by Stanford University Law Library. It includes primary materials on the U.S. military's policy on sexual orientation, from World War I to the present, including legislation; regulations; internal directives of service branches; materials on particular service members' proceedings (from hearing board transcripts to litigation papers and court decisions); policy documents generated by the military, Congress, the Department of Defense, and other offices of the Executive branch; and advocacy documents submitted to government entities

Lambda Legal: State by State

http://www.lambdalegal.org

Select "State by State" from the site's main menu, then click on any state on the U.S. map to learn about specific state and municipal laws related to gay rights issues such as discrimination, hate crimes, and marriage/domestic partnership.

National Gay and Lesbian Task Force

http://www.ngltf.org/library/

The Library includes a variety of Issue Maps that summarize the current status of gay rights concerns, such as adoption, domestic violence laws, civil rights, hate crimes, and marriage.

Data Sites

Frontline: Assault on Gay America

http://www.pbs.org/wgbh/pages/frontline/shows/assault/

This companion site to the television show provides background on Billy Jack Gaither, a gay man who was beaten to death in Alabama in 1999. Includes interviews with his family and his killers, discussion of the history of homophobia, views of religious leaders, and an overview of the "gay gene" debate.

Safe Schools Coalition

http://www.safeschoolscoalition.org

Click on Resources by Topic for links to reports on hate crimes, bullying, harassment, and other problems experienced by gay and lesbian youth.

Sexual Orientation: Science, Education, and Policy

http://psychology.ucdavis.edu/rainbow/

"Provides factual information to promote the use of scientific knowledge for education and enlightened public policy related to sexual orientation and HIV/AIDS." Sections include hate crimes, AIDS, the military, and sexual prejudice. Includes summaries of research studies and fact sheets that "provide an overview of social science theory and empirical research concerning sexual orientation."

Advocacy Sites

—*Against Gay Rights*

American Family Association: Homosexual Agenda

http://www.afa.net/homosexual_agenda/

Family Research Council: Human Sexuality

http://www.frc.org/context.cfm?c=RESEARCH

Traditional Values Coalition

http://traditionalvalues.org

—*Support Gay Rights*

American Civil Liberties Union

http://www.aclu.org

Family Pride Coalition

http://www.familypride.org

Human Rights Campaign

http://www.hrc.org

PFLAG: Parents, Families and Friends of Lesbians and Gays

http://www.pflag.org

Genetic Engineering

Summary

Genetic engineering is defined as the process of taking DNA from one organism and inserting it into another. Early experimentation with gene "splicing" began in the 1970s, when scientists learned that the DNA from some bacteria could recombine with other strains of bacteria. Today scientists are able to transfer genes between larger organisms and different species.

A clone is a "cell, group of cells, or organism that are descended from and genetically identical to a single common ancestor, such as a bacterial colony whose members arose from a single original cell." Technically, the process of cloning is not genetic engineering, since the genetic makeup of the cloned organism is not altered. Cellular manipulation, however, is essential to genetic engineering, to cloning, and also to stem cell research. All of these techniques are broadly referred to as biotechnology, and each is in some way controversial.

"Dolly" the sheep was the first mammal cloned (in 1997) through a technique called somatic cell nuclear transfer (SCNT). At that time, there was concern about application of this technology to clone humans, and President Clinton issued regulations to prohibit use of federal funds for such efforts. He also directed the National Bioethics Advisory Commission (NBAC) to thoroughly review the legal and ethical issues associated with the use of cloning technology to create a human being.

Scientists are interested in both adult stem cells and embryonic stem cells and their potential for therapies or cures of various human diseases. Stem cells are different in several ways from other types of cells. They are unspecialized cells that can renew themselves through cell division. Under certain conditions, they can be induced to become cells with special functions. Stem cells from human embryos can become all cell types of the body because they are pluripotent. They give rise to the multiple specialized cell types that make up the heart, lung, skin, and other tissues. Adult stem cells are generally more limited. In some adult tissues, adult stem cells can generate replacements for cells that are lost through normal wear and tear, injury, or disease.

Keywords
Bioengineering
Biotechnology
Cloning
Designer babies
Gene therapy
Gene transfer
Genetically modified foods
Genome patents
Human genome
Recombinant DNA technology
Stem cells

Keywords
Food safety
Reproductive technologies

124

The use of embryonic stem cells by scientists in research is controversial because they are derived from human embryos that have been created in an in vitro fertilization clinic and then were donated for research purposes. Pro-life advocates believe that destruction of human embryos for experimentation is wrong. Congress has limited stem cell research to use of only a few existing colonies of embryonic stem cells.

Organisms such as bacteria have been genetically engineered to produce vaccines, hormones, and other biological products. Plant and animal genetic makeup is more complex than that of microorganisms. The genetic engineering of plants, also known as crossbreeding or hybridization, has been occurring within plant strains for many centuries. But the insertion of specific genes from other species into plants was not possible until recently.

A genome is an organism's complete set of DNA and is organized into chromosomes. Mapping of various plant and animal genomes, including the human genome, has been completed. This new knowledge of the specific location and functions of each gene segment is fueling much new research and development. Genetically modified foods, from seeds that have been engineered for various traits such as disease resistance or enriched nutritional value, have also become controversial. Some question their safety for human consumption, while others fear the unintended consequences of this technology.

Another facet of genetic engineering involves gene therapy in medicine: replacing defective or missing human genes with normal ones. The first approved gene therapy trials involved children with severe combined immunodeficiency disease. Researchers are also investigating the use of gene therapy for such conditions as hemophilia, Parkinson's disease, diabetes, cancer, and AIDS. The U.S. Food and Drug Administration regulates human gene therapy products.

Finally, new DNA sequences and genetically modified organisms have been patented. Many ethical questions arise about who has the right to own various life forms and whether patenting will inhibit or further the use of these genetic creations in research and development of new therapies and products.

Web Sites

Reference Sites

AgBiotechNet

http://www.agbiotechnet.com

Provides news, reports, chapters from books, abstracts from the scientific literature, and links to other sites on animal and plant biotechnology, transgenics, cloning, biosafety, and genetically modified food.

DOEgenomes.org

http://doegenomes.org

This site is a gateway to a vast amount of information on the human and micro-bial genome programs and an appropriate starting point for most researchers. Provides background, status, news, fact sheets, educational resources, publica-tions, and research information, as well as an overview of the ethical, legal, and social issues related to genetic engineering.

Genethics.ca: The Genetics and Ethics Page

http://genethics.ca

This is a nicely organized gateway to sites and literature on ethical issues related to genetics. Includes a topical menu covering cloning, genetic testing, DNA banking, eugenics, gene therapy, stem cells, xenotransplantation, and other top-ics. Also provides links to news sites, journals, conferences, and discussion groups.

Genetics and Public Policy Center

http://www.dnapolicy.org

The Center is funded by a grant from the Pew Charitable Trusts. It aims to be an objective information source on reproductive genetics issues, such as genetic testing, gene transfer, genes and disease, and reproductive cloning. Topical sec-tions include basic information, useful links, and a bibliography. Also includes data from polls on attitudes toward reproductive genetics.

MEDLINEplus: Genetic Testing/Counseling

http://www.nlm.nih.gov/medlineplus/genetictestingcounseling.html

This research guide from the National Library of Medicine organizes sites into the following categories: general overviews, pictures/diagrams, prevention and screening, research, specific conditions/aspects, law and policy, dictionaries, di-rectories, organizations, and statistics. Also provides a link to retrieve current journal articles on the topic from the MEDLINE database.

National Human Genome Research Institute

http://www.genome.gov

Gateway to information organized in three categories: genetics research, genet-ics applications in health, and policy and ethical concerns. Each category pro-vides a topical overview of important issues along with links to key resources.

Stem Cell Information

http://stemcells.nih.gov

This site from the National Institutes of Health provides resources for those who need an introduction to this topic as well as resources for researchers, including a stem cell registry, news, funding opportunities, and scientific literature.

News Sites

Genome News Network

http://www.genomenewsnetwork.org

Provides news and feature stories written by staff reporters and editors about human medicine, agriculture, microbes, and biotechnology, among other current topics. Describes itself as an "an editorially independent online publication of The Center for the Advancement of Genomics."

Genomics: A Global Resource

http://www.biopad.org

Provides links to news stories on genomics, vaccines, emerging diseases, bioterrorism, and BSE/mad cow disease. Stories are from major news sources (UPI, Reuters, *New York Times*, *Science*, etc.) and university Web sites. Although sponsored by the Pharmaceutical Research and Manufacturers of America (PhRMA) trade group, it provides fair and thorough coverage.

New Scientist: Cloning

http://www.newscientist.com/hottopics/cloning/

This special report provides links to recent and archived articles published in the *New Scientist* on cloning and stem cell technology.

Washingtonpost.com: Gene Research

http://www.washingtonpost.com/wp-dyn/health/specials/genetherapy/

Links to current and archived news stories on this topic as well as some sites for background on the topic

Law/Legislation

Biotechnology and Genetics Law

http://www.megalaw.com/top/biotech.php

Links to relevant statutes, regulations, and related Web sites.

Data Sites

National Bioethics Advisory Commission—Publications

http://www.georgetown.edu//research/nrcbl/nbac/pubs.html

This Georgetown University site provides links to a variety of useful reports from the Commission, including the documents on human stem cell research and human cloning.

President's Council on Bioethics

http://www.bioethics.gov

Presents reports, transcripts, and working papers of the Council on cloning, stem cell research, sex selection, patenting human life, and other topics.

Your Genes, Your Health

http://www.yourgenesyourhealth.org

This is a multimedia guide to common genetic disorders. Describes symptoms, causes, diagnosis, treatment, and sites for more information.

Advocacy Sites

—*Support Aggressive Approach to Genetic Engineering*

CuresNow

http://www.curesnow.org

Genetic Alliance

http://www.geneticalliance.org

Human Cloning Foundation

http://www.humancloning.org

—*Support Restrictions on Genetic Engineering*

Center for Bioethics and Human Dignity

http://www.cbhd.org

Center for Genetics and Society

http://www.genetics-and-society.org

Council for Responsible Genetics

http://www.gene-watch.org

Family Research Council: Human Life and Bioethics

http://www.frc.org/context..cfm?c=RESEARCH

Global Warming

Summary

Many chemical compounds that are naturally found in Earth's atmosphere act as "greenhouse gases." These gases allow sunlight to enter the atmosphere. When sunlight strikes Earth's surface, some is reflected as infrared radiation (heat). Greenhouse gases tend to absorb this radiation as it is reflected back toward space, trapping the heat in the atmosphere and producing a "greenhouse" effect.

Keywords
- Carbon dioxide emissions
- Carbon sequestration
- Climate change
- Greenhouse gases
- Kyoto Protocol
- Ozone

Related Topics
- Energy supply and policy

The greenhouse effect is a natural phenomenon. The problem lies in the fact that atmospheric concentrations of several important greenhouse gases (carbon dioxide, methane, nitrous oxide, and most humanmade gases) have increased by about 25 percent since industrialization began in the nineteenth century. The growth in their concentrations is believed to be caused by human activity. In particular, carbon dioxide emissions have increased dramatically since the beginning of the industrial age, due largely to the burning of fossil fuels and to deforestation

Scientists believe that changes in Earth's climate and biosphere might be induced by the increasing concentrations of these gases, which have the potential to significantly alter the planet's heat and radiation balance. This phenomenon, termed "global warming," has resulted in a rise in average global temperatures of approximately 0.9 degrees Fahrenheit over the past century and could lead to an increasingly warmer climate in the future.

Careful monitoring of the concentrations of those gases in the atmosphere, and analysis of ice cores in Greenland and Antarctica that have captured past concentrations of some of those gases, demonstrate that their global concentrations are increasing. Emissions of carbon dioxide and the other greenhouse gases have not been regulated directly in U.S. pollution control laws such as the Clean Air Act.

Methods for controlling this problem include setting strict emissions standards, reducing fossil fuel use, developing alternative clean energy sources, removing carbon dioxide from emissions, eliminating use of chlorofluorocarbons, and slowing deforestation of Earth. These changes would have far-reaching effects on industries and the economy. Some critics contend that the costs of implementing effective programs would be too high.

Global warming is a worldwide problem, and the solution must be an international one. The most recent international effort to address the greenhouse effect was the Kyoto Protocol, an agreement among industrialized nations to reduce emissions of six greenhouse gases. More than 170 nations signed the treaty, including the United States, the European Union, Canada, and Japan. However, since Congress did not ratify this treaty, the United States is not participating in the global effort. Prospects for approval of the treaty during the Bush administration are dim.

Global warming skeptics argue that natural climate fluctuation, not human activity, is responsible for rising temperatures during the past century. Skeptical scientists also dispute the accuracy of temperature measurements during the past thirty years and advocate placing no limits on the consumption of fossil fuels. Controversial aspects of this topic include the following:

- Cause: Is the current warming trend primarily caused by human activity?

- Extent: How fast and how much future warming will occur?

- Effects: What are the potential impacts?

- Remedies: What are possible solutions for this problem?

Web Sites

Reference Sites

Climate Ark: Climate Change and Renewable Energy Portal

http://www.climateark.org

Provides current news from a variety of sources; an archive of older news stories; and a climate change links directory organized by major categories such as causes, impacts, information, science and research, policy actions, and advocacy.

Encyclopedia of the Atmospheric Environment

http://www.doc.mmu.ac.uk/aric/eae/

This online encyclopedia provides background information on a range of atmospheric issues, including air quality, acid rain, global warming, and ozone depletion.

EPA: Global Warming

http://yosemite.epa.gov/oar/globalwarming.nsf

Sections provide an overview, information on emissions, impacts, actions, official publications, and administration position papers.

NOAA: Paleo Global Warming

http://www.ncdc.noaa.gov/paleo/globalwarming/

National Oceanic and Atmospheric Administration site provides background on global warming, explains scientific techniques for the study of this problem, and provides historical climactic data spanning more than 1,000 years. Includes an image gallery and bibliography.

U.S. Global Change Research Information Office

http://www.gcrio.org

The Research Program was established by the Global Change Research Act of 1990 and is operated by a consortium of federal agencies. The site provides access to information on global change research, adaptation/mitigation strategies and technologies, and educational resources. This site includes bibliographic databases, participating agency Web sites focused on global climate change, and a special section on environmental education and research funding opportunities. Excellent starting point for research.

News Sites

Planet Ark: Reuters World Environment News

http://www.planetark.com/dailynewshome.cfm

Browse daily environmental news stories from around the world; search the news archive by keyword or topic.

WashingtonPost.com: Global Warming

http://www.washingtonpost.com/wp-dyn/nation/specials/science/climatechange/

This special report provides links to current and older news stories from the *Post*.

Yahoo! News: Full Coverage: Climate Change

http://fullcoverage.yahoo.com/fc/

Search Full Coverage for the term "climate". Select the Full Coverage Category for "US: Climate Change" to view news stories, editorials, feature articles, audio/video resources, Web sites, and links to other specialized news sources on this topic.

Law/Legislation

Global Climate Change Briefing Book

http://www.ncseonline.org/nle/crsreports/briefingbooks/climate/

Organizes many resources from the Congressional Research Service (CRS) on this topic, including a compendium of congressional bills and hearings on climate change; texts of international treaties; background information; discussions of the scientific, economic, energy, and legal issues related to the topic; and links to other CRS reports and related sites.

NRDC: Environmental Legislation

http://www.nrdc.org/legislation/legwatch.asp

The National Resources Defense Council (NRDC) is an advocacy organization that provides reports, unpublished research, policy and technical analyses, congressional testimony, and other materials by NRDC's lawyers, scientists, and analysts. Their weekly *Legislative Watch* bulletin tracks movement of environmental bills in Congress.

Pace Law School: Global Warming Central

http://www.pace.edu/lawschool/globalwarming/

Provides background on the legal structure of the UN Framework Convention on Climate Change (UNFCCC) and the Kyoto Protocol, U.S. obligations under the treaties, and actions the U.S. government has taken to meet these obligations, with links to information on what some countries are doing to reduce or stabilize greenhouse gases, as well as other international initiatives.

Sierra Club: Votewatch

http://www.sierraclub.org/votewatch/

The Sierra Club has been monitoring congressional activity on environmental issues since the 106th Congress (1999). It summarizes all of the proposed legislation on this site and provides a complete roster of votes for each bill or amendment.

United Nations Framework Convention on Climate Change

http://unfccc.int

Provides text of the Kyoto Protocol and a variety of related documents, including reports on implementation of the agreement.

Data Sites

EIA Greenhouse Gases Program

http://www.eia.doe.gov/oiaf/1605/frntend.html

This site from the Energy Information Administration presents U.S. data on greenhouse gas emissions. The Energy Policy Act of 1992 created a voluntary reporting program. Utility companies, manufacturers, coal producers, chemical companies, and various trade associations have provided reports included in the database.

Greenhouse Gas Emissions Database

http://ghg.unfccc.int

This searchable Greenhouse Gas Emissions Database provides data by country, type of gas, source of emission, and year (1990–2000). Parties to the UN Framework Convention on Climate Change submit national greenhouse gas inventories for inclusion in the database.

Intergovernmental Panel on Climate Change

http://www.ipcc.ch

The Intergovernmental Panel on Climate Change (IPCC) was established in 1988 by the World Meteorological Organization (WMO) and the United Nations Environment Programme (UNEP) to assess scientific, technical and socioeconomic information relevant for the understanding of climate change. Provides a variety of online publications.

NASA's Visible Earth

http://visibleearth.nasa.gov

This is a directory of images, visualizations, and animations of Earth. Browse by topic or search by keyword (such as ozone, global warming, greenhouse) to view images and descriptions.

Advocacy Sites

—Promote View That Impact of Greenhouse Gases
Not Known or Not Harmful

Center for the Study of Carbon Dioxide and Global Change

http://www.co2science.org/center.htm

CO2 and Climate

http://www.greeningearthsociety.org

Global Climate Coalition

http://www.globalclimate.org

Global Warming: Cooler Heads Coalition

http://www.globalwarming.org

—*Promote Aggressive Action to Prevent Global Warming*

Climate Action Network
http://www.climatenetwork.org

Greenpeace
http://www.greenpeace.org

World Resources Institute
http://www.wri.org

WWF—The Conservation Organization
http://www.panda.org

Gun Control

Summary

At its most basic level, the argument of gun control centers on whether or not individuals have unrestricted rights to carry and own guns. Generally, gun debates have flared up in the political arena after assassination attempts or high-profile school shootings. In 2000, there were 28,663 gun-related deaths in the United States, which averages about eighty per day. Firearm deaths represent one in five injury deaths in our nation. Our gun mortality rate is eight times higher than in other high-income countries. These statistics have caused some scholars to investigate gun ownership in light of public health. Certainly it is an important public policy issue.

The Second Amendment looms large in this contentious public debate. The text of the Amendment reads: "A well-regulated Militia being necessary to the security of a free State, the right of the people to keep and bear Arms shall not be infringed."

Although guns are a hot button political and cultural issue, the Supreme Court has not shown much interest in revisiting the precedent set by the decision in *United States v. Miller,* a case from the middle of the twentieth century, which upheld the right of the federal government to restrict access to certain types of firearms. No federal court has yet struck down a gun control law since the Miller ruling upheld the New Deal legislation, which was the first modern comprehensive federal effort to enact a gun control law.

Those opposed to gun control, who view the Second Amendment as a fundamental individual right, believe citizens have an inherent and unquestioned right to own guns. Most in this camp will acknowledge that there are a few minimal types of regulations permissible to promote public safety and prevent criminals from using firearms. Gun rights activists view gun ownership as a form of personal protection, a right to engage in lawful hunting and sport, or a means of

Keywords
Automatic/semiautomatic weapons
Background checks
Collective right
Concealed weapons
Firearms
Gun licenses
Gun locks
Gun rights
Gun safety
Gun shows
Handguns
Individual right
Right to bear arms
"Safe" guns/smart guns
Second Amendment
United States v. Miller
Waiting period

Related Topics
Civil liberties
School violence

ensuring the government never gains absolute control over its citizenry through means of weapons.

Those who favor gun control argue that this amendment guarantees only a "collective right" of the states to maintain militias, and that the founding fathers never envisioned the levels of gun violence in our society. In contrast to gun rights enthusiasts, gun control activists see individual gun ownership as a privilege, not a right, and that generally guns are a threat to the safety and well-being of citizens. Thus, gun control arguments center on keeping the public safe. Those who favor gun control can vary in their desire for restrictions ranging from complete bans on handguns to requirements for background checks for criminal records on any individual wishing to buy a gun.

There are a number of controversial policy questions in the gun debate. One controversy centers around the right to carry concealed weapons. Do more guns mean less crime or more gun violence? Another debate deals with the issue of safe storage, a concern motivated by accidental deaths of children. There are also raging debates about how to prevent guns from entering the black market and the sale of guns at unregulated gun shows.

Polling data have consistently demonstrated that most Americans believe in a right to own a firearm and the need for more rigorous laws to prevent misuse of firearms. It is also important to recognize that attitudes toward guns vary by region. For instance, owning a gun in New York City is a very different thing than owning one in rural Montana. These differences have made it difficult to formulate a coherent national policy to deal with guns.

Web Sites

Reference Sites

Center for Gun Policy and Research

http://www.jhsph.edu/gunpolicy/

This research center studies gun control as a public health issue. The site includes many research reports available on the public health effects of guns, including national public opinion surveys on gun control. Also included are program reports on separating kids from guns.

Gun Control—Laws and Issues

http://usgovinfo.about.com/cs/guncontrol/

This part of the About.com network provides a comprehensive directory for all issues related to gun control.

Gun Control: National Issues.com

http://www.nationalissues.com/gun_control/

Provides an overview article, pros and cons of the debate, presidential policy, facts and figures, and links to additional resources.

Gun Control vs. Gun Rights

http://www.opensecrets.org/news/guns/

Provides an overview of the controversy, identifies the special interests involved, and tracks the campaign spending done by these special interests.

Second Amendment Research Center

http://www.secondamendmentcenter.org

This is a "comprehensive website, gathering scholarship from all sides of the Second Amendment debate and offering visitors a guided introduction to the controversy. The site will also feature difficult-to-obtain historical materials that shed light on the contemporary arguments." (Description based on press release; site will be available by March 30, 2004.)

News Sites

FirearmNews.com

http://www.firearmnews.com

News from a pro gun rights perspective.

Gun Violence Home Page

http://www.jointogether.org/gv/

News from a gun control advocacy perspective.

Yahoo! News: Full Coverage: Gun Control Debate

http://fullcoverage.yahoo.com/fc/

Search Full Coverage for the term "guns". Select the Full Coverage Category for "Gun Control Debate" to view news stories, editorials, feature articles, audio/video resources, Web sites, and links to other specialized news sources on this topic.

Law/Legislation

Federal Gun Control Legislation Timeline

http://www.infoplease.com/spot/guntime1.html

Outlines major legislation in America on a timeline and gives the reasons the laws were enacted. Covers 1791–1984.

Gun Laws, Gun Control & Gun Rights (JURIST)

http://jurist.law.pitt.edu/gunlaw.htm

This is a comprehensive site for finding legislation relating to guns. Also included is news, presidential positions, general materials on the Second Amendment, books, articles, statistics, reports, and more, providing a one-stop place for finding relevant links to gun control information. There is little summary narrative available, but there are lots of links.

Data Sites

Amfire.com

http://www.amfire.com

Produced by members of the American firearms industry. Provides information for buying guns as well as lists of distributors, statistics regarding firearms, and news.

ATF Online: Firearms

http://www.atf.treas.gov/firearms

This branch of the U.S. Department of Treasury is charged with enforcing federal laws relating to firearms. Contains memos from this department, laws, updates, and a variety of reports relating to firearms laws.

Uniform Crime Reports

http://www.fbi.gov/ucr/ucr.htm

Statistical data on crime gathered and issued by the FBI, including the role of guns in these crimes.

Advocacy Sites

—For Gun Control

Brady Center to Prevent Gun Violence

http://www.bradycenter.org

Gun Control Truth

http://www.secondamendmentfacts.com

Gun Free Kids

http://gunfreekids.policy.net

Handgun Epidemic Lowering Plan (HELP) Network

http://www.helpnetwork.org

—For Gun Rights

Americans for Gun Safety (AGS)

http://ww2.americansforgunsafety.com

Armed Females of America

http://www.armedfemalesofamerica.com

Gun Owners of America

http://www.gunowners.org

National Rifle Association (NRA)

http://www.nra.org

Hate Groups and Crimes

Summary

According to the Federal Bureau of Investigation (FBI), a hate crime (also called a bias crime) is a criminal offense committed against a person or property that is motivated in whole or in part by the offender's bias against a race, religion, disability, sexual orientation, or ethnicity/national origin. Hate crimes are directed against members of a specific group because of their membership in that particular group. Hate speech, however, is not criminal and is protected under the First Amendment.

A report issued by the American Psychological Association (APA) states, "Hate crimes are message crimes. They are different from other crimes in that the offender is sending a message to members of a certain group that they are unwelcome." Most of those committing hate crimes act alone, in pairs, or as members of a small group. Many perpetrators are under the age of twenty. One common trait is membership in a hate organization, such as neo-Nazi or Ku Klux Klan groups.

Keywords
Anti-Semitism
Bigotry
Christian identity movement
Crimes against minorities
Domestic terrorism
Homophobia
Intolerance
Ku Klux Klan
Matthew Shepard
National Church Arson Task Force
Neo-Nazi groups
Skinheads
White power

Related Topics
Censorship
Civil liberties
Gay rights
Race relations

Hate crimes take many different forms: a swastika or hateful words painted on a wall, a burning cross, threatening telephone messages, physical assaults, and in some cases, murder. The Hate Crimes Statistics Act of 1990 includes these offenses in the definition of a hate crime: murder; non-negligent manslaughter; forcible rape; aggravated assault; simple assault; intimidation; arson; and destruction, damage, or vandalism of property. According to FBI annual hate crime statistics, the most frequently targeted groups are African Americans, Jewish Americans, gay men and lesbians, and Asian Americans.

"Violence against black Americans has a long and tragic history in the United States, starting with slavery and continuing with lynchings, firebombings, cross burnings, and assassinations. From 1882 to 1968, a reported 4,743 people were lynched; of those, the vast majority were black" (*Hate Crimes: A Reference Handbook*).

FBI statistics indicate that approximately 85 percent of attacks against individuals or institutions that occur because of their religion were directed against Jewish Americans. This trend may be changing since the September 11, 2001, terrorist attack on the United States. In 2001, anti-Islamic religious bias incidents grew by 1,600 percent over the previous year.

Before passage of the Hate Crime Statistics Act in 1990, official U.S. government data on antigay violence was not collected. Current statistics vary, with FBI data showing fewer incidents than those reported by the National Gay and Lesbian Task Force (NGLTF), which has been collecting its own data since 1985. Gay rights organizations have consistently claimed that antihomosexual hate crimes are vastly underreported.

Current federal law allows prosecution of a hate crime only if the crime was motivated by race, religion, national origin, or color. It does not include sexual orientation, gender, or disability status. In addition, the assailant must intend to prevent the victim from exercising a federally protected right. The status of hate crime laws in the states is varied. Twenty-one states include mental and physical disability in their lists. Twenty-four states include sexual orientation. Seven states have no hate crime law.

Expansion of the law to cover these new groups has been controversial. Those who support expanding current law believe that protecting a group under hate crimes legislation will make the public aware that the group is vulnerable and is in need of protection. They believe that civil rights legislation had a chilling effect on racial bigotry in the United States and hope that expanding hate crimes laws will have a similar effect on homophobia.

Those who oppose special legislation argue that hate crimes legislation is redundant, since these offenses are already punishable under the law. Some in this group, who believe that homosexuality is a choice rather than biologically predetermined, also argue that hate crime legislation should only apply to personal characteristics that are beyond the individual's control, such as gender, race, national origin, color, and disability.

Web Sites

Reference Sites

Hate Crimes Today: An Age-Old Foe in Modern Dress

http://www.apa.org/pubinfo/hate/

This site, from the American Psychological Association (APA), provides a research-based overview of hate crimes and examines the effects on victims and the various reasons why people commit hate crimes. It also considers the role of the economy in hate crimes and proposes some possible solutions for this problem. Includes a bibliography.

The Hate Directory

http://www.hatedirectory.com

This very comprehensive document is available in PDF format, with clickable links to sites listed in the directory. Includes almost 100 pages of hate group listings, organized by type: Web sites, FTP sites, mailing lists, discussion groups, chat, racist Web rings, racist Internet games, Web hosting services used by these groups, and organizations combatting hate on the Internet. Both currently active and inactive sites are listed.

News Sites

Civilrights.org—Issues

http://www.civilrights.org/issues/

Provides current news and other resources (reports, speeches, testimony at congressional hearings, court decisions) on a variety of political, legal, economic, and social justice topics, including hate crimes, poverty, welfare reform, housing, immigration, labor, and employment.

Washingtonpost.com: Hate Crimes

http://www.washingtonpost.com/wp-dyn/nation/specials/socialpolicy/hatecrimes/

Special report links to current and archived stories on this topic as well as backgrounders on famous hate crime cases.

Yahoo! News: Full Coverage: Hate Crimes

http://fullcoverage.yahoo.com/fc/

Search Full Coverage for the term "hate crime". Select the Full Coverage Category for "US: Hate Crimes" to view news stories, editorials, feature articles, audio/video resources, Web sites, and links to other specialized news sources on this topic.

Law/Legislation

Hate Crime Legislation

http://www.religioustolerance.org/hom_hat1.htm

Site from Ontario Consultants on Religious Tolerance presents a detailed summary of both points of view on extending hate crime laws to cover attacks on gays and lesbians; also provides a summary of legislative activity in the United States and Canada.

Hate Crimes Laws

http://www.adl.org/99hatecrime/intro.asp

Provides detailed analysis from the Anti-Defamation League, with recommendations. Click the link for State Hate Crime Laws to view a U.S. map and a detailed chart comparing the status of various hate crime statutory provisions in the states.

Lambda Legal: State by State

http://www.lambdalegal.org

Select State by State from the site's main menu, then click on any state on the U.S. map to learn about specific state and municipal laws related to gay rights issues such as discrimination, hate crimes, and marriage/domestic partnership.

National Gay and Lesbian Task Force

http://www.ngltf.org/library

The Library includes a variety of Issue Maps that summarize the current status of gay rights concerns, such as adoption, domestic violence laws, civil rights, hate crimes, and marriage.

NCJRS: Hate Crime Resources—Legislation

http://www.ncjrs.org/hate_crimes/legislation.html

Summarizes the current federal legislation governing hate crimes.

Data Sites

Amnesty International: Library: Sexual Orientation

http://web.amnesty.org/library/eng-347/index

Provides an international perspective on hate crimes against gays and lesbians, with news and reports of violence based on sexual orientation from many countries.

Anti-Violence Project

http://www.avp.org/publications/reports/reports.htm

Reports on anti-lesbian, gay, bisexual, and transgender violence collected by member organizations of the National Coalition of Anti-Violence Programs. Summarizes and presents data on national trends along with some local reports from cities and states.

FBI: Uniform Crime Reports

http://www.fbi.gov/ucr/ucr.htm

This is a key source for data on hate crimes collected by federal and state law enforcement agencies.

Frontline: Assault on Gay America

http://www.pbs.org/wgbh/pages/frontline/shows/assault/

This companion site to the television show provides background on Billy Jack Gaither, a gay man who was beaten to death in Alabama in 1999. Includes interviews with his family and his killers, discussion of the history of homophobia, views of religious leaders, and an overview of the "gay gene" debate.

Hate Crimes Research Network

http://www.hatecrime.net

This site from the Department of Sociology of Portland State University in Oregon is designed to link academic research done by sociologists, criminologists, psychologists, and other academics on the topic of bias motivated crime. Includes texts, bibliographies, and links to other research sites. The goal is to create a common pool of research and data to understand the phenomenon of hate crimes.

Hate on Display: A Visual Database of Extremist Symbols, Logos and Tattoos

http://www.adl.org/hate_symbols/default.asp

This database provides an overview of many symbols frequently used by neo-Nazis, the Ku Klux Klan, racist skinheads, racist prison gangs and other hate or extremist groups or movements.

Safe Schools Coalition

http://www.safeschoolscoalition.org

Click on Resources by Topic for links to reports on hate crimes, bullying, harassment, and other problems experienced by gay and lesbian youth.

Sexual Orientation: Science, Education, and Policy

http://psychology.ucdavis.edu/rainbow/

"Provides factual information to promote the use of scientific knowledge for education and enlightened public policy related to sexual orientation and HIV/AIDS." Sections include hate crimes, AIDS, the military, and sexual prejudice. Includes summaries of research studies and fact sheets that "provide an overview of social science theory and empirical research concerning sexual orientation."

Advocacy Sites

—*Promote Hate*

David Duke

http://www.duke.org

National Association for the Advancement of White People

http://www.naawp.org

StormFront

http://www.stormfront.org

—*Promote Tolerance*

Anti-Defamation League (ADL)

http://www.adl.org

Partners Against Hate

http://www.partnersagainsthate.org

Simon Wiesenthal Center

http://www.wiesenthal.com

Southern Poverty Law Center

http://www.splcenter.org

Health Policy

Summary

During the twentieth century, the United Nations recognized access to healthcare as a basic human right. As a share of its economy, the United States spends more money on healthcare than any other nation in the world, yet the healthcare needs of many Americans are not being fully met. Access to quality healthcare depends in large part on the availability of insurance coverage. Many factors affect the availability of health insurance, including employment status, income, and age.

The National Center for Health Statistics reported that in 2000, 40.5 million Americans (16.8 percent of the population) under age sixty-five lacked health insurance; 12.4 percent of children under eighteen had no coverage. The major source of coverage for those under sixty-five is employer-sponsored group health insurance. Thirty-nine million people were enrolled in the Medicare program for senior citizens. Another publicly funded program, Medicaid, provides coverage for low-income adults and children.

Keywords
Healthcare financing
Healthcare rationing
Health insurance
HMOs
Managed care
Medicaid
Medical liability reform
Medical privacy
Medicare
Patient bill of rights
Prescription drug coverage
Privatization
State Children's Health Insurance Program (SCHIP)
Universal health insurance coverage

Related Topics
Welfare reform

The cost of providing health insurance has been steadily rising. Beginning in the late 1980s, employers began to enroll their employees in managed care programs (also known as health maintenance organizations or HMOs). Managed care programs keep a tighter control on costs and utilization of services and emphasize the importance of preventive care. Before doctors can perform some procedures, they must first get approval from the patient's healthcare system for the expenses to be covered. Some HMOs have been accused of maximizing their profits at the expense of quality patient care.

Federal legislation has helped those who change jobs to keep their insurance coverage in place. In 1996, President Clinton signed the Health Insurance Portability and Accountability Act, which stipulated that workers who had previous insurance coverage were immediately eligible for coverage of preexisting health conditions. This law also guaranteed that employees could keep existing coverage after they left their jobs.

The Medicare program is divided into two parts. Part A, also known as Hospital Insurance (HI), is financed by a payroll tax and covers care provided in hospitals, nursing facilities, and hospices, and some home health services. Part B, also known as Supplementary Medical Insurance (SMI), is financed through a combination of monthly premiums and general tax revenues. It provides optional additional coverage for doctor's visits and other outpatient services.

The coverage provided by Medicare is not comprehensive. It does not currently cover prescription drugs, long-term nursing care, or basic vision, dental, and hearing-related care. Medicare recipients must purchase supplemental policies from insurance companies to cover these expenses. In late 2003, Congress passed, and President George W. Bush signed, legislation that amends the Medicare program to add some prescription drug coverage for senior citizens, beginning in 2006.

Another federal program, Medicaid, provides health insurance for low-income families with children and people with disabilities, long-term (nursing home) care for senior citizens and disabled individuals, and supplemental coverage for low-income Medicare beneficiaries for services not covered by Medicare. Medicaid is an entitlement program jointly financed by the states and the federal government. Federal funding for Medicaid comes from general revenues.

The Medicaid benefit package is defined by each state based on broad federal guidelines. There is much variation among state Medicaid programs regarding not only which services are covered but also the amount of care provided. Since its inception in 1965, Medicaid enrollment and expenditures have grown substantially State fiscal crises have put more strain on the Medicaid program as states look for ways to reduce these costs.

Although each type of health insurance program discussed here has its own issues and constituencies, most concerns relate to methods of managing programs and controlling costs. The factions are organized into those who favor more federal and state government control over provision of health services and those who want more private sector involvement in management of these programs.

Some analysts believe that the only way to control rapidly increasing costs is through rationing healthcare, by putting limits on the amount and kind of care people can receive. Those who argue against rationing fear that the elderly, poor, and chronically ill, those who are entirely dependent on federal programs, would suffer tremendously from cutbacks in care. They believe that improving the efficiency of the U.S. healthcare system would save enough money to make healthcare available to all.

Web Sites

Reference Sites

Centers for Medicare and Medicaid Services

http://cms.hhs.gov

Provides overviews of the federal health insurance programs, related laws and regulations, state waivers and demonstration programs, forms, publications and manuals, and a glossary of terms.

Duke Health Policy CyberExchange

http://www.hpolicy.duke.edu/cyberexchange/

Excellent guide to health policy sites, with links organized into categories. Covers key health policy issue areas such as public health, health expenditures, health coverage, health delivery systems, regulation, as well as health care system profiles and comparisons. Links to a wide variety of other health information sources (agencies, organizations, industry groups).

HealthFinder—Your Guide to Reliable Health Information

http://www.healthfinder.gov

This site is a service of the U.S. Department of Health and Human Services together with other federal agencies. It links to carefully selected information and Web sites from over 1,700 health-related organizations. Search for a topic, or browse by category. Provides information on diseases and conditions, doctors, dentists, public clinics, hospitals, long-term care, nursing homes, health insurance, prescriptions, health fraud, Medicare, Medicaid, and medical privacy.

MEDLINEplus: Health Insurance

http://www.nlm.nih.gov/medlineplus/healthinsurance.html

This research guide from the National Library of Medicine organizes sites into the following categories: general overviews, research, specific conditions/aspects, dictionaries, directories, law and policy, organizations, and statistics. Also provides a link to retrieve current journal articles on the topic from the MEDLINE database.

News Sites

Kaiser Network.org

http://www.kaisernetwork.org

See the Daily Reports for news summaries on health policy and reproductive health issues. The Kaiser Foundation provides brief abstracts of stories appearing in a variety of news sources on abortion, pregnancy, childbirth, family planning, and politics/policy related to these topics. These daily reports are also archived; the archive can be searched by keyword and date.

Stateline.org

http://www.stateline.org/index.do

Managed by the Pew Center on the States, the site was "founded in order to help journalists, policy makers and engaged citizens become better informed about innovative public policies." This is an excellent resource for news on issues of importance to states, such as welfare and social policy, land use and growth, and environment and energy. Browse by topic or by state; search for keywords.

Yahoo! News: Full Coverage: Health Care

http://fullcoverage.yahoo.com/fc/

Search Full Coverage for the term "health care." Select the Full Coverage Category for "US: Health Care" to view news stories, editorials, feature articles, audio/video resources, Web sites, and links to other specialized news sources on this topic.

Law/Legislation

Health Law

http://www.megalaw.com/top/health.php

This site provides links to state statutes on health, federal sites, journals, advocacy organizations, professional and trade groups, research, and policy sites.

Health Privacy

http://www.healthprivacy.org

The Health Privacy Project site offers an overview of health consumer privacy rights, summaries of state health privacy statutes, federal regulations and proposed legislation on health privacy, articles, reports, and links to other sites on this topic.

Data Sites

Agency for Health Care Research and Quality (AHRQ)

http://www.ahcpr.gov

AHRQ provides evidence-based information on healthcare outcomes, quality, cost, use, and access. Site provides data sources, survey information, and research findings organized by topic, such as managed care, mental health, rural health, etc.

Dartmouth Atlas of Health Care

http://www.dartmouthatlas.org

The Atlas project from Dartmouth University Medical School focuses on the accurate description of how medical resources are distributed and used in the United States. The Atlas documents serious defects in the quality of care now provided in the fee-for-service Medicare system, variations in healthcare, and end-of-life care. Provides a series of national, state, and topical reports.

Georgetown University: Health Policy Institute

http://ihcrp.georgetown.edu

Provides research papers on issues relating to healthcare financing, the uninsured, federal health insurance reforms, quality of care and outcomes research, mental health services research, and the impact of changes in the healthcare market on providers and patients.

National Academy for State Health Policy

http://www.nashp.org

This nonprofit organization conducts policy analyses and produces information sources on access for the uninsured, managed care, chronic and long-term care, Medicaid, children's health, and cost containment.

National Center for Health Statistics: FASTATS

http://www.cdc.gov/nchs/fastats/

Choose links to health expenditures or health insurance coverage to view data summaries and links to more comprehensive statistical data sources.

RAND Health

http://rand.org/health/

Provides research summaries, publications, and survey data related to current health policy concerns, such as healthcare organization, economics and finance, quality of care, international health, public health, needs of vulnerable populations, etc. Browse full text publications by topic or search the abstracts to locate useful ones.

Urban Institute: Assessing the New Federalism

http://newfederalism.urban.org

This nonpartisan research organization project aims to analyze the devolution of responsibility for social programs from the federal government to the states. Researchers monitor program changes and fiscal developments related to healthcare, welfare, and childcare. Key components of the project include a household survey, studies of policies in thirteen states, and a welfare rules data-base with information on all states and the District of Columbia.

Advocacy Sites

—*Support Expanding Private Role in Healthcare Coverage*

American Association of Health Plans

http://www.aahp.org

Americans for Free Choice in Medicine

http://www.afcm.org

Council for Affordable Health Insurance

http://cahionline.org/cahi_index.shtml

Health Insurance Association of America

http://www.hiaa.org

—*Support Expanding Government Role in Healthcare Coverage*

Families USA

http://www.familiesusa.org

National Coalition on Health Care

http://www.nchc.org

Our Future.org: Health Care

http://www.ourfuture.org/issues_and_campaigns/healthcare/

Physicians for a National Health Program

http://www.pnhp.org

Homeland Defense

Summary

On January 24, 2003, the U.S. Department of Homeland Security came into existence. The formation of this new department was the most significant reorganization of the federal government since 1947 when the military branches were moved into one Department of Defense. This reorganization was in direct response to the terrorist acts of September 11, 2001, in the belief that more and worse such attacks were likely. In the words of President George W. Bush at the signing of the bill, this new department "will analyze threats, will guard our borders and airports, protect our critical infrastructure, and coordinate the response of our nation for future emergencies."

The Department has five major directorates:

Keywords
Anthrax
Airport security
Arab Americans
Border patrol
Department of Homeland Security
High rise buildings
Homeland Security Act of 2002
Nuclear power plants
Police and fire departments
Port and maritime security
Sky marshals
Smallpox vaccine
Threat advisory levels
Travel security
U.S. Patriot Act

Related Topics
Civil liberties
Immigration
National defense
Terrorism

- Border and Transportation Security

- Emergency Preparedness and Response

- Science and Technology

- Information Analysis and Infrastructure Protection

- Management

Additional agencies that report to the Secretary of Homeland Security are the U.S. Coast Guard, U.S. Secret Service, Bureau of Citizenship and Immigration Services, Office of State and Local Government Coordination, Office of Private Sector Liaison, and Office of Inspector General.

Although most people in the United States were united behind the abstract notion of protecting our borders during the initial aftermath of the September 11 attacks, the discussion of creating a Department of Homeland Security was not without controversy. There was concern about trying to merge too many disparate functions into one department. It was feared that too large a department would exacerbate the problems of bloating and bureaucratic inefficiencies that it was in fact attempting to counteract. There was also concern that the creation of this new department would cause everyone to necessarily focus on issues of reorganization rather than on immediate issues of finding out and preventing further terrorist acts. There was disagreement about exactly how many federal employees would be affected, and there were predictions of great turf battles and labor disputes. Conservatives who loathed big government saw a mammoth.

Homeland defense differs from national defense in the sense that the concern is for protecting life and property on our own shores and does not extend to national interests globally. However, the two issues cannot be divorced from each other. A few months into the existence of the new department, controversy arose over whether the administration was addressing the two concerns in proper balance. Some would argue that protection of our own shores should happen more swiftly and with more funding than aggressive actions against nations whose role in terrorism is unclear. The burden of additional security measures has tended to fall on cities at a time of economic recession. Fire and police departments are seen as the first line of defense and response in the wake of a terrorist act, yet many of these municipal departments are facing budget cuts. In the meantime, boosting of the military budget has also happened in conjunction with federal tax cuts.

Some suggestions for improving homeland security from opponents of the current administration have included increased funding, creation of a domestic intelligence agency separate from the FBI, increasing the funding for the Americorps volunteer program and training these individuals to protect communities in the wake of a terrorist attack, and the creation of a community defense service that would rely heavily on community volunteers to act in a time of crisis.

Apart from organizational and funding issues are concerns of policy and actions enacted by the government. For instance, there is much controversy regarding the U.S. Patriot Act, which gives sweeping new powers to both domestic law enforcement and international intelligence agencies in an effort to improve our ability to find terrorists on our soil. Critics argue that it also greatly limits the civil liberties of Americans and destroys the exact rights America seeks to retain.

There are a variety of controversies regarding air safety. The United States is instituting a Sky Marshal program that many deem unnecessarily expensive. Another program has included arming pilots, which critics claim means requiring pilots to do something they are not trained for, may not be good at, and that might provide new sets of flying dangers. Other concerns revolve around changes in immigration policy and international student visas. There are concerns that the more tightly we are protected, the more our civil liberties of privacy, free expression, and freedom to move about are hindered. There are concerns about racial profiling against Arab Americans in efforts to identify terrorists. There have also been criticisms of the threat advisories that the Department of Homeland Security issues. Some feel they are alarmist, give no direction to citizens on how to act, add financial burdens on local governments to take unnecessary action, and are changed without any information as to why the change has happened.

Web Sites

Reference Sites

Brooking Institute Project on Homeland Security

http://www.brookings.edu/dybdocroot/fp/projects/homeland/homeland.htm

Examines the budget, organization, economics, and key events of the homeland security reorganization plan.

CNN.com—A Massive Federal Makeover

http://www.cnn.com/2002/US/11/20/facts.homeland/

This is a factsheet on issues surrounding the creation of the Department of Homeland Security and has links to updates on the issue and key questions on the controversy.

News Sites

Homeland Security Actions—White House

http://www.whitehouse.gov/homeland/

Provides the latest news related to the Department of Homeland Security and other actions related to homeland security taken by the White House.

Yahoo! News: Full Coverage: Terrorism

http://fullcoverage.yahoo.com/fc/

Search Full Coverage for the term "terrorism". Select the Full Coverage Category for "US: Terrorism" to view news stories, editorials, feature articles, audio/video resources, Web sites, and links to other specialized news sources on this topic. All articles about homeland security are listed on the terrorism page.

Law/Legislation

U.S. Anti-Terrorism Laws (JURIST)

http://jurist.law.pitt.edu/terrorism/terrorism3.htm

Covers recent and pending legislation; relevant links to the U.S. Code; related Executive orders, decisions, and declarations; regulations; and state laws that pertain to terrorism and security issues.

Data Sites

CFR: Homeland Security

http://www.cfr.org/reg_issues.php?id=4∥1

Provides access to articles (including from the journal *Foreign Affairs*), opinions, transcripts, and related links.

Chemical and Biological Information Analysis Center

http://www.cbiac.apgea.army.mil

Provides lots of information regarding defense against chemical or biological weapons that could be of use to communities threatened by a terrorist attack.

Homeland Security: Center for Defense Initiatives

http://www.cdi.org/program/issue/index.cfm?ProgramID=39&issueid=59

Provides policy reports on various aspects of homeland security, including the Department of Homeland Security, the Sky Marshal program, port and maritime security, various threats, and various weapons issues.

Homeland Security: The CATO Institute

http://www.cato.org/defense-studies/homeland-security.html

Includes a variety of policy papers from this organization as well as opinion pieces by researchers that have appeared in other publications.

Institute for Homeland Security

http://www.homelandsecurity.org

Provides a variety of data regarding homeland security, including full text access to the *Journal of Homeland Security*. The virtual library link provides portal access to all sorts of information, including statistics, policy, and threats.

U.S. Department of Homeland Security

http://www.dhs.gov

This is the official Web site of the federal department. While still not well populated, the site provides up-to-date news relating to the five directorates of the office.

Advocacy Sites

—*Preparedness Sites*

American Red Cross: Homeland Security Advisory System

http://www.redcross.org/services/disaster/beprepared/hsas.html

Homeland Defense

http://hld.sbccom.army.mil

Ready.gov

http://www.ready.gov

Survive a Nuclear Attack

http://www.surviveanuclearattack.com

—*Critical of Homeland Security Efforts*

Department of Homeland Security (parody site)

http://www.depthomelandsecurity.com

Office of Homeland Security (parody site)

http://securethehomeland.com

Repeal the Patriot Act Now!

http://www.repealnow.com

Homelessness

Summary

Throughout history, homeless people have lived among us. In many societies, homeless people were viewed as lazy and deserving of their fate. Some people thought that society should intervene to reduce homelessness. They established poorhouses, where the homeless were sent and made to do difficult, unpleasant work, to reform their lazy habits and convince them to get regular jobs. Poorhouses failed to reduce homelessness and

Keywords
Affordable housing
Gentrification
Homeless shelters
Housing choice voucher program
Housing trust funds
Low-income housing
Panhandling laws
Section 8 housing

Related Topics
Fair wages
Welfare reform

went out of use by the early 1900s. By this time, in the United States many factory workers received little pay for long hours of work. Homelessness in large cities became more common.

Attitudes toward the homeless began slowly to change. Social scientists studied homeless people and discovered that most homeless people wanted to work and earn enough money to pay for housing and other things. Attitudes changed even more during the Great Depression. As millions lost their jobs and homes, it was easy to understand how good people could end up homeless. People felt that the government should help the homeless and poor.

During the presidency of Franklin D. Roosevelt, many laws intended to reduce homelessness and poverty were enacted. The Social Security Act of 1935 established programs to provide government funds directly to the elderly and to children of single mothers, to help alleviate poverty and homelessness. The United States Housing Act of 1937 established federal government programs to develop housing projects (referred to as Section 8 projects) and to help low-income people get home loans. Later in the century, the McKinney Homeless Assistance Act of 1987 helped to develop the homeless service system in the United States.

Social researchers today believe that homelessness is primarily a result of poverty and lack of affordable housing, not character defects of the individuals who become homeless. But gaining an accurate count of the U.S. homeless population is difficult. Since homeless people are unable to respond to phone or mail surveys, researchers have had to develop new methods for collecting data. The difficulty of accurately counting the homeless also means that the exact size of the homeless population is controversial.

In 1990, the U.S. census counted homeless persons in emergency shelters, street locations, youth shelters, and shelters for abused women. Homeless advocacy groups contended that the methods were inadequate and the results too low. According to a 1996 Urban Institute research study, on any given day at least 800,000 people are homeless in the United States, including about 200,000 children in homeless families. A twenty-five-city survey released by the U.S. Conference of Mayors in 2002 indicates that approximately 44 percent of homeless people are working and 40 percent are families with children. This survey found that requests for emergency food assistance increased an average of 19 percent over the previous year. Requests for emergency shelter assistance grew an average of 19 percent in the eighteen cities that reported an increase, the steepest rise in a decade.

Mental disabilities or job loss may increase vulnerability to homelessness, but they cannot explain the high number of people who fall into homelessness every year. Urban Institute research attributes the rise in homelessness to changing housing markets and local zoning restrictions that exclude low-income housing, dramatic reductions in federally supported housing over the past twenty years, dwindling employment opportunities for people with a high school education or less, and the removal of institutional supports for people with severe mental illness. Housing market trends indicate that the situation is getting worse. Current housing costs, coupled with low-wage jobs and economic contraction, could push even the working poor out of their homes.

Many factors contribute to the lack of affordable housing, including abandonment of decaying housing units and conversion, when low-income or government-subsidized units are converted to other purposes, such as condominiums, offices, retail stores, or warehouses. Research indicates that many lost units are unavailable to low-income renters because owners have "opted-out" of their government contracts to cash in on a more lucrative, high-cost rental market. This process is called gentrification.

As the numbers of homeless increase, many U.S. cities are applying legal sanctions to homeless people who live on the streets to prevent panhandling in business districts and around tourist areas, camping in parks, sleeping in doorways or on sidewalks, or simple loitering. These laws demonstrate that public tolerance for homeless people is waning. City officials also contend that the new ordinances force homeless individuals to seek the mental health and substance abuse treatment services that they often need.

Advocates for the homeless argue that such laws rob homeless people of their civil rights and their dignity. Critics also argue that by forcing police to round up homeless people, these city ordinances waste resources. The government should use its economic resources to address the causes of homelessness, such as low wages and lack of affordable housing. Advocates believe that effective means to combat the housing and homelessness problems include

- housing trust funds, rental assistance programs, and access to funds for paying back rent and security deposits;
- programs that encourage developers to build or renovate affordable properties; and
- programs to help families develop financial management skills.

Web Sites

Reference Sites

HOMELESS: Web Links on Homelessness

http://csf.colorado.edu/homeless/

Provides archives of the International HOMELESS discussion list and organized links to a wide variety of sites on topics such as housing, homeless shelters, health and medical services, children, memories of homelessness, and regional resources.

Homelessness

http://www.financeprojectinfo.org/WIN/homeless.asp

This organized directory of links includes announcements, organizations, federal and multistate programs, state and local programs, service and technical assistance providers, and general publications.

National Resource Center on Homelessness and Mental Illness

http://www.nrchmi.com

The Center provides fact sheets; reports; annotated bibliographies; a referral list of organizations that provide services to the homeless; and links to other sites on homelessness, mental health, and housing.

News Sites

NPR: Housing First

http://www.npr.org/news/specials/housingfirst/

The year-long special reporting project, begun in 2002, explores the housing dilemmas of Americans with special needs. Exclusive Web elements of the Housing First coverage include in-depth background reports on key interest groups, photos, videos, maps, graphics and artwork, Web-only audio and interviews, and a virtual library of resources and links on related topics.

Yahoo! News: Full Coverage: Homelessness

http://fullcoverage.yahoo.com/fc/

Search Full Coverage for the term "homelessness". Select the Full Coverage Category for "US: Homelessness" to view news stories, editorials, feature articles, audio/video resources, Web sites, and links to other specialized news sources on this topic.

Law/Legislation

McKinney Act

http://www.nationalhomeless.org/mckinneyfacts.html

This fact sheet provides a brief history of the McKinney Act, describes its content and evolution, and summarizes recent trends in McKinney Act legislation and funding.

National Housing Law Project

http://www.nhlp.org

This site provides "information packets" on public housing, Section 8 vouchers, homeownership, and HUD rental housing. Tracks legislation, regulations, and court decisions of interest.

Data Sites

Homelessness Programs and the People They Serve

http://www.urban.org/url.cfm?ID=310291

This Urban Institute report presents findings from a national survey of homeless assistance providers and clients, conducted in 1996 and published in 1999, and is considered a landmark study on this topic. Provides a detailed overview of characteristics of homeless clients, makes comparisons to those who were formerly homeless, and describes assistance programs.

Housing and Community Development KnowledgePlex

http://www.knowledgeplex.org

Thissite funded by the Fannie Mae Foundation provides a Knowledge Library, with articles and reports on a variety of topics, including homelessness and affordable housing. Includes news stories on affordable housing and housing policy from Lexis/Nexis.

HUD USER Publications

http://www.huduser.org/publications/pdrpubli.html

The U.S. Department of Housing and Urban Development (HUD) provides full text of reports, executive summaries, case studies, and guidebooks; publications are organized into topical groups, such as homelessness, affordable housing, housing policy, and public housing.

Joint Center for Housing Studies

http://www.jchs.harvard.edu

The Joint Center at Harvard University investigates, evaluates, and reports on emerging housing issues and community development policies. The Center's annual report, *State of the Nation's Housing,* identifies and analyzes demographic, economic, and social trends. It also publishes working papers, conference proceedings, and other research notes.

U.S. Census Bureau: Housing Topics

http://www.census.gov/hhes/www/housing.html

Provides data from the American Housing Survey on home ownership, housing affordability, vacancy data, and market absorption of apartments.

Advocacy Sites

—*Promote Affordable Housing*

Corporation for Supportive Housing

http://www.csh.org

National Housing Trust

http://www.nhtinc.org

National Low Income Housing Coalition

http://www.nlihc.org

—*Promote Policies to End Homelessness*

National Alliance to End Homelessness

http://www.naeh.org

National Coalition for Homeless Veterans

http://www.nchv.org

National Coalition for the Homeless

http://www.nationalhomeless.org

Immigration

Summary

The United States has a proud history of being "a nation of immigrants," a "melting pot," an "experiment in cultures." The Statue of Liberty stands in the New York harbor as an icon of pride welcoming the "huddled masses." These are all positive images conjured up by the notion of bringing foreigners into our midst. However, immigration has always had moderate and extreme critics.

There are two kinds of immigration: legal and illegal. Legal immigrants comprise about 700,000 to 900,000 people entering the United States annually. There are approximately 275,000 people who enter the United States illegally each year. In all, it is estimated that there are about 5 million illegal immigrants residing in the United States. Most policymakers and activists recognize the problem that illegal immigration poses, but not all agree on the methods of curtailing it. Increased border patrol is the method most often used.

There is less agreement on the issue of legal immigration. Those who favor and encourage immigration do so for a variety of reasons. Immigrants often have highly technical skills otherwise lacking in our society. Immigrants also fill low-paying jobs and allow companies to keep production costs low. Apart from labor issues, many favor a generous immigration policy because they see that immigrants provide a blend of assimilation along with increased cultural awareness and diversity to our country. Others support immigrants seeking asylum here because of human rights violations suffered in their home countries. Some believe it reflects our ideals and humanitarian concern to allow such people to stay.

Those opposed to open immigration policies are so for a variety of reasons. Labor organizations argue that immigrants take low-skilled jobs, leaving few opportunities for native-born workers. Some states with large immigrant populations argue that the cost of educating and providing medical care for immigrants and their children is too high for them to bear. Environmentalists may

Keywords
Assimilation
Border patrol
Common culture
Deportation
Economic cost of immigration
Illegal immigrants
Illegal Immigration Reform and
 Immigrant Responsibility Act
International students
Legal immigrants
Separatism
Pluralism
Visas

Related Topics
Diversity
Terrorism

argue that the rapid growth of the American population is depleting natural re-sources and cannot be sustained. Curtailing immigration is one way of slowing population growth. Culturally, some would argue that increasingly immigrants are not assimilating or becoming Americanized but instead are retaining their own cultures and fragmenting society. Finally, there are those who argue that immigrants are more likely to fail in our society, leading them to lives of crime or dependence on social programs.

Recent legislation affecting immigrants has included the Welfare Reform bill, which denies a welfare safety net to immigrants, and the Illegal Immigration Reform and Immigrant Responsibility Act, which increases the number of pa-trols on the border and makes the requirements for legal immigrants to bring their families here more stringent. Even more recently, the terrorist attacks of September 11, 2001, have had an effect on immigration policies and attitudes, with increased suspicion and surveillance of immigrants coming from the parts of the world where terrorism is suspected of originating. This has also affected international student visas. Some of the September 11 terrorists learned skills used to carry out their acts of aggression here in the United States. There is con-cern that international students can take technical skills back to their countries and use them to construct weapons systems for use against America.

Web Sites

Reference Sites

Center for Immigration Studies
http://www.cis.org

Provides extensive narrative and links to reports on all issues of U.S. immigra-tion. Read recent news reports or browse through any of the following topics: current numbers, history, legal immigration, illegal immigration, terrorism and national security, wages and poverty, citizenship and assimilation, population and environment, black Americans, government and politics, costs, refugees and asylums, and guest workers.

Peopling North America: Populations Movements and Migration
http://www.ucalgary.ca/applied_history/tutor/migrations/

This is an historical documentary of various groups that came to North America.

Public Agenda Online: Immigration
http://www.publicagenda.org

Select ""Immigration" from the list of Issue Guides. Provides an overview of the issue; frames the debate; and provides news, facts, and other data. An excellent starting point.

News Sites

AILA: The Professional Organization for Immigration Lawyers

http://www.aila.org

As the title says, this is the home of the organization for immigration lawyers. A news reader is provided on the top level page with news of all recent legal issues related to immigration.

Yahoo! News: Full Coverage: US Immigration

http://fullcoverage.yahoo.com/fc/

Search Full Coverage for the term "immigration". Select the Full Coverage Category for "US: Immigration" to view news stories, editorials, feature articles, audio/video resources, Web sites, and links to other specialized news sources on this topic.

Law/Legislation

Federal Publications: Immigration

http://west.thomson.com/fedpub/immigrat.asp

Provides weekly updates to changes in immigration law. Click on the "current update" link for the most recent information.

Immigration Law (JURIST)

http://jurist.law.pitt.edu/sg_immig.htm

Provides access to news, books, legislation, cases, associations, and more on the subject of immigration law.

LLRX: Immigration Law on the Web

http://www.llrx.com/features/immigrat.htm

This is a research guide for finding legal information online.

U.S. Commission on Immigration Reform (now dissolved)

http://www.utexas.edu/lbj/uscir/

Provides historical background to examination and reform of U.S. immigration laws. Includes various reports issued by the organization and testimony given before Congress.

Data Sites

Foreign-Born Population (U.S. Census Bureau)

http://www.census.gov/population/www/socdemo/foreign.html

The Census Bureau offers extensive statistics and analysis of the characteristics of the demographic and socioeconomic characteristics of the foreign-born population in the United States. Many reports offer comparisons to the native-born population.

Migration Information Source

http://www.migrationinformation.org

Provided by the Migration Policy Institute, this site looks at migration as an international concern but contains a special "U.S. in Focus" section. Provides recent news as well as full scholarly articles on timely issues.

Population Reference Bureau

http://www.prb.org

Provides data of all kinds on the world's population. From the home page, click on "Migration" for articles, datasheets, and reports on the world's migration issues. Some are U.S. concerns; others apply to different countries.

TRAC INS

http://trac.syr.edu/tracins/

Although a change to the site address to reflect the change in the department's name will likely occur, this site tracks spending, enforcement, staffing, and other trends of the federal immigration service. TRAC is a governmental monitoring service at Syracuse University.

U.S. Citizenship and Immigration Services

http://uscis.gov

This organization, formerly the Immigration and Naturalization Service (INS), changed its name upon its reorganization into the Department of Homeland Security. This source is useful for current policies and procedures relating to immigration into the United States.

Advocacy Sites

—Pro-Immigrant/Immigration

Future of Freedom Foundation Immigration Project

http://www.fff.org/issues/immigration.asp

Immigrant's Rights—ACLU

http://www.aclu.org/ImmigrantsRights/ImmigrantsRightsMain.cfm

National Immigration Forum

http://www.immigrationforum.org

National Network for Immigrant and Refugee Rights

http://www.nnirr.org

—Anti-Immigrant/Immigration

Americans for Immigration Control

http://www.americanimmigrationcontrol.com

Coalition for the Future American Worker

http://www.americanworker.org

H1B (Technical Visa Program) Info

http://www.h1b.info

Project U.S.A.

http://www.projectusa.org

U.S. Border Control

http://www.usbc.org

VDARE

http://www.vdare.com

National Defense

Summary

Since the fall of the Soviet Union in December 1991, America has been considered the sole remaining superpower of the planet. This interesting distinction provides positives and negatives for concerns of national defense.

National defense, viewed broadly, is the job of keeping America safe, strong, and secure. When thinking broadly about defense, a variety of American interests in the global community need to be considered. This may include not only issues of military concern, but social, political, and economic ones as well. As with a variety of issues covered in this book, September 11, 2001, had a profound effect on the issue of national defense. For instance, in its effort to destroy terrorist organizations in an act of self-defense, America has been involved in nation building. This underscores the complexity of defense and that it goes beyond the issue of homeland defense covered elsewhere in this book.

Keywords
America's global role
Diplomacy
Foreign policy
Globalization
Humanitarianism
Intelligence
Military spending
Peacemaking
Promoting democracy
Rogue states
Strategic alliances
Superpower

Related Topics
Homeland defense
Terrorism
Weapons

There are various competing concerns in national defense. One perspective is to look at the strength of the nation in terms of domestic issues taking priority over other concerns of defense. Advocates of this view believe the United States. should act militarily only when our direct interests are threatened; otherwise we should focus on domestic issues. For instance, some may say that reducing taxes to shore up the economy is of higher importance than building better defense systems or a larger military.

A somewhat opposite view is to see the United States as the promoter of democracy and the protector of human rights. Advocates of this view see this as the most practical way to promote a peaceful planet and expand global markets. This perspective requires the United States. to be actively engaged in world events, advocating and sometimes fighting for democracy, deposing dictators, or interfering with human rights violators. It opens the door for a very aggressive U.S. role in world events. If our national defense entails a role as an important player in world stability, we must increase our concern for international ethnic violence or civil war, which could spiral out of control and threaten our interests.

Sometimes the concern for such issues comes from international organizations we belong to such as the United Nations or NATO. For example, when the nation of Yugoslavia disintegrated in the 1990s it left a fragile, ethnically diverse population struggling to shift power. The United Nations first stepped in to assist with humanitarian needs resulting from the struggle. Eventually NATO stepped in when realities of ethnic cleansing came to light, and many of our troops were involved in peacekeeping efforts.

Such a struggle highlights that national defense is not as simple as looking after our own interests, but that broader questions of foreign policy come into play. For instance, what is our relationship with the international organizations we belong to? We have joined with larger organizations for reasons of international stability, but sometimes they ask us to take actions that do not directly affect us. How do we influence their activities, and how do we allow them to influence our actions? When is it appropriate for our nation to step in where oppression or ethnic cleansing is occurring? When do we take such actions unilaterally, and when do we seek to build coalitions? What values and concerns do we want to define us in the international community?

Again, September 11, 2001, has infused national defense policies with a variety of new concerns. National defense is not as simple as how our government deals with other governments. Terrorist organizations are not nation-bound and create a whole new level of threat to our national defense. Terrorism caused America to go to war with both Afghanistan and Iraq. While there was not much dissent among Americans regarding our action in Afghanistan—where perception was that we were going after parties immediately responsible for the attacks—there has been much more disagreement about the invasion of Iraq. The reason for invading was concern that this rogue nation, which did not cooperate in the international community, was producing weapons of mass destruction (WMDs). The concern was that this government either might use them against us or might sell them to terrorists who would. Aside from the threat of WMDs was concern about atrocities its leader, Saddam Hussein, committed against the people of Iraq.

There has been no shortage of debate about this most recent act of national defense. Can rogue governments producing WMDs be contained, or must they be disrupted? What level of certainty must we have about the production of WMDs before taking actions against a nation? How can we sustain an aggressive attack on terrorists and countries who harbor them? How do we determine and verify that a nation is harboring terrorists? What steps do we take to protect ourselves at home, and at what cost? Is it appropriate to oust a leader of a nation just because of atrocities against its people, or must there be a verified threat against our own well-being?

The answers to these questions and more shape how we define and carry out national defense.

Web Sites

Reference Sites

Defense Strategy Review Page

http://www.comw.org/qdr/

Provides lists of the various issues concerning current defense issues, analyzes the policies, and provides alternatives to these policies. An excellent way to discover competing ideas for achieving national security.

Frontline: The War Behind Closed Doors

http://www.pbs.org/wgbh/pages/frontline/shows/iraq/

This Frontline documentary examines the people and conflicts that went into finally making the "grand strategy" to go to war with Iraq. This documentary helps to explain the Bush administration's political strategy for national defense.

Public Agenda: America's Global Role

http://www.publicagenda.org

Select "America's Global Role" from the list of Issue Guides. Provides a framework of the issue of America's global role, outlines the various perspectives that exist, and gives facts, figures, and opinion data related to this topic, which is closely interwoven with issues of national defense.

News Sites

Washingtonpost.com: National Security

http://www.washingtonpost.com/wp-dyn/nation/nationalsecurity/

Provides daily news on all aspects of national security from *Washington Post* reporters.

Yahoo! News: Full Coverage: U.S. Armed Forces

http://fullcoverage.yahoo.com/fc/

Search Full Coverage for the term "armed forces". Select the Full Coverage Category for "US: Armed Forces" to view news stories, editorials, feature articles, audio/video resources, Web sites, and links to other specialized news sources on this topic.

Law/Legislation

FindLaw Legal News: International

http://news.findlaw.com/legalnews/international/

Provides news headlines of international concern, many having to do with issues of national security.

Thomas

http://thomas.loc.gov

Search "national security" for updated legislation regarding this issue.

Data Sites

Annual Defense Report

http://www.defenselink.mil/execsec/adr_intro.html

From the Department of Defense, this report is presented to Congress and the president each year. Includes topics such as America's role in the world, fighting the war on terror, defense policy goals, and efforts to modernize forces. Reports are available back to 1995.

Atlantic Monthly: Foreign Policy

http://www.theatlantic.com/politics/foreign/foreign.htm

This is an archive of articles published in the *Atlantic Monthly* having to do with issues of national security and foreign policy.

Council on Foreign Relations

http://www.cfr.org

This is a nonpartisan group that "is dedicated to increasing America's understanding of the world and contributing ideas to U.S. foreign policy. " The Web site is full of in-depth reports, opinion pieces, links to other sites, and articles from their premier journal *Foreign Affairs*.

DoctrineLink

http://www.fas.org/man/doctrine.htm

From the Federation of American Scientists, this site purports to be "the most comprehensive online guide to military doctrine currently available."

Institute for National Strategic Studies

http://www.ndu.edu/inss/insshp.html

Working under the Secretary of Defense, this organization conducts research, strategic gaming, conferences, and publications.

National Security: The Center for Science and Technology Online

http://www.tecsoc.org/natsec/natsec.htm

Examines various technological challenges of national security, including cyberwarfare.

National Security Strategy of the United States

http://www.whitehouse.gov/nsc/nss.html

From the White House, this document provides the governing principles and overall goals for national security from the current administration.

U.S. Department of State

http://www.state.gov

Provides data from the department responsible for diplomatic relationships with other countries. Provides information about other countries, living abroad, and a host of international issues that infuse the diplomatic process.

Where to Find Military Information

http://library.nps.navy.mil/home/militaryinfo.htm

Links to sites giving information on the budget, history, organization, and more about the U.S. military.

Advocacy Sites

—*Decrease Military/Increase Domestic and Humanitarian Efforts*

Friends Committee on National Legislation

http://www.fcnl.org

Nonviolence.org

http://www.nonviolence.org

Returned Peace Corp Volunteers for a Better World

http://www.rpcv.org

—*Increase Military/Greater American Global Role*

Democrats for National Security

http://www.demsfornatsec.org

National Defense Industrial Association

http://www.ndia.org

Project for the New American Century

http://www.newamericancentury.org

Prisons

Summary

At the end of 2000 there were over 2 million people incarcerated in America; no country has a larger prison population. This is an interesting distinction for the nation billing itself as the "home of the free." Incarceration rates for the United States were about one in every 109 men and one in every 1,695 women. The cost of housing a prisoner is about $20,000 per year. In the 1990s about $27 billion was spent on building new prisons.

These staggering numbers can be supplemented with even more staggering detail. The cost of punishing criminals has certainly become a major concern for our nation. While one would assume that the large numbers of incarcerations signal a society out of control, crime rates have not risen as rapidly.

Keywords
Antiprison movement
Drug courts
Incarceration rates
Juvenile inmates
Lock 'em up
Mandatory sentences
Mental illness and prisons
Parole policies
Prison overcrowding
Prison population
Privatization of prisons
Tough-on-crime policies
Treatment or jail time

Related Topics
Death penalty
Drug policy
Substance abuse

Prison growth has largely been attributed to tough-on-crime policies, most of which have grown out of the drug wars. Thirty-one percent of prisoners are serving time for drug offenses. Seventy percent of all criminals are in jail for nonviolent offenses. Sixty percent reported being on drugs or alcohol at the time of their arrest.

Some suggest that tough-on-crime policies are largely political and prey on Americans' fears, while not being based on adequate research or information as to their effectiveness. Indeed, it is difficult to find advocacy organizations that stand for such policies. There is debate about whether nonviolent drug offenders should receive mandatory sentences, removing discretion for the punishment from the judge hearing the case. There is disagreement over whether certain offenders can be rehabilitated and made fit to be part of society again. There are differences of opinion as to when to punish the crime or when to treat the criminal. And then there are questions about whether it is appropriate to keep building new prisons to overcome issues of overcrowding, and when or where funding should be redirected instead to prevent as many people as possible from ending up in prison. While "tough-on-crime" policies seem to be the prevailing norm for handling crime, it is challenging to find organized groups who advocate such policies. Therefore, to find information supporting that viewpoint it is necessary to do some general searching on such phrases as "tough on crime" or "lock them up".

There are a number of controversies regarding prison populations. For instance, a number of mentally ill Americans are incarcerated and are not receiving treatment for the illness that caused their unlawful behavior. Race is another issue of debate when it comes to considering prison populations. Disproportionate numbers of blacks and Hispanics are incarcerated, sparking debates about the reasons. Imprisoned juveniles remain a cause for controversy. Some believe that giving juveniles prison sentences only turns them into hardened criminals who will eventually be let loose on society once again. Those advocates point to successes of treatment programs for young offenders and contend that treatment and work programs are much more appropriate sentences for youth.

Another debate is whether to privatize prisons. Some would argue that it is not appropriate for private companies to be in the business of incarcerating Americans. There is concern that there will be lower quality standards if prisons are privatized, and that private companies will have a financial stake in keeping the jails well populated. However, it has also been shown that private prisons can save local governments money.

Web Sites

Reference Sites

Debt to Society: Mother Jones

http://www.motherjones.com/prisons/

This is an investigative report on the reasons for vast prison populations in America. Includes a wealth of statistical data, an atlas of incarceration, and a large database of prison organizations and advocacy groups.

Incarcerated America: HRW Backgrounder

http://www.hrw.org/backgrounder/usa/incarceration/

This is a background report on incarceration rates in America. This report includes lots of statistical data as well as references to other research on the topic.

Jailing the Mentally Ill

http://bach.americanradioworks.org/features/mentally_ill/

This online documentary outlines the problem of the mentally ill ending up in prison. Includes information one when someone should go to jail versus a mental institution, facts about the insanity defense, a photo essay, statistics, and links to other resources.

Private Prisons

http://www.ucc.uconn.edu/~logan/

Provides outlined links to the issues and arguments, studies and reports, data, and sample contracts. While the opinions in the issues and arguments section favor privatization of prisons, this paper provides useful detail about the issues involved in the debate.

News Sites

Correctional News Online

http://www.correctionalnews.com

Provides updated news for the correction professional, including prison policies, activities, and commercial products that are needed by prisons. Users can sign up for a free subscription to the print magazine.

Yahoo! News: Full Coverage: U.S. Prisons

http://fullcoverage.yahoo.com/fc/

Search Full Coverage for the term "prisons". Select the Full Coverage Category for "US Prisons" to view news stories, editorials, feature articles, audio/video resources, Web sites, and links to other specialized news sources on this topic.

Law/Legislation

LII: Law about . . . Prisons and Prisoner Rights

http://www.law.cornell.edu/topics/prisoners_rights.html

Provides an overview of federal and state laws governing prisons and prisoners as well as current information on laws being debated and enacted.

Data Sites

Bureau of Justice Statistics

http://www.ojp.usdoj.gov/bjs/

Includes statistics on crime and sentencing. Includes a report called "Prisoners in 2001."

Competitive Corrections Research Project

http://www.rppi.org/privatization/ccrp/

From the Reason Institute, this site provides research publications, links to other online sources, and a list of books on the topic of private prisons.

Corrections.com

http://www.corrections.com

This is a commercial site for news, information, and resources of interest for those in the corrections industry.

DOJ: Prison and Parole Information

http://www.usdoj.gov/prisoninfo.htm

Provides information for individuals and communities such as parole policies, lists of prisons nationally, how to get inmate information, inmate services, and information about prisoner re-entry into society.

Federal Bureau of Prisons

http://www.bop.gov

Includes a prisoner locator search and information about the Bureau.

Prison Activist Resource Center

http://prisonactivist.org

Provides links to all sorts of prison-related issue sites. Includes a directory of organizations involved in prison-related activism and activities.

Prison Diaries: NPR All Things Considered

http://www.npr.org/programs/atc/prisondiaries/

Provides audiotapes recorded over a six-month period by inmates and correctional officers, giving a sense of daily life in prison.

The Sentencing Project

http://www.sentencingproject.org

This organization "promotes reduced reliance on incarceration and increased use of more effective and humane alternatives to deal with crime. It is a nationally recognized source of criminal justice policy analysis, data, and program information. Its reports, publications, and staff are relied upon by the public, policymakers and the media."

Advocacy Sites

—Pro-Treatment Options/Alternatives to Sentencing

American Corrections Association

http://www.aca.org

Center for Community Alternatives
http://www.communityalternatives.org

Center on Juvenile and Criminal Justice
http://www.cjcj.org

Criminal Justice Policy Foundation
http://www.cjpf.org

Families Against Mandatory Minimums
http://www.famm.org

—Pro-Mandatory Sentencing/Tough-on-Crime Policies

American Legislative Exchange Council
http://www.alec.org

—Against Privatization of Prisons

American Federation of State, County and Municipal Employees (AFSCME)
http://www.afscme.org

CorpWatch: Prison Industry
http://www.corpwatch.org/issues/PII.jsp?topicid=119

Race Relations

Summary

Unlike the topic "diversity" in this book, the topic "race relations" not only addresses issues of race but also assumes a sense of division and a need for mending. While only the most extreme in society advocate official policies of discrimination and segregation, the reality of racial tension still exists. Most discussions about race relations today center around how the history and lingering realities of racial disparities should be addressed. Traditionally, racial clashes in America have been between whites and African Americans. This clash was highlighted in the 1992 Los Angeles riots. However, other racial tensions have occurred in history, such as when Japanese Americans were interned during World War II. More recently, the terrorist attacks of September 11, 2001, have caused increased tensions between Arab immigrants and Arab Americans and the rest of society. Hispanics are rapidly becoming the "majority minority" in America. It is projected that within this century whites will cease to be the majority race in the United States, a statistic many believe will change the nature of racial relations.

A variety of recent events have profiled the problems that exist in race relations. Most recently, two days of rioting occurred in Benton Harbor, Michigan, when a black man died while fleeing white police, a scenario not at all new to America. Crowds are angered because they perceive a white police state oppressing disadvantaged black neighborhoods. There is a sense that local governments and police employ racial profiling, which is a programmatic means of singling out one race (generally blacks) in certain neighborhoods for suspicion and monitoring, assuming that this group is the most likely to commit crimes. This is generally done based on statistics of past crimes. While even the president has issued a statement condemning racial profiling, some suggest that stronger measures need to be taken to prevent it. In addition, there are studies highlighting the disparities that exist in prison sentences for minorities.

Keywords
- Confederate flag
- Discrimination
- Los Angeles riots (1992)
- Majority race
- Police brutality
- Prejudice
- Racial disparities
- Racial profiling
- Racial violence
- White privilege

Related Topics
- Diversity
- Hate groups and crimes
- Immigration
- Reparations for slavery

Some neighborhoods, again almost exclusively African American or other minority, find that police brutality is epidemic. There is a sense that a few officers are generally responsible for these acts, but too often police departments do nothing to prevent or punish such activity. It is often felt that acts of brutality are motivated by racism on the part of individuals involved. Two high-profile cases that have highlighted the controversy in the past decade are the Rodney King beatings in Los Angeles and the Abner Louima case in New York.

Racial tension was again highlighted recently in South Carolina when a group demanded that the state stop flying the confederate flag atop the state Capitol in Columbia. As a historical symbol of slavery, African Americans believe it should no longer be allowed to fly next to other current government symbols. In 2000 a bill to remove it caused great controversy, with opponents claiming that it was an important symbol of their heritage.

The economic reality that racial minorities are more likely than whites to live in poverty cannot be ignored when examining why tensions still exist. Charges of racism inherently arise when it comes to such economic issues as welfare reform, home loan policies, and get-tough policies on drug use and crime.

Racial minorities often feel a sense of discrimination when the media do not represent them fairly or equally. Media images are seen as important in shaping the values and expectations of young people. If only the majority race is depicted in media, or if minorities are only portrayed in a negative light, minorities may feel devalued or sense the need to conform to majority mores.

Web Sites

Reference Sites

Public Agenda Online: Race

http://www.publicagenda.org

Select "Race" from the list of Issue Guides. Provides an overview of the topic, recent news stories, facts and data, resources for more information, and public opinion data.

Race Relations: About.com

http://racerelations.about.com

Provides access to a variety of articles and links on all aspects of race relations. Be prepared for annoying pop-up ads.

Race Watch

http://www.zmag.org/racewatch/racewatch.htm

Part of a social change consortium, this site intends to improve racial relations. It is rich with links to sites on all aspects of racial relations, including those pertaining to specific racial groups.

Understanding Prejudice

http://www.understandingprejudice.org

Provides a wealth of readings, links, organizations, and material from experts on the topic of prejudice. Although this is a companion Web site to a book, there is much valuable information available here for free.

News Sites

Yahoo! News: Full Coverage: African Americans

http://fullcoverage.yahoo.com/fc/

Search Full Coverage for the term "African Americans". Select the Full Coverage Category for "US African Americans" to view news stories, editorials, feature articles, audio/video resources, Web sites, and links to other specialized news sources on this topic. You may wish to also search for these related topics:

> U.S.> Arab and Muslim Americans
>
> U.S.> Latinos and Hispanics
>
> Law enforcement issues

Law/Legislation

NOLO

http://www.nolo.com

On the home page search "race" for useful articles that summarize U.S. law on issues of race. Each article summarizes U.S. law, gives strategies for action, and provides links to related articles and recent news stories about litigation regarding racial issues. Legal contexts for race legislation include employment, adoption, housing discrimination, and police misconduct.

Data Sites

Crosspoint Anti Racism

http://www.magenta.nl/crosspoint/

This is a searchable directory of organizations involved in antiracism activities worldwide.

Frontline: LAPD Blues

http://www.pbs.org/wgbh/pages/frontline/shows/lapd/bare.html

This is a documentary about the troubled Los Angeles police department after the Rodney King beating. Examines allegations of profiling, brutality, and other injustices against the department.

How Race Is Lived in America

http://www.nytimes.com/library/national/race/

This is a series of researched articles by the *New York Times*.

Online NewsHours—Race Relations Reports

http://www.pbs.org/newshour/bb/race_relations/race_relations.html

This is a collection of news stories done by PBS news involving issues of race. This list is current and dates back to 1995.

Salon Directory: Racial Issues

http://dir.salon.com/topics/racial_issues/index.html

This is a collection of over 100 articles that have appeared online in *Salon Magazine* related to racial issues.

U.S. Census Bureau

http://www.census.gov

This is the site for official demographics, trends, and population reports.

Advocacy Sites

—*Promoting Racial Minorities*

Arab American Institute

http://www.aaiusa.org

Issues and Views: On the Frontline of Dissent since 1985

http://www.issues-views.com

National Counsel of La Raza

http://www.nclr.org

National Urban League

http://www.nul.org

The Official Website of the National Association for the Advancement of Colored People

http://www.naacp.org

Tomas Rivera Policy Institute

http://www.trpi.org

—Police Brutality/Profiling

Lamberth Consulting

http://www.lamberthconsulting.com

October 22nd Coalition

http://www.october22.org

—Racism in Society/Culture

Center for Equal Opportunity (conservative)

http://www.ceousa.org

FAIR's Racism Watch Desk

http://www.fair.org/racism-desk/

Network of Alliances Bridging Race and Ethnicity

http://www.jointcenter.org/nabre/

Racial Equality: ACLU (liberal)

http://www.aclu.org/RacialEquality/RacialEqualitymain.cfm

Racism and Human Rights

http://www.hrw.org/campaigns/race/

White Privilege: an antiracism resource

http://www.whiteprivilege.com

Reparations for Slavery

Summary

The slave trade began in the 1600s in the Americas, long before the United States was a country. Enslaving African descendants was allowed to continue in the United States until President Abraham Lincoln signed the Emancipation Proclamation in 1862. Even after freedom was granted to slaves and all Americans of African descent, and after the Thirteenth Amendment outlawing slavery was enacted, African Americans continued to be treated poorly by society through discriminatory practices that were sometimes legal and institutional, and sometimes personal and covert. It is generally accepted that this history of mistreatment is the root cause of poorer conditions for African Americans in society today. Some seek to find a way to repair this damage by asking for reparations for slavery.

Keywords
Conditions for black Americans
Emancipation Proclamation
Forty acres and a mule
Holocaust reparations
Reparations Assessment Group
Reparations for race riots
Representative John Conyers
Thirteenth Amendment

Keywords
Diversity
Race relations

In 1988 Japanese Americans interned by the United States during World War II were awarded $20,000 apiece and given a formal apology by the U.S. government. Survivors of the Jewish Holocaust have received over $60 billion from the German government for the atrocities committed against them and for the slave labor they were required to provide. While the issue of reparations for slavery of African Americans seems a modern cause, the first effort to repay slaves was mostly unsuccessfully undertaken by Union General William T. Sherman (the "40 acres and a mule" solution) in 1865, with several failed efforts following over the years. During the Civil Rights Movement of the 1960s, an increased effort to renew this cause began. The recent awards benefiting Japanese American and Holocaust survivors have again brought the issue to the fore. Representative John Conyers (D. Mich.) has introduced a slavery reparations bill in every session of Congress since 1989. Florida and Oklahoma have set precedents by providing reparations to individuals who suffered during race riots in their states in the first half of the twentieth century.

Different polls provide different results about the level of support for this idea. Generally, a majority of African Americans believe there should be reparations for slavery, and a majority of whites believe there should not be such reparations. Four million Africans and their descendants worked as slaves in

America. The number of African Americans now living in the United States is over 35 million, making this the largest group in history that would benefit from such a program, and also making it potentially the most expensive such undertaking ever.

Those who support reparations for slavery believe that this money is back pay for 250 years of slave labor. Advocates say that it was the labor of these slaves that fueled the American economy, making it a wealthy nation, so therefore it is unjust that their descendants suffer the most poverty. Some say African Americans also deserve consideration for the post-slavery years in which they endured oppressive discrimination. Others claim that whites have been able to pass down the economic gains they have obtained, whereas blacks, due to oppression and discrimination, have not, thus exacerbating the disparities that exist between the races today. Therefore, even though slavery has been illegal for over 100 years, supporters of reparations state that there should be no time limit to their claim. Awards received by Holocaust survivors and interned Japanese Americans strengthen their claim. Proponents believe reparations are needed to put this chapter in history behind us and move forward.

Those who oppose reparations argue that there should in fact be a statute of limitations to this claim. There are no former slaves currently living to receive the reparations. Those who did own slaves are also dead and cannot be punished for this misconduct. Only their innocent descendants can be made to pay. In addition, there are newer immigrants to America who had no stake and no ancestry in the slave business who would be forced to pay part of these reparations. Some opponents believe that reparations would insult the achievements of blacks who have gone far in society through their own efforts and abilities. Some feel that making these payments would only serve to further damage the relationships of whites and blacks in this nation, rather than repair them.

Web Sites

Reference Sites

Reparations Central

http://www.reparationscentral.com

Although this is a pro-reparations site, it is useful for providing the context for the issue, recent news articles, legislative updates, links to other sites, and online articles.

Slavery Reparations: About.com

http://racerelations.about.com/cs/reparations/

Provides history, background, recent legislation, and opinion articles.

News Sites

Google News

http://news.google.com

Search for "reparations and slavery".

Yahoo! News

http://news.yahoo.com

Search for "slave reparations" or "reparation and slavery". There is no news portal available for this topic via the Full Coverage service.

Law/Legislation

Congressman John Conyers, Jr: Major Issues: Reparations Page

http://www.house.gov/conyers/news_reparations.htm

Outlines the legislative activity related to reparations undertaken by Conyers, including an outline of his viewpoint, actions taken, and news related to Conyers and reparations.

Findlaw's Writ: Sebok: A New Dream Team
Intends to Seek Reparations for Slavery

http://writ.corporate.findlaw.com/sebok/20001120.html

This is a two-part article examining legal aspects of seeking reparations for slavery.

Data Sites

African American Reparation Action Network

http://www.angelfire.com/super/freedom/

Presents one proposed act citing dollar figures and who would be eligible.

Avalon Project: Statutes of the United States Concerning Slavery

http://www.yale.edu/lawweb/avalon/statutes/slavery/slmenu.htm

Provides primary source documents related to slavery. Use the search feature to find items relating to reparations.

Black Reparations.com

http://www.blackreparations.com

Includes online surveys, discussions, and articles.

Advocacy Sites

—*Pro-Reparations*

CURE: Caucasians United for Reparations and Emancipation
http://www.reparationsthecure.org/june03/

N'CORBRA (National Coalition of Blacks for Reparations in America)
http://www.ncobra.com

Ubuntu
http://www.ubuntu.tv/

—*Against Reparations*

Issues and Views: On the Frontline of Dissent since 1985
http://www.issues-views.com

National Center for Public Policy Research/Slavery Reparations Resource Center
http://www.nationalcenter.org/Reparations.html

We Won't Pay
http://www.wewontpay.com

Reproductive Technologies

Summary

Scientists and doctors have developed a variety of new technologies to assist reproduction for infertile couples who want to have children. Others, such as single people, postmenopausal women, and gay partners, also use them. Since 1978, when the first test-tube baby was born in England, fertility has become a multibillion-dollar industry, one that has created tens of thousands of babies.

All of the techniques for dealing with infertility share a common feature: Conception of the child does not involve sexual intercourse. Sometimes fertility drugs can be used to stimulate egg production, so that women can experience a normal pregnancy. One common outcome of this method is multiple pregnancies. The rate among women treated with fertility drugs can be as high as 25 percent. There are also more risks to the health of the fetuses in this situation. Physicians may recommend that some of the fetuses be aborted during the first few months of pregnancy, to enhance development of the others.

Keywords
Artificial insemination
Assisted reproduction
Designer babies
Donor eggs
Embryo transfer
Fertility drugs
Gamete intrafallopian tube transfer
Human cloning
In vitro fertilization
Infertility
Sex selection
Surrogacy
Test-tube baby

Related Topics
Abortion
Adoption
Genetic engineering

Artificial insemination, where sperm is placed in the female reproductive tract using a medical instrument, is a common procedure. There are two major kinds of artificial insemination: artificial insemination husband (AIH), which uses the semen of the woman's partner; and donor insemination (DI), which uses the semen of someone else.

Another popular technique used to help infertile couples become pregnant is in vitro fertilization (IVF) and embryo transfer. The term *in vitro* is Latin for "in glass," and this is where conception occurs. These fetuses are often referred to as "test tube babies." With IVF, fertilization takes place outside the mother's body. Ripe eggs are removed from the woman's ovaries and incubated with sperm to create an embryo. After it goes through the first phases of development, the embryo is transferred into the woman's uterus. If one of the partners is unable to produce eggs or sperm, people known to the couple may donate them, or they may be acquired through fertility clinics. Success rates for IVF depend on a patient's age and other factors, but average between 20 and 30 percent.

Couples undergoing IVF must also decide how many eggs to fertilize, whether they want to create and freeze embryos for future use, and how to dispose of any unused frozen embryos. Former spouses have waged custody battles over frozen embryos.

Gamete intrafallopian tube transfer (GIFT) is another technique used to help couples with infertility problems. This technique involves placing eggs and sperm in the woman's fallopian tubes. In this case, the fertilization takes place inside the woman's body. GIFT is a more complex procedure but has a success rate that is about twice that of in vitro fertilization.

Surrogacy is an arrangement in which a woman carries a baby through pregnancy and then gives the child to another person when the baby is born. A surrogate mother is often paid to carry a baby and give birth. Surrogacy may involve a couple or a single person who needs help to have a baby. In surrogacy, the embryo must be implanted in the surrogate mother using in vitro fertilization techniques.

Many ethical issues and controversies surround these new technologies. Assisted reproduction permits the selection of embryos based on various genetic traits. These fetuses are sometimes called "designer babies." Screening involves removing and analyzing a single cell from an embryo. Some clinics offer to screen in vitro embryos for genetically transmitted diseases. The rejected embryos are discarded or donated to research. Selection of embryos based on gender is not common in the United States. It occurs, for the most part, in developing countries where families believe it is best to have sons rather than daughters.

Many infertile couples choose reproductive technologies because they really want to have a child that is related to them. Some people also feel very strongly that they want to experience pregnancy and childbirth. Critics of this approach believe that it is better to adopt a child than to use reproductive technologies to get pregnant. They contend that although adoption can be emotionally difficult, it provides a home and family for a child who is already in the world.

Web Sites

Reference Sites

Genetics and Public Policy Center

http://www.dnapolicy.org

The Center is funded by a grant from the Pew Charitable Trusts. It aims to be an objective information source on reproductive genetics issues, such as genetic testing, gene transfer, genes and disease, and reproductive cloning. Topical sections include basic information, useful links, and a bibliography. Site also includes data from polls on attitudes toward reproductive genetics.

International Council on Infertility Information Dissemination (ICIID)

http://www.inciid.org

Provides consumer-targeted infertility information that covers cutting-edge technologies and treatments. Includes fact sheets, reproductive news and research summaries, a directory of professionals providing treatment, and discussion forums.

MEDLINEplus: Infertility

http://www.nlm.nih.gov/medlineplus/infertility.html

This research guide from the National Library of Medicine organizes information and links into categories such as news, overviews, diagnosis/symptoms, coping, pictures, research, statistics, treatment, law/policy, and organizations.

Reproductive Health Gateway

http://www.rhgateway.org

This project, managed by Johns Hopkins University, provides access to publications of a wide variety of health organizations. May be searched by keyword or browsed by topic.

Virtual Hospital: Assisted Reproductive Technologies

http://www.vh.org/adult/patient/obgyn/assistedreproductivetechnology/

This online textbook for patients explains common procedures, such as gamete intrafallopian transfer (GIFT), in vitro fertilization, embryo cryopreservation, and several others.

News Sites

ASRM: Headlines in Reproductive Medicine

http://www.asrm.org/news.html

The American Society of Reproductive Medicine provides links to daily news stories in a variety of online newspapers and sites; links are retained for the current and previous week.

New Scientist: Cloning

http://www.newscientist.com/hottopics/cloning/

This special report provides links to recent and archived articles published in the *New Scientist* on cloning and stem cell technology.

Yahoo! News: Full Coverage: Fertility and Pregnancy

http://fullcoverage.yahoo.com/fc/

Search Full Coverage for the term "fertility". Select the Full Coverage Category for "Health: Fertility and Pregnancy" to view news stories, editorials, feature articles, audio/video resources, Web sites, and links to other specialized news sources on this topic.

Law/Legislation

Legal Overview of Surrogacy Laws by State

http://www.surrogacy.com/legals/map.html

This map, last updated in 1997, shows which states recognize surrogacy, which criminalize the practice, and which have no laws on this subject. Check the state family law code for a particular state to determine whether there have been changes since this chart was prepared.

Data Sites

CDC: Assisted Reproduction Technology Reports

http://www.cdc.gov/nccdphp/drh/art.htm

Provides data on prevalence of various techniques and success rates, mandated by the Fertility Clinic Success Rate and Certification Act.

Frontline: Making Babies

http://www.pbs.org/wgbh/pages/frontline/shows/fertility/

This companion site to the television program examines new reproductive technologies. Includes interviews with infertility and bioethics specialists, videos of several procedures, and a discussion of human cloning.

Advocacy Sites

—*Support Restrictions on Reproductive Technologies*

Center for Bioethics and Human Dignity

http://www.cbhd.org

National Right to Life

http://www.nrlc.org

U.S. Conference of Catholic Bishops

http://www.usccb.org/prolife/issues/

—Support Expanded Use of Reproductive Technologies

Association of Reproductive Health Professionals

http://www.arhp.org

OPTS: The Organization of Parents Through Surrogacy

http://www.opts.com

RESOLVE: The National Infertility Association

http://www.resolve.org

School Reform

Summary

The most recent presidential platform was no different than most in listing educational reform as an administrative priority. At least since the 1983 report *A Nation At Risk* was published, public school reform has been on the public agenda, with few disagreeing that reform is needed. The most recent education reform bill, the No Child Left Behind Act, is but another federal attempt at reforming education.

However, traditionally education has not been managed federally in the United States, and most reform efforts are debated at the local level. The largest debate that exists on the topic is *how* to reform it. Reform efforts do tend to fall into four broad categories.

Keywords
Charter schools
Education reform
Educational financing/funding
Educational standards
Home schooling
No Child Left Behind Act
Proficiency tests
School choice
School improvement
Teaching methods
Vouchers

Related Topics
Church and state
School violence

First, many believe that if high standards are set for students, they live up to the expectations. The argument assumes that the way to set standards and know if students are reaching them is through proficiency testing. Standards also allow professionals to ensure every child is getting an appropriate education. This is the reform most emphasized in the No Child Left Behind Act. Opponents of this view argue that an emphasis on the proficiency testing required to enact standards hinders creative and real-world approaches to learning that mean more to students than scores on a test. The pressure for schools to ensure children perform well on tests causes them to teach for the test instead of teaching students how to think. In addition, a large bureaucracy is required to administer, assess, and maintain such a program.

Next, some would argue that a student-centered approach to teaching is what matters most. Advocates believe that teaching students to analyze material, grouping diverse achievement levels together, and emphasizing discussion is important for producing critical thinkers who learn well to interact with a variety of their peers. Opponents claim that this method has not been effective in improving student performance where it has been used and that it allows students to too much choice in their academic undertakings, often leading them to choose the easiest route to a degree.

A third argument blames school failure on inadequate or uneven funding. Often, the schools of disadvantaged children receive the least amount of funding when it could be argued that they need the most assistance. Advocates say that with better funding schools can hire better and more motivated teachers. Opponents of this argument do not like the idea of changing funding for schools from local to more centralized entities, which would be needed to ensure even funding. They claim that citizens in one district might be forced to pay for waste in another district. They also claim that schools need to be more efficient with the budgets they have, and that families are failing the students, not the schools.

Finally, there are those who would argue that public education should be subject to the same market forces as exist in business. By offering choices to students and parents, you increase competition. This competition will force schools to conform to the most successful methods or disappear. Opponents to this argument contend that education is not a business and should not be subject to the same market forces. Using public funds to send children to more popular private schools depletes the money available to improve the public schools already available. Private schools have the ability to pick and choose which students they will educate, always leaving the bottom of society to be dealt with by a demoralized and underfunded public system.

Aside from the various reform proposals are other social concerns that are part of the success formula, such as crime, drug use, discipline, and demographics. These concerns must also be considered when incorporating methods of reform.

Unlike other topics in this book, the advocacy groups listed below are not grouped by bias but are listed alphabetically with a brief statement of their biases and goals.

Web Sites

Reference Sites

AFT: K-12:Issues in Education

http://www.aft.org/edissues/Issues.htm

Provides a definition of, and this labor organization's stand on, each issue.

Education Commission of the States

http://www.ecs.org

See "education issues" for issue briefs that provide an overview of the educational issue, subtopics, and links to related issues.

National Education Association

http://www.nea.org

Although this is an advocacy site for public education, it contains a vast wealth of data of every kind relating to educational issues and school reform.

Public Agenda Online: Education

http://www.publicagenda.org

Select "Education" from the list of Issue Guides. Provides an outline of the reform issue and the various methods being examined by policymakers. Frames the debate by providing pros and cons, public opinion data, facts and figures, and links to useful resources.

News Sites

Yahoo! News: Full Coverage—U.S.—Education

http://fullcoverage.yahoo.com/fc/

Search Full Coverage for the term "education". Select the Full Coverage Category for "US Education" to view news stories, editorials, feature articles, audio/video resources, Web sites, and links to other specialized news sources on this topic.

Education Week

http://www.edweek.org

This newspaper for education professionals covers all news of educational interest.

CNN Education

http://www.cnn.com/EDUCATION/

This is CNN's permanent page for up-to-date information about schools and learning. The bottom of the page provides educational materials for teachers to use current events in the classroom.

Law/Legislation

No Child Left Behind

http://www.nclb.gov

This is the official home page for the current presidential initiative to improve education at the federal level.

LII: Law About . . . Education

http://www.law.cornell.edu/topics/education.html

Provides an overview of the legal issues relating to education, federal laws, state laws, and links to other key resources.

Data Sites

Brown Center on Educational Policy (Brookings Institute)

http://www.brookings.edu/browncenter

Provides in-depth research reports from this center within the Brookings Institute.

CNN Specials: Back to Schools

http://www.cnn.com/SPECIALS/2002/back.to.school/

This is a journalistic look at what changes are happening in American schools.

Education Issues

http://www.nasbe.org/Educational_Issues/Educational_Issues.html

Provides policy briefs, reports, and journal articles from the National Association of State Boards of Education. Included are reports related to school choice as well as school safety.

ERIC Resources

http://www.eric.ed.gov

Provides access to a variety of research tools from the U.S. Department of Education, including a database of scholarly articles, clearinghouse data and reports, and ERIC Digests, and an online reference service.

National Center for Education Statistics

http://nces.ed.gov

Includes federal statistics on education in the United States.

National School Boards Association

http://www.nsba.org/site/index.asp

This is a comprehensive site for school news, data, board policies, and legislation.

Progressive Policy Institute: Education

http://www.ppionline.org/ppi_ka.cfm?knlgAreaID=110

Provides research reports on reform issues, primarily about charter schools.

U.S. Department of Education

http://www.ed.gov/index.jsp

Provides up-to-date education news, legislation, federal policy, and data. Includes resources for parents, teachers, and administrators as well as budget and administrative information about the Department of Education. Information on school violence is available under the Education Resources link.

Advocacy Sites

—*Various Reforms As Indicated*

Council for Basic Education

http://www.c-b-e.org/

Works to promote high standards in grades K–12.

Educators for Social Responsibility

http://www.esrnational.org/home.htm

Promote a welcoming school environment, character education, and conflict resolution skills.

Fair Testing

http://www.fairtest.org/

An advocacy organization working to "end the abuses, misuses and flaws of standardized testing."

Heritage Foundation: Education

http://www.heritage.org/research/education/

Advocates a free market approach to reform.

Home School Legal Defense Association

http://www.hslda.org/Default.asp?bhcp=1

Defends the right of parents to direct the education of their children.

School Violence

Summary

The devastating and well-publicized incidents of gun violence in Jonesboro, Arkansas; Paducah, Kentucky; and Littleton, Colorado have raised public awareness of school violence and given parents as well as society cause for alarm. Bullying, disagreements, and other instances of unrest in schools that used to be written off as harmless are getting increased attention.

School violence is not always as sensational as the shooting sprees that have gained national attention. The Center for the Prevention of School Violence defines school violence as "any behavior that violates a school's educational mission or climate of respect or jeopardizes the intent of the school to be free of aggression against persons or property, drugs, weapons, disruptions, and disorder."

Keywords
Bullying
Drug-free schools/Student
  drug use
Gay teens
Hazing
Juvenile delinquency
Juvenile offenders
School shootings
Weapons at school
Zero tolerance policies

Related Topics
Gun control
Hate groups and crimes

Bullying is only one factor that has been identified as contributing to antisocial behaviors in schools. While all students are subject to bullying for a variety of reasons, gay teens sometimes experience harassment specifically because of being gay. Other factors that are not under school control also contribute to violence within the schools; child abuse and neglect, a culture of violence in communities, easy access to guns, and economic or social injustice are also contributing factors. And what is most often overlooked as a cause of violence are simple day-to-day routines and annoyances children face in school daily.

Less than 1 percent of homicides of children happen in schools, and in general the number of violent school acts has diminished. However, many would argue that any incident of school violence is doubly harmful. Not only can it hurt or kill students, the very threat or perceived threat of it can reduce children's ability to learn. Some studies have documented student and teacher absentee rates that are directly correlated to fear of violence.

Many strategies for keeping schools safe exist. Some of these tactics have been proven to work within schools, even if they do not get at the root of the problem causing the antisocial behavior. Introduced in the 1990s, following the example of zero tolerance drug policies, some school districts have adopted zero tolerance weapons policies. Zero tolerance policies have been criticized for being too harsh and not considering the circumstances of the individual situation. As is the case with zero tolerance drug policies, it is difficult to find advocates for the policies, but more possible to find examples of it. Other prevention methods that have been and are used are metal detectors, uniforms, and use of law enforcement personnel in schools.

Alternatively, approaches involving cooperation, mediation, education, and conflict resolution techniques have risen to the surface. In North Carolina a student-based problem-solving model proved effective in one high school. Another approach, the Resolving Conflict Creatively Program (RCCP), shows evidence that early school-based violence prevention initiatives can work and should be included in communities' efforts to prevent violence among children and youth.

Web Sites

Reference Sites

The Hamilton Fish Institute on School and Community Violence

http://www.hamfish.org

This nonpartisan institute, which exists to study issues of school violence and provide input to policymakers, provides strategies for dealing with school violence, trends and data, factors leading to violence, legal sources, and links to a variety of resources for understanding school violence. Begin by using the "topics" pull down list.

NCJRS: In the Spotlight: School Safety

http://www.ncjrs.org/school_safety/summary.html

Includes a summary of the issue of school safety/violence, facts and figures, legislation, research reports, links to other sites, and more. Developed by the National Criminal Justice Reference Service.

When Kids Kill

http://whyfiles.org/065school_violence/index.html

This online documentary by a group of academic scholars looks at some of the high-profile school shooting sprees and why these happened. Facts about school violence, opinions from psychologists, and the answers that gun safety can provide are examined. A bibliography of published articles and online Web sites is also provided.

News Sites

Yahoo! News: Full Coverage: School Violence

http://fullcoverage.yahoo.com/fc/

Search Full Coverage for the term "school violence". Select the Full Coverage Category for "US School Violence" to view news stories, editorials, feature articles, audio/video resources, Web sites, and links to other specialized news sources on this topic.

Law/Legislation

LII: Law About . . . Education

http://www.law.cornell.edu/topics/education.html

Provides an overview of the legal issues relating to education, federal laws, state laws, and links to other key resources.

School Law

http://www.nsba.org

Select the "School Law" option on the top left of the screen. Provides clips of recent legal news stories, lists of Supreme Court hearings related to schools, and a list of legislation by "issue". This site is provided by the National School Board Association.

Data Sites

Center for the Prevention of School Violence

http://www.ncdjjdp.org/cpsv/

With data laid out in the format of a school floor plan, this site gives strategies to implement throughout school buildings to ensure safety.

Education Issues

http://www.nasbe.org/Educational_Issues/Educational_Issues.html

Provides policy briefs, reports, and journal articles from the National Association of State Boards of Education. Included are reports related to school choice as well as school safety.

HRW: Hatred in the Hallways

http://www.hrw.org/reports/2001/uslgbt/

This is a Human Rights Watch report on bullied gay, lesbian, and transgendered teens.

Indicators of School Crime and Safety, 2000

http://nces.ed.gov/pubs2001/crime2000/

Provides school crime statistics from the National Center for Education Statistics. Includes victimization data, fatalities, and data about school environments.

Monitoring the Future

http://www.monitoringthefuture.org/

Includes online research of teens regarding drug use, smoking, and other actions deemed unsafe.

OJJDP School Violence Resources

http://ojjdp.ncjrs.org/resources/school.html

From the U.S. Department of Justice, this site provides access to a variety of strategy and research reports.

The Safety Zone

http://www.safetyzone.org

This is a clearinghouse for school safety information.

School Safety and Security Center

http://www.keepschoolssafe.org/index.htm

Provides safety literature and resources for parents, schools, and students on how to keep schools safe.

U.S. Department of Education

http://www.ed.gov/index.jsp

Provides up-to-date education news, legislation, federal policy, and data. Includes resources for parents, teachers, and administrators as well as budget and administrative information about the Department of Education. Information on school violence is available under the Education Resources link.

Advocacy Sites

—Welcoming Environment/Mediation Training

Fight Crime: Invest in Kids

http://www.fightcrime.org/

National Alliance for Safe Schools

http://www.safeschools.org/

SAVE: Students Against Violence Everywhere

http://nationalsave.org/

—Zero Tolerance/Police Intervention

Manhattan Institute

http://www.manhattan-institute.org

National Association of School Resource Officers

http://www.nasro.org

Smoking

Summary

Smoking costs the United States approximately $150 billion each year in healthcare costs and lost productivity. Cigarettes contain at least forty-three distinct cancer-causing chemicals. Smoking is directly responsible for 87 percent of lung cancer cases and causes most cases of emphysema and chronic bronchitis. Approximately 440,000 people in the United States die each year from smoking-related illnesses, and an additional 1,000 deaths occur each year due to smoking-related fires.

About 90 percent of all smokers start while under the age of twenty-one, making underaged smoking not only bad for youth but also the largest contributing factor to all smoking habits. Efforts to reduce teen smoking include controlling advertising most likely to appeal to youth, working with stores to keep cigarettes out of the hands of youth, working with youth to help them manage stress and other factors that contribute to cigarette addiction, educating youth on the health risks of smoking, and lobbying the media for less glamorized use of cigarettes on TV and in the movies. Even so, an estimated 2 million American youths start a smoking habit each year.

Tobacco is a nearly $400 billion industry in the United States; it spends over $9 billion each year in advertising. Groups that work to control tobacco often refer to the tobacco industry as "Big Tobacco." In 1954 the tobacco industry itself created a research group first called the Tobacco Industry Research Council, later changing its name to the Tobacco Research Council. This organization no longer exists, but it generated much controversy about the scientific findings it put forth.

Tobacco control refers to efforts to ensure smoke-free air, limit youth access, tax cigarettes, and prevent additional use by banning advertising or controlling the type of advertising being done. The battle against secondhand smoke began when a stewardess successfully persuaded Congress to ban smoking on

Keywords
Anti-tobacco movement
Attorneys General Masters Tobacco
  Settlement Agreement
Big tobacco
Cost to society
Politics of tobacco
Safer cigarettes
Secondhand smoke/ETS/
  environmental tobacco smoke
Smoking bans
Smokeless tobacco
Tobacco litigation
Underaged smokers

Related Topics
Corporate accountability
Substance abuse

airplanes in 1990. Since that time smoke-free areas have become the norm in restaurants, workplaces, and most public buildings. Contention continues about whether to ban smoking in such places as bars. Even so, efforts to reduce the numbers of children and adults subjected to secondhand smoke in their homes, cars, and other private venues continue. Advertising dollars have been spent trying to educate parents and others about the effect their smoking has on children.

Tobacco litigation has been a prominent issue, with the debate being whether tobacco companies know that nicotine in cigarettes is addictive. Company executives continuously deny that they knowingly withheld this information from consumers and argue that their customers have a right to buy cigarettes if they choose to do so. This has raised many issues of corporate responsibility in making so many Americans dependent on such a harmful product while never being held financially, criminally, or legally responsible for any deaths related to smoking. Although tobacco companies don't win legal cases, they tend to not lose by employing delaying tactics that cost the plaintiff too much time and money, thus making them drop the case. In November 1998 the largest settlement in tobacco litigation was reached; it is called The Attorneys General Masters Tobacco Settlement Agreement. This settlement has required tobacco companies to do some odd campaigning against smoking on television, radio, and via their Web sites.

Some groups are lobbying to have Congress place cigarettes under the control of the FDA. Other efforts have focused on creating a "safer" cigarette by limiting the amount of nicotine and other chemicals that can be added to the cigarette. Other issues that remain strongly contentious are advertising campaigns launched by tobacco companies targeting groups that are seen as more vulnerable and the exportation of cigarettes to countries that do not have regulations or educational programs to protect and enlighten citizens about the health risks of smoking.

Web Sites

Reference Sites

ACS: Tobacco and Cancer

http://www.cancer.org/docroot/PED/ped_10.asp?sitearea=PED&level=1

Provides information on the harmful effects of tobacco, quitting tips, legislation, teens and smoking, and the American Cancer Society supported "Great American Smokeout."

Tobacco Control: Key Resources

http://galen.library.ucsf.edu/collres/reflinks/tobacco/

From the organization that owns and provides access to the Tobacco Control Archives, this page provides access to those archives as well as a variety of other information resources on tobacco. Includes links to encyclopedic information, general smoking information, as well as statistics, news, and other types of information on tobacco.

Tobacco Reference Guide

http://new.globalink.org/tobacco/trg/

In book-like form, this site provides organized facts and quotes about tobacco, including the usage problem, history of tobacco, all the ailments caused by tobacco smoking, economics of tobacco, and a variety of miscellaneous facts and links to resources. The author is a medical doctor.

TobaccoPedia: An Online Tobacco Encyclopedia

http://www.tobaccopedia.org

Provides portal access to all forms of information regarding tobacco.

Yahoo Health Encyclopedia: Tobacco Use—Smoking and Smokeless Tobacco

http://health.yahoo.com/health/dc/002032/0.html

Provides an overview of tobacco information, its effects, chemicals in cigarettes, and health risks.

News Sites

Tobacco.org

http://tobacco.org

This is the most comprehensive site for daily updates to news from around the country and the world related to tobacco, smoking, and litigation news.

Yahoo! News Full Coverage: Smoking

http://fullcoverage.yahoo.com/fc/

Search Full Coverage for the term "smoking or tobacco". Select the Full Coverage Categories for "Smoking" and "Tobacco Lawsuits" to view news stories, editorials, feature articles, audio/video resources, Web sites, and links to other specialized news sources on this topic.

Law/Legislation

LII: Law About . . . Alcohol, Tobacco, and Controlled Substances

http://www.law.cornell.edu/topics/alcohol_tobacco.html

Provides an overview of laws that govern these topics as well as recent court cases, federal law, and state law.

State Legislated Actions on Tobacco Issues

http://slati.lungusa.org

From the American Lung Association, this guide to state legislation is up to date and comprehensive. Additional smoking information can be accessed from this page.

Data Sites

American Lung Association—Tobacco Control

http://www.lungusa.org/tobacco/

Fact sheets on smoking, secondhand smoke, smoking among other adults, as well as other data and statistics are available from this sight.

CDC's STATE: State Tobacco Activities Tracking and Evaluation

http://www2.cdc.gov/nccdphp/osh/state/

This electronic data warehouse contains up-to-date and historical state-level data on tobacco use prevention and control. The STATE System is designed to integrate many data sources to provide comprehensive summary data and facilitate research and consistent interpretation of the data.

Tobacco Control

http://tc.bmjjournals.com

This online journal with peer-reviewed articles considers all aspects of tobacco prevention and control.

Tobacco Documents Online

http://tobaccodocuments.org

Provides searching and full-text access to primary source documents related to tobacco, tobacco companies, and smoking.

Tobacco Industry Tracking Database

http://www.tidatabase.org

This bibliographic database provides over 11,000 entries dating back to 1960 on all aspects of tobacco and smoking. Provided by a pro-control group.

Advocacy Sites

—*For Tobacco Control/Nonsmokers' Rights*

Americans for Non-Smokers Rights

http://www.no-smoke.org

Big Tobacco Sucks

http://www.bigtobaccosucks.org

Campaign for Tobacco-Free Kids

http://tobaccofreekids.org

Infact

http://www.infact.org

—*Against Tobacco Control/For Smokers' Rights*

FORCES

http://www.forces.org

International Tobacco Growers Association

http://www.tobaccoleaf.org

Tobacco Associates

http://www.tobaccoassociatesinc.org

Substance Abuse

Summary

Substance abuse and dependence cuts across all lines of race, culture, educational, and socioeconomic status, leaving no group untouched by its devastating effects. A recent survey estimated that about 13.0 million citizens of the United States had used an illegal substance in the month preceding the study. Substance abuse is an enormous public health problem, with far-ranging effects throughout society. In addition to the toll substance abuse can take on one's physical health, substance abuse is considered to be an important factor in a wide variety of social problems, affecting rates of crime, domestic violence, sexually transmitted diseases (including HIV/AIDS), unemployment, homelessness, teen pregnancy, and failure in school. One study estimated that 20 percent of the total yearly cost of health care in the United States is spent on the effects of drug and alcohol abuse.

Keywords
Addiction
Alcoholism
Binge drinking
Chain smoking
Children of addition
Club drugs
Detoxification
Drug abuse
Inhalant abuse
Intravenous drug use
Needle exchange programs
Parity for substance abuse
  (insurance)
Street drugs
Substance dependence
Twelve steps
Underaged drinkers

Related Topics
Drug policy
Smoking
Welfare reform

(From the *Gale Encyclopedia of Medicine* via FindArticles).

Part of the controversy currently surrounding this topic is that some believe too much attention regarding substance abuse is given to the issue of illicit drugs, ignoring the abuses of legal substances. Some also feel that more attention should be given to the issue of treatment, not simply punishment and fixing the damage caused by abuse. There has been an increased effort to destigmatize substance abuse as a moral failing and instead look at the biological and medical nature of chemical dependencies. Other major initiatives have been undertaken to ensure that substance abuse and mental health are covered as other treatable diseases by medical insurance plans (parity). Club drugs have become a new enticement for young people, adding to binge drinking problems found among college age and younger people. Alcohol marketing and advertising are coming under increased criticism in light of the fact that fully 50 percent of the alcohol industry's income comes from abusive use of their product (drinking by minors and excessive adult drinking).

Recent research examines other potential aspects of substance abuse policy, including the link between gambling and eating disorders and substance abuse. It is estimated that 30 to 40 percent of all new HIV infections are caused by injection drug use. An issue being examined is how to incorporate HIV/AIDS treatment and prevention in the criminal justice system to treat the medical needs of those incarcerated because of illicit substance abuse. There are those who are wondering whether better policies of drug prevention and treatment aimed at juveniles can help to break the cycle of juvenile criminalization. Substance abuse has also been linked to welfare reform, as many welfare recipients are unable to work due to substance abuse problems. In addition, substance-abusing parents cause 70 percent of the nation's child welfare cases, raising questions about when state agencies should intervene on a child's behalf.

The role of religion in treating substance abuse is another interesting policy dilemma. Faith-based initiatives appear to be a natural connection, as research has shown that religion can tremendously aid people fighting substance abuse who are also receiving professional therapy. However, most clergy are ill prepared to handle substance abuse issues, and most mental healthcare professionals fail to take advantage of God, religion, or spirituality in their treatments.

A host of other issues can be examined. Substance abuse in schools adds 10 percent more to the cost of education by means of class disruption and violence, special education, teacher turnover, truancy, property damage, counseling, and more. States spend over 13 percent of their budgets on substance abuse problems. Ninety-six percent of that money goes to fix the wreckage of abuse problems; only 4 percent goes to prevention and treatment. Binge drinking on college campuses leads to rioting, sexual abuse, lower academic achievement, and a whole host of other problems. Controversies over treatment versus punishment abound.

In summary, substance abuse is a highly complex social policy issue that affects the healthcare, economic, educational, welfare, religious, and family systems in our nation. Aside from the nation's drug policy, abuse of all kinds of substances—legal and illegal—is an issue requiring public policy action.

Web Sites

Reference Sites

Principles of Drug Addiction Treatment

http://www.nida.nih.gov/PODAT/PODATindex.html

This report from the NIH provides comprehensive information on treatment strategies, categories of programs available in the United States, scientifically based approaches to treatment, and answers to a variety of questions. Also included is a list of other resources to consult.

Substance Abuse Home Page: Join Together Online

http://www.jointogether.org/sa/

This site provides an overview of this complex issue, a list of hot topics related to substance abuse, related resources, news, and legislative updates. The group providing this information supports community-based efforts to reduce, prevent, and treat substance abuse across the nation.

News Sites

Alcohol Research Center

http://alcoholresearch.lsumc.edu

Provides up-to-the-minute news feeds on "Alcohol in the News."

Yahoo! News: Full Coverage: Substance Use and Abuse

http://fullcoverage.yahoo.com/fc/

Search Full Coverage for the term "substance abuse or alcoholism". Select the Full Coverage Categories for "Substance Use and Abuse" or "Alcohol and Alcoholism" to view news stories, editorials, feature articles, audio/video resources, Web sites, and links to other specialized news sources on this topic.

Law/Legislation

LII: Law About . . . Alcohol, Tobacco, and Controlled Substances

http://www.law.cornell.edu/topics/alcohol_tobacco.html

Provides an overview of laws that govern these topics as well as recent court cases, federal law, and state law.

Data Sites

Addiction Resource Guide

http://www.addictionresourceguide.com

This is "a comprehensive directory of addiction treatment facilities online."

Center on Addiction and Substance Abuse

http://www.casacolumbia.org

A wealth of research is provided giving insights into the varied implications of substance abuse in society.

Go Ask Alice: Alcohol, Nicotine and Other Drugs

http://www.goaskalice.columbia.edu/Cat2.html

Provides candid questions and frank answers from Columbia's Health online question and answer service.

National Institute on Drug Abuse

http://www.nida.nih.gov

This federal institute is charged with researching the scientific aspects of drug abuse and ensuring that the data are distributed to policymakers and healthcare professionals. The Web site provides a wealth of scientific data.

NCADI: National Clearinghouse for Alcohol and Drug Information

http://www.health.org

This national clearinghouse provides information about drugs, the policy issues, links to resources, news, and related databases.

Substance Abuse and Mental Health Services Administration

http://www.samhsa.gov

SAMHSA is the federal agency charged with improving the quality and availability of prevention, treatment, and rehabilitative services to reduce illness, death, disability, and cost to society resulting from substance abuse and mental illnesses. This site provides lots of data on dependencies and education and prevention programs. Access several clearinghouses of information through this portal as well.

Advocacy Sites

—More Treatment/Medical Plan Coverage

Hazelden

http://www.hazelden.org

NAADAC: The Association for Addiction Professionals

http://www.naadac.org

—Alcohol Industry Accountability

FACE Project

http://www.faceproject.org

MADD

http://www.madd.org

—Club Drugs/Youth Problems

NIDA—Club Drugs.org

http://www.clubdrugs.org

Project GHB

http://www.projectghb.org

Teen Pregnancy

Summary

Teens are more likely now than they were in the past to have premarital sex and, as a result, to bear children out of wedlock. According to surveys conducted on a regular basis, by the time teenagers reach the age of sixteen, 39 percent of females and 45 percent of males are sexually active. Other surveys of teenagers indicate that social or peer pressure and a belief that "everyone is doing it" are primary motivations for teen sexual activity. Only a small proportion mentioned being in love with their partners or wanting to feel grown up. Some studies suggest a link between substance abuse and sexual activity.

Adults tend to agree that it is preferable for teenagers to delay sex until adulthood, because the risks of premarital sex—AIDS and other sexually transmitted diseases as well as pregnancy—are so high. Teen pregnancy is also closely linked to a range of social issues, such as welfare dependency, child well-being, and responsible fatherhood. Only 56 percent of teen mothers ever graduate from high school. A female who begins parenting in her teens makes half the lifetime earnings of a woman who has her first child at twenty or later. Children of teen mothers are often born into poverty and thus face many disadvantages. Preventing teen pregnancy is not simply a reproductive health issue.

Although there has been a drop in adolescent pregnancy rates over the last twenty-five years across the developed world, U.S. teenagers have higher pregnancy rates, birthrates, and abortion rates than adolescents in other developed countries. The Alan Guttmacher Institute notes that some 900,000 Americans younger than twenty become pregnant every year. More than three-quarters of pregnancies among teenagers each year are unintended, and more than one-quarter end in abortion. "The primary reasons why U.S. teenagers have the highest rates of pregnancy, childbearing and abortion among developed countries is less overall contraceptive use" (Guttmacher Institute, *Teenage Sexual and Reproductive Behavior in Developed Countries*, 2001).

Keywords
Abstinence
Adolescent pregnancy
Birth control
Contraception
Premarital sex
Sex education
Unmarried fathers
Unmarried mothers

Related Topics
Abortion
Adoption
Welfare reform

Contrasting ideologies play an important role in the debate about how to prevent teenage pregnancy. Those who believe teenage sex is wrong support programs that advise teens to say no to sex. This is known as abstinence-only sex education. The welfare reform law enacted in 1996 created the Abstinence Education Program, which provides federal grants to states for abstinence education activities such as mentoring and counseling designed to promote abstinence from sexual activity until marriage. State agencies may administer abstinence education programs or they may provide grants to other public and private agencies, including faith-based organizations.

Some question the effectiveness of abstinence-only sex education. They argue that when students take virginity pledges and then fail to keep them, they are unprepared to protect themselves against pregnancy or infection and are much less likely to use contraceptives. These advocates support comprehensive or "abstinence plus" sex education programs that include discussion of the value of abstinence but also teach teens to protect themselves against pregnancy and sexually transmitted diseases by using condoms or other forms of contraception if they do decide to become sexually active.

Web Sites

Reference Sites

MEDLINEplus: Teenage Pregnancy

http://www.nlm.nih.gov/medlineplus/teenagepregnancy.html

This research guide from the National Library of Medicine organizes sites into the following categories: general overviews, coping, diagnosis, prevention and screening, research, specific conditions/aspects, dictionaries, directories, organizations, and statistics. Also provides a link to retrieve current journal articles on the topic from the MEDLINE database.

National Campaign to Prevent Teen Pregnancy

http://www.teenpregnancy.org

This organization describes itself as a "nonprofit, nonpartisan initiative supported almost entirely by private donations." Its goal is to reduce the teen pregnancy rate by one-third between 1996 and 2005. The "Research, Resources and Information" section of the site includes literature reviews and reports on topics such as evaluating abstinence programs, welfare reform, and the role of men and boys in pregnancy prevention. Also presents survey data on adult and teen attitudes about sex, abstinence, contraception, and a range of other topics.

Planned Parenthood: Teen Issues

http://www.plannedparenthood.org/teens/

Provides useful information on both abstinence and birth control as a means of preventing pregnancy, as well as sexuality and options for coping with unintended pregnancy.

Reproductive Health Gateway

http://www.rhgateway.org

This project, managed by Johns Hopkins University, provides access to publications of a wide variety of health organizations. May be searched by keyword or browsed by topic.

Resource Center for Adolescent Pregnancy Prevention

http://www.etr.org/recapp/

"ReCAPP provides practical tools and information to effectively reduce sexual risk-taking behaviors." Includes information on programs and curriculum, research abstracts, statistics, and links to other resources.

News Sites

Yahoo! News: Full Coverage: Fertility and Pregnancy

http://fullcoverage.yahoo.com/fc/

Search Full Coverage for the term "fertility". Select the Full Coverage Category for "Health: Fertility and Pregnancy" to view news stories, editorials, feature articles, audio/video resources, Web sites, and links to other specialized news sources on this topic.

Law/Legislation

U.S. Social Security Act, Sec. 510

http://www.ssa.gov/OP_Home/ssact/title05/0510.htm

This section of the federal law (PL 104-193) guarantees $50 million annually over five years beginning in FY 1998 for abstinence-only education grants to the states. The law contains an eight-point definition of abstinence-only education that sets forth specific messages to be taught.

Data Sites

Alan Guttmacher Institute

http://www.agi-usa.org

The Institute provides publications, policy reports, and data, including state fact sheets, on abortion, teen pregnancy, contraception, sexual behavior, and diseases. Fact sheets are updated monthly.

CDC: Reproductive Health Information Source

http://www.cdc.gov/nccdphp/drh/

The Centers for Disease Control (CDC) collect health statistics from the states and other sources and provide various data reports, fact sheets, and tables on reproductive health, unintended pregnancy, and assisted reproductive technology topics. Most statistical information on other Web sites is derived from CDC data.

HRSA: Abstinence Education

http://mchb.hrsa.gov/programs/adolescents/abstinence.htm

This site provides a fact sheet and an annual report for Section 510 Abstinence Education grants to the States; it includes data for the SPRANS Community Based Abstinence Education grant program.

National Center for Health Statistics: Teen Births

http://www.cdc.gov/nchs/fastats/teenbrth.htm

This site provides access to recent statistical reports on teen births as well as more comprehensive overviews, showing trends over time, and links to other data sites.

State Sexuality Education Policy

http://www.agi-usa.org/pubs/spib_SSEP.pdf

Report from the Guttmacher Institute (in PDF format) lists state requirements for teaching about abstinence, contraception, HIV and sexually transmitted diseases, and parental consent requirements.

Advocacy Sites

—*Promote Abstinence*

Abstinence Clearinghouse

http://www.abstinence.net

It's Great to Wait: Sexual Abstinence Until Marriage

http://www.greattowait.com

Not Me, Not Now

http://www.notmenotnow.org

Straight Talk

http://www.straight-talk.com

—*Promote Comprehensive Sex Education Programs*

Advocate for Youth: Rights, Respect, Responsibility

http://www.advocatesforyouth.org

CFOC's Teen Sexuality Education

http://www.cfoc.org

National Organization on Adolescent Pregnancy, Parenting and Prevention

http://www.noappp.org

SIECUS: Sexuality Information and Education Council of the U.S.

http://www.siecus.org

Terrorism

Summary

Certainly the September 11, 2001, attacks on the World Trade Center and the Pentagon provide Americans with a modern-day definition of terrorism that has put this issue, in some form or another, on the front page of most American newspapers daily. While the issue is not new to America or the world, September 11 certainly defines America's current understanding of and response to terrorism. The attacks have been compared to the Pearl Harbor attack of World War II, mostly because there have been so few large-scale attacks against our country on our own soil.

The official U.S. response to the 2001 attacks has been the declaration of a "war on terror." Initially this included hunting down Osama bin Laden and all Al-Qaeda operatives who claimed responsibility for the attacks. Because bin Laden and Al-Qaeda were based in Afghanistan and harbored by the ruling Taliban government, the U.S. attack included dismantling that government in the process. America next turned its attention to Saddam Hussein in Iraq, believing he was secretly compiling weapons of mass destruction (WMD) that he might use against us or sell to terrorists who might use them against us. Rumblings about Iran's involvement with WMDs and terrorism are making it unclear whether future conflict will happen there.

Americans have been divided in their support of the war on terror. Those who support it feel that a tough, no-tolerance approach will send the message that others should not consider such actions against us. There is belief that the next attack will be more destructive, killing more people, and that it is necessary to take a proactive approach to finding terrorists and WMDs before this can happen. Those who oppose this response believe that such retaliation will incite further terrorist actions, will alienate potential allies, and is not sustainable. Alternate responses they advocate include diplomacy, homeland security, and

Keywords
Al-Qaeda
Anti-Americanism
Arms trade
Bioterrorism
Dirty bombs
Eco-terrorism
Military tribunals
Operation Enduring Freedom
Responding to terrorism
September 11, 2001
Terrorist networks
War on terror
Weapons of mass destruction (WMD)
World Trade Center

Related Topics
Civil liberties
Homeland security
Immigration policy
National defense
Race relations
Weapons

increased intelligence efforts. Some groups, although few, advocate public dialog toward understanding the animosity provoking the attacks to find peaceful responses. The war on terror becomes more complex as time goes on and the United States takes preemptive actions.

Domestic complications of the war on terror have included charges of racism and anti-Muslim sentiment because the organizations involved in terror against the United States are Middle Eastern and Islamic, thus turning the spotlight on related American communities. While the government has made a concerted effort to separate out the issues, not all are convinced it is being done successfully. Additional criticism of an uncontrolled response against terrorism is that American values of privacy and free speech and other civil liberties are being undermined at the cost of seeking out every potential threat.

The war on terror produces foreign relations complications. Some would insist that America, as a democratic superpower, is superior by nature and has a moral responsibility to secure the world against terrorist organizations through war when necessary and democratization when possible. Others shun preemptive strikes they view as imperialistic and do not agree that our role is to spread democracy throughout the world but instead to affirm the differences that exist worldwide and define policies that allow us to peacefully coexist.

Another interesting component of America's foreign relations in regard to terrorism is the role that the Israeli–Palestinian conflict plays in our relationship with other Middle Eastern countries. This conflict, along with the side we take, complicates our relationship with Muslim countries in the region. In addition, our relationships with countries like Saudi Arabia, Egypt, and Pakistan cannot be avoided, yet they add more layers of complication.

The issue of how to handle captured suspected terrorists is also a point of debate. The United States proposes the use of military tribunals rather than the regular court system for trying suspects of terrorism. Military tribunals do not protect the constitutional rights of citizens in the way regular courts do and will likely receive criticism from the international community. However, military tribunals have been used during wartime in the past, and some see them as necessary for dealing with enemies of the state.

Web Sites

Reference Sites

Frontline: The Roots of Terrorism
http://www.pbs.org/wgbh/pages/frontline/roots/

Includes the companion Web sites of seven Frontline special investigations that examined events leading to the September 11 attack.

Global War on Terrorism (U.S. Air Force)

http://www.au.af.mil/au/awc/awcgate/cps-terr.htm

Provides portal access to almost every topic related to America's struggle with terrorism.

Public Agenda Special Report: Terrorism

http://www.publicagenda.org/specials/terrorism/terror.htm

This site provides an overview, facts, perspectives, public opinion, resources, and links to related topics covered by the institute, such as America's global role, immigration, and Internet policy.

Terrorism: Questions and Answers

http://www.terrorismanswers.com/

Introductory and comprehensive views of terrorism are explained by the Council on Foreign Relations.

Terrorism: The Center for Defense Information

http://www.cdi.org/program/index.cfm?programid=39

Provides outlined information regarding terrorism from this institute, including news, arms trade, foreign policy, homeland security, legislation, U.S. targets, terrorist networks, and U.S. policy.

News Sites

DefenseLink News

http://www.defenselink.mil/news/

Up-to-date coverage of military activity, which at the time of this writing is involved in counterterrorist activities.

Yahoo! News Full Coverage: Terrorism

http://fullcoverage.yahoo.com/fc/

Search Full Coverage for the term "terrorism". Select the Full Coverage Categories for "Terrorism" to view news stories, editorials, feature articles, audio/video resources, Web sites, and links to other specialized news sources on this topic.

Law/Legislation

Terrorism Law and Policy (JURIST)

http://jurist.law.pitt.edu/terrorism.htm

Information on U.S. antiterrorism laws, terrorism and civil liberties, and world antiterrorism laws, as well as expert perspectives on events.

Thomas: Legislation Related to the Attacks of September 11

http://thomas.loc.gov/home/terrorleg.htm

This specially maintained page within Thomas tracks continuing legislation related to the September 11 attacks.

Data Sites

Alternative Resources on the U.S. "War Against Terrorism"

http://www.pitt.edu/~ttwiss/irtf/Alternative.html

Provided by a division of the American Library Association, this list provides resources that counter opinion and policy of the U.S. government.

Congressional Reports: Joint Inquiry into the Intelligence Community Activities Before and After the Terrorist Attacks of September 11, 2001

http://www.gpoaccess.gov/serialset/creports/911.html

Provides the full text of the 872-page report completed by the Senate Select Committee on Intelligence and the House Permanent Select Committee on Intelligence looking into how the attacks were allowed to happen. The report presents the joint inquiry's findings and conclusions, an accompanying narrative, and a series of recommendations.

FBI War on Terrorism

http://www.fbi.gov/terrorinfo/terrorism.htm

Provides links to FBI publications and companion Web sites.

RAND Research Area: Terrorism

http://www.rand.org/terrorism_area/

This is a collection of articles by "hot topic" related to terrorism that have appeared in RAND publications as well as in the regular media. Also contains a list of recent RAND publications on terrorism.

Response to Terrorism (U.S. Department of State)

http://usinfo.state.gov/topical/pol/terror/

Provides descriptions of various governmental counterterrorism initiatives, patterns of global terrorism, recent news about terrorism, a chronology of events, and international efforts to control terrorism.

September 11 Digital Archive

http://www.911digitalarchive.org/

Includes e-mail, photos, video, audio, and documents that were collected and relate to the September 11 attacks. Also provides a portal to other September 11 Web sites.

Terrorism: Polling Report.com

http://www.pollingreport.com/terror.htm

Provides results of surveys regarding the war on terrorism.

Terrorism Research Center

http://www.terrorism.com

Provides portal information to country profiles, terrorist profiles, significant events, news, books, Web sites, and other information related to terrorism. Some data are proprietary to this independent organization; other information is in the public domain.

Advocacy Sites

—Domestic Policy Responses

American-Arab Anti-Discrimination Committee

http://www.adc.org

Families of September 11

http://www.familiesofseptember11.org

Muslims Against Terrorism

http://www.matusa.org

—Foreign Policy Responses

Peaceful Tomorrows

http://www.peacefultomorrows.org

Not in Our Name

http://www.notinourname.net

War on Terror: Amnesty International (concern for human rights)

http://www.amnestyusa.org/waronterror

Water Resources

Summary

Water is the most common and important substance on Earth, covering almost three-fourths of its surface. However, much of Earth's water is saline and thus not available for drinking, farming, and industrial use. Only about 3 percent is freshwater. Freshwater sources include rivers and streams as well as underground aquifers (groundwater). Half of all the drinking water in the United States comes from groundwater, which is also used extensively for irrigation.

Keywords
Aquifers
Freshwater
Water conflict
Water conservation
Water privatization
Water rights
Water supply
Water for profit

Related Topics
Energy supply and policy
Farmland

Availability of adequate supplies of freshwater varies not only from region to region but also from year to year within regions, depending on rainfall. Natural phenomena known as El Niño and La Niña influence weather and precipitation. El Niño is a naturally occurring disruption of the ocean-atmosphere system in the tropical Pacific Ocean that affects weather conditions around the globe. It causes increased rainfall across the southern part of the United States, warmer than normal temperatures in the north central states, and cooler than normal temperatures in the southeastern and southwestern United States. The effects of La Niña on climate tend to be the opposite of El Niño.

Freshwater supply and use in the United States is monitored and reported by the U.S. Geological Service (USGS). The Ogallala aquifer is the largest single source of underground water in the United States. This aquifer provides water to portions of eight western states: Colorado, Kansas, Nebraska, New Mexico, Oklahoma, South Dakota, Texas, and Wyoming. Like many aquifers in the West, this source of underground water is rapidly being depleted because its water supply is being extracted by thousands of wells at a faster rate than can be replenished through annual rainfall. On almost every continent, many major aquifers are being drained faster than their natural rate of recharge. This problem is most severe in India, China, the United States, North Africa, and the Middle East.

Some regions of the United States do not have adequate water supplies at the same time that other areas may be experiencing floods. For example, the American West, from the Rocky Mountains to the California coast, is arid, with a limited and inconsistent supply of water. Urban growth also puts stress on water supplies. Conflicts over water supplies between urban and rural areas, especially in the Western United States, have become more frequent.

In the United States, state laws and regulations establish how an individual, company, or other organization obtains and protects water rights. When water rights are disputed, the question is usually resolved in the courts. When the water involved crosses state boundaries, states may enter into various agreements for water sharing. When agreement cannot be reached between states, the matter is usually settled in federal courts, or in some cases by an act of Congress.

Another source of conflict is privatization of the water supply. According to *Fortune* magazine, water is now big business. " It promises to be to the 21st century what oil was to the 20th." Private companies are replacing publicly owned and regulated utility companies in some areas. In some U.S. cities, the municipal water and sewer facilities are old and in need of expensive repairs. Some cities have contracted with private water companies as an alternative to repairing systems. Often the cost of water rises dramatically when private companies replace public utilities. In some developing countries where there is no existing water utility service, private companies have also found business opportunities.

Web Sites

Reference Sites

EPA: Water

http://www.epa.gov/water/

Site categories include groundwater and drinking water, water science, wastewater management, wetlands, oceans, and watersheds. Each category contains a nontechnical overview of the topic and consumer-oriented publications as well as more technical reports, regulations, and data.

UNESCO Water Portal

http://www.unesco.org/water/

Provides links to UN programs on water resources, recent publications, data, news, and events related to freshwater supplies around the world. Includes links to a library of water-related photos and an international glossary of hydrology. The portal also includes a directory (links and brief descriptions) of water-related sites that can be browsed by theme or by geographic region.

USGS: Water Resources of the United States

http://water.usgs.gov

This U.S. Geological Survey portal provides links to water data; publications (factsheets, reports, news releases); technical resources related to groundwater, surface water, and water quality; and links to various government water program sites

News Sites

Planet Ark: Reuters World Environment News

http://www.planetark.com/dailynewshome.cfm

Browse daily environmental news stories from around the world; search the news archive by keyword or topic.

The Water Barons

http://www.icij.org/water/

This special project from The Center for Public Integrity, an organization of investigative journalists, provides ten articles that describe water privatization efforts and controversies around the world. The introduction notes that "explosive growth of three private water utility companies in the last 10 years raises fears that mankind may be losing control of its most vital resource to a handful of monopolistic corporations."

Yahoo! News: Full Coverage: Water Issues

http://fullcoverage.yahoo.com/fc/

Search Full Coverage for the term "water". Select the Full Coverage Category for "World: Water Issues" to view news stories, editorials, feature articles, audio/video resources, Web sites, and links to other specialized news sources on this topic .

Law/Legislation

FAOLEX

http://faolex.fao.org/faolex/

Describes itself as "the world's largest electronic collection of national laws and regulations, as well as treaties, on food, agriculture and renewable natural resources." Topics include agriculture, animals, environment, fisheries, food, forestry, land, plants, water, and wildlife. Legal texts are summarized and indexed in English, French, or Spanish. Useful for international or comparative perspective on these topics.

International Water Law Project

http://www.internationalwaterlaw.org

This site is provided by the Pacific Institute, a nonprofit research organization. It offers treaties, articles, news stories, and case law related to this topic.

NRDC: Environmental Legislation

http://www.nrdc.org/legislation/legwatch.asp

The National Resources Defense Council (NRDC) is an advocacy organization that provides reports, unpublished research, policy and technical analyses, congressional testimony, and other materials by NRDC's lawyers, scientists, and analysts. Their weekly *Legislative Watch* bulletin tracks movement of environmental bills in Congress.

Safe Drinking Water Act

http://www.epa.gov/safewater/sdwa/sdwa.html

This Act was originally passed by Congress in 1974 and was later amended in 1986 and 1996. It regulates the public drinking water supply and protects rivers, streams, reservoirs, and groundwater wells. It authorizes the Environmental Protection Agency (EPA) to set and monitor national health-based standards for drinking water.

Sierra Club: Votewatch

http://www.sierraclub.org/votewatch/

The Sierra Club has been monitoring congressional activity on environmental issues since the 106th Congress (1999). It summarizes all of the proposed legislation on this site and provides a complete roster of votes for each bill or amendment.

Data Sites

Ground Water Atlas of the United States

http://capp.water.usgs.gov/gwa/

This site provides an online version of the printed publication produced by the U.S. Geological Survey. It provides geologic and hydrologic data about important aquifers (underground water sources) in the United States. Chapters in the atlas are written for use by nonspecialists and contain many illustrations.

NRCS: State of the Land

http://www.nrcs.usda.gov/technical/land/

This site, from USDA's Natural Resources Conservation Service, provides data and analysis on land use, soil erosion, water quality, water supply, wetlands, and other issues regarding the conservation and use of natural resources.

WaterWatch

http://water.usgs.gov/waterwatch/

This site from the U.S. Geological Survey provides maps and graphs of water resources conditions. Select a category (such as real-time stream flow or drought conditions) and a geographic area to generate maps, plots, or tables from the database. Use the "Additional Information" links at the top to jump to other government water data sites.

Advocacy Sites

—Support Privatization or Outsourcing of Water Services

Center for Free Market Environmentalism: Water

http://www.perc.org/publications/water.php

Water and Wastewater Program

http://www.rppi.org/water/

World Bank: Private Sector Development

http://www.worldbank.org/privatesector/transaction/

—Promote Conservation of Water Resources

Freshwater Society

http://www.freshwater.org

Nature Conservancy: Freshwater Initiative

http://nature.org/initiatives/freshwater/

Water in the West

http://www.waterwest.com

Weapons

Summary

War has been an unfortunate and prominent reality of history. In fact, estimates indicate that in the 3,000 years of recorded history there have been fewer than 300 years of a conflict-free planet. In light of this reality, the production, proliferation, and enhancement of weapons has been an issue for societies to contend with over time. Questions that come to mind are: How much money should a nation spend on weapons in light of the other financial burdens of its society? Who should be allowed to have weapons? What sorts of weapons should societies have? What levels of testing, placement, and stockpiling of weapons should be allowed? These and other questions need to be examined on the national and global level. The tension for each nation lies in having the ability to protect itself versus proliferation to the point that is harmful to the existence of humankind.

The weapons of greatest threat to the planet are nuclear weapons. With the capability to utterly destroy entire nations, if not the planet, these weapons have required the most attention in recent times. In the 1960s and 1970s the tensions were largely between the United States and the Soviet Union. Treaties such as SALT and START were negotiated through the 1980s to keep both nations in check. With the dismantling of the Soviet government concern grew over the retention of these weapons by small republics that would not observe treaties created by superpowers. Increasingly, concern has grown over how to keep these weapons from countries that refuse to participate in international discussions or treaties (rogue states), or even worse, from terrorist organizations interested in destroying governments but which do not represent a government

Keywords

Anthrax
Anti-Ballistic Missile (ABM) Treaty
Arms control
Biological weapons
Chemical weapons
Dirty bomb
Disarmament
Intercontinental ballistic missiles (ICBMs)
Land mines
Missile defense
MOAB (Mother of All Bombs)
Nuclear disarmament
Nuclear test ban
Nuclear weapons
Ricin
Rogue states
Smallpox
Strategic Defense Initiative (SDI)
Weapons of mass destruction

Related Topics
Homeland defense
National defense
Terrorism

themselves. If such an organization were to destroy a major city in the United States, what sort of response would we make? What sort of deterrent is there to keep such an organization from using such a weapon? Currently, the greatest controls over nuclear weapons are the cost of making them, the controls over the materials required to make them, and controls employed by governments to know to whom they are selling materials. There is great fear that these deterrents are unsustainable, not foolproof, and that in time nuclear weapons will make it into the hands of a terrorist organization determined to use them.

Because of the difficulty in creating nuclear weapons, it is known that some nations and terrorist groups have been working to develop other forms of weapons that can cause widespread destruction (weapons of mass destruction, or WMDs). These sorts of weapons include chemical and biological weapons, which can infect or contaminate large numbers of people with chemical burns or illnesses on a large scale. Some of the toxins of concern are anthrax, sarin, ricin, and smallpox. The largest deterrent to use of such substances to date has been the inability to effectively "weaponize" them, or put them in a form in which they can be launched and effectively detonated and spread. The 1925 Geneva Convention banned use of chemical weapons in warfare but does not ban biological weapons and is certainly not recognized by terrorists or rogue states. "Dirty bombs," or those containing radiological material, are seen as yet another mass destruction alternative to nuclear bombs.

Use of antipersonnel landmines has also attracted international attention. Retreating armies bury these mines to deter the advance of the enemy. The problem for society is that they are often left behind even after a war is over and detonate on unsuspecting children and other civilians as they are trying to rebuild after war and get on with their lives.

One other major controversy in current weapons issues is the creation of long-range (even intercontinental) missiles and defense shields. Long-range missiles allow an enemy to attack a nation from a far distance and without the advance warning. Some propose use of technology and weapons to build a sort of national shield that would be able to detect and destroy such missiles before they reach their intended target or populated area. President Reagan proposed such a defense system in the 1980s, calling it a Strategic Defense Initiative (SDI). His critics called it "Star Wars" because they deemed the concept science fiction. Critics also balked at the amount of money that would have been required to create such a system, which would have been taken from what seemed to be more doable and necessary social and defense projects. This debate continues today. President George Bush has retired the ABM treaty and has resumed funding research in this area.

Web Sites

Reference Sites

Arms Control Association: Subject Resources

http://www.armscontrol.org/subject/

Covers issues such as biological weapons, chemical weapons, missile defense, and landmines. Each issue provides access to key documents (treaties, factsheets, etc.) of current importance to the issue, as well as articles by this organization analyzing the situation.

Avoiding Armageddon

http://www.pbs.org/avoidingarmageddon/

This is an in-depth investigation into the collision of terrorism and weapons of mass destruction. Provides a primer on WMDs. Includes personal testimonies and interactive lessons.

Ballistic Missile Defense Project: The Claremont Institute

http://www.claremont.org/projects/missiledefense

Through the use of Quick Time movies, this interactive Web site addresses what threat exists from ballistic missiles, how it affects Americans, how it would work, and why we do not yet have a defense system. This site is pro-missile defense.

CNN.com Biological and Chemical Weapons

http://news.yahoo.com/fc?tmpl=fc&cid=34&in=world&cat=biological_weapons_and_warfare

This is a tutorial on "what they are and what they do".

NOVA Online: Bioterror

http://www.pbs.org/wgbh/nova/bioterror/

Provides an investigation of the history, development, and future use of biological weapons. Includes interviews with two biowarfarers who were on opposite sides of the Cold War. Companion Web site for a NOVA documentary.

NTI Issues and Analysis

http://nti.org/e_research/e3_issues.html

Provides issue briefs on a variety of weapons-related issues such as missile defense, biological weapons, and chemical weapons. This site is supports nonproliferation.

News Sites

Yahoo! News Full Coverage: Biological and Chemical Weapons

http://fullcoverage.yahoo.com/fc/

Search Full Coverage for the term "biological and chemical weapons". Select the Full Coverage Categories for "Biological and Chemical Weapons" to view news stories, editorials, feature articles, audio/video resources, Web sites, and links to other specialized news sources on this topic. Full coverage pages for "Anthrax" and "Nuclear Weapons" are also available.

Law/Legislation

International and Comparative Law (JURIST)

http://jurist.law.pitt.edu/sg_il.htm

Use this portion of the Jurist legal site for finding international news and treaties of which arms control may be a part.

Data Sites

ABM/Missile Defense

http://www.heritage.org/Research/MissileDefense/

Provides reports, opinions, and interactive tutorials from this conservative think tank, which supports missile defense as a primary way of protecting the nation.

Carnegie Endowment: Treaties and Agreements

http://www.ceip.org/files/nonprolif/resources/treaties.asp

Includes text, overviews, and news about weapons treaties.

Center for Non-Proliferation Studies

http://cns.miis.edu/

Data, tutorials, country profiles, publications, and subscription databases are available, with information on all sorts of WMDs including nuclear, missile, chemical, and biological weapons.

Disarmament Resources in the United Nations System

http://www.un.org/partners/civil_society/m-disarm.htm

The United Nations has been a major force in the international effort to disarm nations and reduce weapons proliferation. This site has descriptions of their efforts, data on countries, treaties, institutes, and links to related international organizations involved in arms control.

Henry L. Stimson Center

http://www.stimson.org

Provides research articles on tactics for working toward nonproliferation. Click on "projects" to find summaries of issues related to various weapons and controlling them in various parts of the world.

How Nuclear Bombs Work

http://www.howstuffworks.com/nuclear-bomb.htm

Presents clear, scientific information on the physics, design, and other aspects of nuclear bombs. Click on "lots more information" for descriptions of other weapons of mass destruction such as dirty bombs and MOAB.

National Nuclear Security Administration

http://www.nnsa.doe.gov

This unit oversees nuclear weapons development and non-weapon use of nuclear energy in the United States. The site provides access to policy statements, open letters, speeches, congressional testimony, budget information, and more.

Advocacy Sites

—Nonproliferation

Council for a Livable World

http://www.clw.org

Institute for Defense and Disarmament Studies

http://www.idds.org

Nuclear Threat Initiative

http://nti.org

Zero-Nukes.org

http://www.zero-nukes.org

—Pro-Defense Initiatives

FIT-AIM-ACT Campaign for America's Defense

http://www.fitaimact.org

Frontiers of Freedom

http://www.ff.org

High Frontier

http://www.highfrontier.org

Missile Defense Agency

http://www.acq.osd.mil/bmdo/bmdolink/html/

Welfare Reform

Summary

In August 1996, President Clinton signed the Personal Responsibility and Work Opportunity Reconciliation Act, also known as the welfare reform law. This law ended the Aid to Families with Dependent Children (AFDC) program and replaced it with a new program, Temporary Assistance for Needy Families (TANF).

The impetus for welfare reform came from the states. In 1994, Wisconsin implemented a program called Wisconsin Works, which based aid on recipients' efforts to secure employment. The thrust of the 1996 welfare reform act transfers control over welfare spending to the states, allowing them to initiate programs similar to Wisconsin's.

Keywords
Aid to Families with Dependent Children (AFDC)
Entitlement program
Food stamp program
New federalism
State block grants
TANF reauthorization
Temporary Aid to Needy Families (TANF)
Welfare dependency
Welfare to work
Workfare

Related Topics
Fair wages
Health policy
Homelessness
Teen pregnancy

AFDC was an entitlement program that guaranteed benefits to all recipients whose income and resources were below state-determined eligibility levels. These state tests of financial need were subject to federal guidelines. Unlike AFDC, TANF is not an entitlement program. TANF is a federal block grant program, in which the federal government allocates a "block" of funds to each state to use for this general purpose. The states have the authority to determine eligibility requirements and benefit levels. In practice, many states have based their TANF programs in part on their earlier practices.

The welfare reform law also contains provisions to reduce out-of-wedlock births, especially among teen mothers. Teen mothers tend to have less education and fewer job skills, and they traditionally place a large burden on the welfare system. To be eligible for TANF benefits, unmarried teenage parents are required to remain in high school and to live in an adult-supervised setting. The federal food stamp program, which is administered by the U.S. Department of Agriculture, remains available to help low-income individuals and families and is not affected by current welfare reform laws.

Those who support increased state control over welfare programs believe that state governments are better suited to assist their poor than is the federal government. By combining dozens of federal welfare programs into block grants to the states, welfare reform can serve low-income people more efficiently. Many felt that the old entitlement system did not reward hard work and that it discouraged the stability of two-parent families. Some charged that the program actually harmed recipients by creating "welfare dependency."

Others believe that the welfare-to-work system merely pushes welfare recipients deeper into poverty, since many are working in low-wage service-sector jobs. They are concerned about the five-year lifetime limit on benefits for adults in the TANF program, especially in areas with high unemployment. Others worry that many women will be unable to compete for and hold onto jobs because of a lack of skills and inadequate childcare. They also argue that, given the lack of federal oversight, during an economic downturn states would slash cash payments and services, destroying the financial safety net for the poor.

More than five years has passed since welfare reform first became law. The 1996 law, which expired in 2002, combined with a strong economy to reduce welfare rolls. A number of public and private organizations have studied the impact of this legislation on poor families. Congress is considering some modifications to the law, based on this experience. Congressional factions differ on how to refine and reauthorize the law.

Proposals put forward in 2003 by Republicans limit the amount of time that welfare recipients can spend in education and training programs and also restrict people to five years of benefits over their lifetimes. This bill continues to ban illegal immigrants from aid programs and offers a modest increase in childcare spending. Democrats propose even more money for childcare and for the states to run their basic assistance programs. They would also allow states to continue benefits for people longer than five years if they are complying with welfare rules.

Web Sites

Reference Sites

Administration for Children and Families: Welfare Reform

http://www.acf.hhs.gov/programs/ofa/welfare/

This site from the U.S. Department of Health and Human Services is useful for locating official policy documents, research data, and laws/regulations related to federal welfare reform and the TANF program.

Public Agenda Online: Poverty and Welfare

http://www.publicagenda.org

Select "Poverty and Welfare" from the list of Issue Guides. The site includes sections that provide an overview of issues, alternative viewpoints, data, recent news, public opinion surveys, etc.

Welfare Information Network

http://www.financeprojectinfo.org/win/

This site is a clearinghouse for information, policy analysis, and technical assistance related to welfare, workforce development, and other human and community services. Includes summaries of TANF State Plans for many topics, such as waivers, time limits, childcare and family support services, teen parent programs, and work activities, enabling comparisons of how states are handling these issues.

News Sites

Civilrights.org—Issues

http://www.civilrights.org/issues/

Provides current news and other resources (reports, speeches, testimony at congressional hearings, court decisions) on a variety of political, legal, economic, and social justice topics, including hate crimes, poverty, welfare reform, housing, immigration, labor, and employment.

Stateline.org

http://www.stateline.org/index.do

Managed by the Pew Center on the States, the site was "founded in order to help journalists, policy makers and engaged citizens become better informed about innovative public policies." This is an excellent resource for news on issues of importance to states, such as welfare and social policy, land use and growth, environment, energy, and healthcare. Browse by topic or by state; search for keywords.

Yahoo! News: Full Coverage: Welfare Reform

http://fullcoverage.yahoo.com/fc/

Search Full Coverage for the term: "welfare reform". Select the Full Coverage Category for "US: Welfare Reform" to view news stories, editorials, feature articles, audio/video resources, Web sites, and links to other specialized news sources on this topic.

Law/Legislation

Summary: Final Rule: TANF Program

http://www.acf.dhhs.gov/programs/ofa/exsumcl.htm

Summarizes the regulatory changes put into effect by passage of the Personal Responsibility and Work Opportunity Reconciliation Act of 1996 (P.L. 104-193).

Data Sites

Institute for Research on Poverty

http://www.ssc.wisc.edu/irp/

This nonprofit, nonpartisan institute at the University of Wisconsin-Madison investigates the causes and consequences of poverty and social inequality. Site includes a Welfare Reform Research Database. Search or browse by subject term to find links to topical reports on welfare reform issues produced by a variety of organizations.

National Conference of State Legislatures: Welfare Reform

http://www.ncsl.org/statefed/welfare/welfare.htm

Includes news, policy analysis, and data related to state implementation of welfare reform.

Research Forum on Children, Families, and the New Federalism

http://www.researchforum.org

This site, produced by Columbia University's National Center for Children in Poverty, features a searchable database of summaries of large- and small-scale research projects; key topics pages; resources pages; and lists of recent publications related to welfare reform, child and family well-being, and community/neighborhood issues.

Urban Institute: Assessing the New Federalism

http://newfederalism.urban.org

This nonpartisan research organization project aims to analyze the devolution of responsibility for social programs from the federal government to the states. Researchers monitor program changes and fiscal developments related to healthcare, welfare, and childcare. Key components of the project include a household survey, studies of policies in thirteen states, and a welfare rules database with information on all states and the District of Columbia.

U.S. Census Bureau: Poverty
http://www.census.gov/hhes/www/poverty.html

Provides federal definition and poverty guidelines, reports from the latest Census, historical studies, and other special reports.

Welfare, Children and Families: A Three-City Study
http://www.jhu.edu/~welfare/

This is a Johns Hopkins University research project to evaluate consequences of welfare reform for children and families in three cities: Boston, Chicago, and San Antonio.

Advocacy Sites

—Promote Further Restrictions on Welfare Benefits

Cato Institute
http://www.cato.org

Heritage Foundation
http://www.heritage.org

Welfare Reform Works
http://www.whitehouse.gov/infocus/welfarereform/

—Promote More Generous Welfare Benefits

Center for Law and Social Policy
http://www.clasp.org

Jobs for the Future
http://www.jff.org

National Campaign for Jobs and Income Support
http://www.nationalcampaign.org

World Trade

Summary

Since nations first began trading with one another, governments have tried to control the flow of goods into their lands, usually through tariffs or through quotas limiting the amount of imports. Tariffs are taxes imposed on imported goods to protect industries within a country from competitors, Today, most of the world's industrialized nations support free trade and the elimination of trade barriers, claiming that such protectionist measures amount to economic discrimination. Those who back free trade argue that removing trade barriers represents the best way to ensure a worldwide improvement in the standard of living. Eliminating tariffs pushes the overall price of consumer goods much lower, they argue, allowing households to get the goods they need more cheaply.

Keywords
European Union
Fair trade
Free trade
GATT
G-8 nations
Global economy
Globalization
International business
International trade
Multinational corporations
NAFTA
Permanent normal trade relations
(PNTR)
Protectionism
Tariff protection
Trade barriers
Transnational corporations

Related Topics
Fair wages

Critics of free trade argue that by removing trade barriers, governments encourage companies to move their production facilities to countries where wages are lower or to lower the wages of their current workers to better compete. Reduction of tariffs rewards nations whose industries underpay their workers to keep costs down. Meetings of the International Monetary Fund (IMF), World Bank gatherings, and summits of the Group of Eight (G-8) leaders have recently drawn large groups of protesters, and at times these protests have become violent.

These protesters support "fair trade," an equitable and fair partnership between marketers in North America and producers in Asia, Africa, Latin America, and other parts of the world. A fair trade partnership works to provide low-income artisans and farmers with a living wage for their work.

Twentieth-century international trade agreements that have lowered barriers include the General Agreement on Tariffs and Trade (GATT) and the North American Free Trade Agreement (NAFTA). NAFTA, which was launched in 1994, removed barriers to trade and investment among Canada, Mexico, and the United States. Labor and environmental groups argue that NAFTA has enriched international corporations but has resulted in U.S. job losses, as companies relocate to Mexico where labor costs are lower. Despite the controversial track record of NAFTA, the proposed Free Trade Area of the Americas (FTAA) would extend NAFTA to an additional thirty-one countries and 400 million people.

Globalization describes the ongoing global trend toward the freer flow of trade and investment across borders and the resulting integration of the international economy. Historically, many businesses and corporations have included operations outside their national borders to provide raw materials, manufacture products, and expand markets. However, international trade agreements promoted by industrialized nations since the 1980s have accelerated the pace of globalization.

Critics of globalization claim it results in unemployment and the loss of jobs in developed countries. Supporters believe that globalization contributes to growth, and that unemployment is mainly due to governments' failure to adopt sound economic policies. They argue that it raises the productivity and living standards of people in developing countries by offering access to foreign capital, global export markets, and advanced technology.

Controversy also surrounded the entrance of China into the World Trade Organization and granting of special trade status to a country that has historically violated the human rights of its workers. The cornerstone principle of the World Trade Organization is that members provide each other unconditional Most Favored Nation trade status, now called Permanent Normal Trade Relations (PNTR) in U.S. trade law. In 2000, President Clinton signed legislation extending permanent normal trade relations to mainland China. Conservatives and business groups like the U.S. Chamber of Commerce and the Business Roundtable, which believe it will help expand sales of U.S. goods in China, supported this bill. It was opposed by Democrats and by unions, human rights advocates, and environmentalists, who argue that it will cost American jobs and remove any motivation for China to improve conditions for workers.

Web Sites

Reference Sites

G8 Information Centre

http://www.g7.utoronto.ca

University of Toronto Library provides this site on the group of eight (G-8) industrialized nations, which meet regularly for summits on macroeconomic management, international trade, and relations with developing countries. Site includes factsheets, news, research, summit documents, and policy analysis.

Global Trade Negotiations Home Page

http://www.cid.harvard.edu/cidtrade/

From Harvard University's Center for International Development, this site provides trade news; issue areas with overviews and links to important resources; and other links to research papers, research institutes, think tanks, and trade organizations. Site does not advocate any specific trade policies or support any particular ideology.

The Globalization Website

http://www.emory.edu/SOC/globalization/

This site, developed by a sociology professor at Emory University, provides a useful overview of the debates related to globalism, articles on issues and theories, reviews of key books, brief biographies of important people, and links to organizations and data sources. Excellent starting point for exploring the many facets of globalization.

News Sites

Globalization Issues: Blog

http://globalization.about.com./blog/

Provides links to current stories on this topic from a variety of news sources.

Yahoo! News: Full Coverage: WTO and International Trade

http://fullcoverage.yahoo.com/fc/

Search Full Coverage for the term "WTO". Select the Full Coverage Category for "Business: WTO and International Trade" to view news stories, editorials, feature articles, audio/video resources, Web sites, and links to other specialized news sources on this topic.

Law/Legislation

Guide to Global Trade Law

http://www.hg.org/trade.html

Includes links to supranational organizations (United Nations, European Union, GATT, NAFTA), texts of some recent treaties, relevant U.S. law, regulations, and agencies related to trade

Lex Mercatoria: Treaties and Organizations

http://www.jus.uio.no/lm/treaties.and.organisations/lm.chronological.html

Provides texts of modern and historical international trade treaties, conventions, and model laws, organized chronologically.

Revised Guide to International Trade Law Resources on the Internet

http://www.llrx.com/features/trade3.htm

This guide, produced by a law librarian at Georgetown University, offers instruction on researching trade law and an annotated guide to good sources, organized in these categories: starting points, international agreements, international organizations, U.S. government resources, dispute settlement, country guides, statistics, and commentary/analysis.

Data Sites

Office of Trade and Economic Analysis: Data and Analysis

http://www.ita.doc.gov/td/industry/otea/

This U.S. Department of Commerce site provides a wealth of U.S. trade data. Foreign Trade Highlights presents cumulative data tables on U.S. international trade in goods and services. Monthly update reports are available, as are links to other data sites and organizations.

Pew Global Attitudes Project

http://people-press.org/pgap/

This project is a series of worldwide public opinion surveys that focus on a changing world, specifically regarding globalization, democratization, modernization, and, in countries with significant Muslim populations, the role of Islam in public policy.

United Nations: Comtrade

http://unstats.un.org/unsd/comtrade/

This database provides detailed statistics by country on commodities exported or imported. Although this is a subscription database, free guest access is provided; guests may not export data tables.

U.S. Census Bureau: Foreign Trade Statistics

http://www.census.gov/foreign-trade/www/

Provides data tables on U.S. trade in goods and services, imports, and exports by country, and tables showing state exports by country and commodity.

YaleGlobal Online Magazine

http://yaleglobal.yale.edu

YaleGlobal Online is a publication of the Yale Center for the Study of Globalization. The magazine publishes original articles and multimedia presentations; it also republishes important articles from other publications. Browse articles by topic (economy, globalization, trade, labor, politics, etc.) or by region.

Advocacy Sites

—*Oppose Globalization*

Centre for Research on Globalization

http://globalresearch.ca

Fair Trade Watch

http://www.naftalawsuit.uswa.org

International Forum on Globalization

http://www.ifg.org

Public Citizen: Global Trade Watch

http://www.citizen.org/trade/

—*Support Globalization*

Business Roundtable

http://www.brtable.org

International Chamber of Commerce: Case for the Global Economy

http://www.iccwbo.org/home/menu_case_for_the_global_economy.asp

United States Council for International Business

http://www.uscib.org

USA*Engage

http://www.usaengage.org

Appendix A

Opinion Magazines

This is a representative list of magazines, available online in whole or in part, which look at issues of public importance to Americans. While there are hundreds more, these were selected because of their stature, cross-representation, and the number of articles they provide for free online. Check with your local library for access to any articles that are cited but not available on the Web site.

Use these sites to gain political perspectives on issues. The list has been divided by political bias to afford an easy way to find opposing viewpoints on a topic. Liberal and conservative publications will often have a persuasive perspective. Neutral or nonpartisan publications may take a persuasive approach on a topic or may focus more heavily on research findings. By viewing an issue from all "sides," you will gain fuller insight into the topic.

Conservative or Libertarian Focus

The American Conservative

http://www.amconmag.com

Publisher: American Conservative, LLC

Description: A different spin on conservative politics, guided by Pat Buchanan's political viewpoint.

American Enterprise

http://www.TAEmag.com

Publisher: American Enterprise Institute for Public Policy Research

Description: Contains articles on economics, foreign policy, law, social policy, regulation, politics, public opinion, and media.

The American Spectator

http://www.spectator.org

Publisher: American Spectator

Description: National magazine of politics and culture.

Frontpage Magazine

http://www.frontpagemag.com

Publisher: Center for the Study of Popular Culture

Description: Covers political news from a conservative perspective.

Hoover Digest

http://www.hooverdigest.org

Publisher: Hoover Institution

Description: Designed for the informed reader who seeks important commentary on current public policy issues; includes a compilation of the recent work of Hoover Institution's scholars.

Human Events

http://www.humaneventsonline.com

Publisher: Eagle Publishing, Inc.

Description: Provides political news and analysis from a conservative viewpoint.

Insight on the News

http://www.insightmag.com

Publisher: Washington Times Corporation

Description: Reports on and analyzes the week's news from a conservative viewpoint.

National Review

http://www.nationalreview.com

Publisher: National Review, Inc.

Description: Discusses national and international issues from a conservative viewpoint.

The New American

http://www.thenewamerican.com

Publisher: American Opinion Publishing Inc.

Description: For constitutional conservatives and economic libertarians; focuses on political science, social opinion and economic theory.

Reason

http://www.reason.com

Publisher: Reason Foundation

Description: Libertarian journal of opinion providing commentary on current affairs, economics, and issues.

The Weekly Standard

http://www.weeklystandard.com

Publisher: News America, Inc.

Description: Provides a forum for conservative perspectives on political issues.

Against the Current

http://solidarity.igc.org/contATC.html

Publisher: Solidarity

Description: Provides a socialist viewpoint on issues. One goal is to promote dialogue among activists, organizers, and serious scholars on the Left.

Liberal or Progressive Focus

Alternative Press Review

http://www.altpr.org

Publisher: A A L Press

Description: Aimed at people interested in the alternative press, alternative culture, and politics.

The American Prospect

http://www.prospect.org

Publisher: The American Prospect, Inc.

Description: Offers political and social commentary from a liberal perspective.

Dissent

http://www.dissentmagazine.org

Publisher: Foundation for the Study of Independent Social Ideas, Inc.

Description: Contains features and articles about politics in the United States, social and cultural commentary, and detailed coverage of European politics.

In These Times

http://www.inthesetimes.com

Publisher: Institute for Public Affairs

Description: Presents a leftist viewpoint along with frequent discussions of strategies for the Democratic party; strong coverage of labor and the women's movement.

Monthly Review

http://www.monthlyreview.org

Publisher: Monthly Review Foundation

Description: Review of culture, politics, and society from a socialist perspective.

Mother Jones

http://www.motherjones.com

Publisher: Foundation for National Progress

Description: Progressive periodical featuring high-quality investigative reporting, political commentary, and features.

The Nation

http://www.thenation.com

Publisher: The Nation Company, L.P.

Description: Covers foreign affairs, local and national politics, education, and law.

The New Republic

http://www.thenewrepublic.com

Publisher: New Republic

Description: Commentary on current political, social, economic, and cultural issues in the United States and around the world.

TomPaine.common Sense

http://www.tompaine.com

Publisher: Florence Fund

Description: Fosters national debate on controversial public issues in the United States by presenting ideas, opinions, and analyses often overlooked by the mainstream media.

Utne

http://www.utne.com

Publisher: Lens Publishing Co., Inc.

Description: Provides a digest of materials reprinted from alternative and independent media.

The Washington Monthly

http://www.washingtonmonthly.com

Publisher: Washington Monthly, LLC

Description: Covers politics and government, with articles about the White House, Congress, and other current affairs.

Neutral or Diverse Focus

The Atlantic Monthly

http://www.theatlantic.com

Publisher: Atlantic Monthly Co.

Description: Provides insight and commentary on the latest social and political issues.

Commentary

http://www.commentarymagazine.com

Publisher: American Jewish Committee

Description: Focuses mainly on contentious social and political issues.

Commonweal

http://www.commonwealmagazine.org

Publisher: Commonweal Foundation

Description: Reviews public affairs, religion, literature, media, and the arts.

Foreign Policy

http://www.foreignpolicy.com

Publisher: Carnegie Endowment for International Peace

Description: Journal of political science and international relations.

The Futurist

http://www.wfs.org/futurist.htm

Publisher: World Future Society

Description: This is a journal of forecasts, trends, and ideas about the future. The magazine strives to serve as a neutral clearinghouse of ideas.

Issues in Science and Technology

http://www.nap.edu/issues/

Publisher: Issues in Science and Technology

Description: A journal of ideas and opinions, exploring the policy implications of developments in science, technology, and health.

National Journal

http://nationaljournal.com/about/njweekly/stories/

Publisher: National Journal Group, Inc.

Description: Provides nonpartisan analysis of politics, policy, and government.

New Perspectives Quarterly

http://www.digitalnpq.org

Publisher: Blackwell Publishing, Inc.

Description: Examines social and political thought on economics, environment, politics, culture, and critical issues.

The New Yorker

http://www.newyorker.com

Publisher: Conde Nast Publications Inc.

Description: Contains fiction; poetry; cartoons; longer essays; articles; and profiles of artists, writers, politicians, and other notables.

Newsweek

http://www.newsweek.com

Publisher: Newsweek, Inc

Description: Reports on current political, national, and international business and economic and cultural events. Analyzes trends in society, the arts, lifestyles, technology, and health through articles and commentary.

The Public Interest

http://www.thepublicinterest.com

Publisher: The National Interest, Inc.

Description: Addresses domestic policy issues, including education, welfare, housing, and poverty.

Salon

http://www.salon.com

Publisher: Salon Media Group

Description: Electronic magazine covering notable political and cultural news and issues.

Slate

http://www.slate.com

Publisher: Microsoft Corporation

Description: Opinion and commentary on political, cultural, economic, and social issues of note.

Time

http://www.time.com/time/

Publisher: Time, Inc

Description: Reviews the news of the week and provides in-depth analyses from multiple perspectives.

US News & World Report

http://www.usnews.com

Publisher: U S News & World Report, Inc.

Description: Reports on and analyzes current events and issues in the United States and throughout the world from multiple perspectives. Covers business and financial news and issues, as well as social and technological trends.

The Wilson Quarterly

http://www.wilsonquarterly.com

Publisher: Woodrow Wilson International Center for Scholars

Description: Nonpartisan magazine ranges over many issues in politics and policy, culture, religion, science, and other fields.

World Press Review

http://www.worldpress.org

Publisher: Stanley Foundation

Description: Selects, translates, and reprints articles from international publications that provide analysis and commentary on world politics, business, science, and culture.

Appendix B

Think Tanks

This is a representative list of think tanks or research institutes that look at issues of public importance to Americans. Although there are hundreds more, these organizations were selected because of their stature, cross-representation, and the number of publications they provide for free online.

Use these sites to gain political perspectives on issues. The list has been divided by political bias to afford an easy way to find opposing viewpoints on a topic. Liberal and conservative organizations will often have a persuasive perspective. Neutral or nonpartisan organizations may take a persuasive approach on a topic or may focus more heavily on research findings. By viewing an issue from all "sides," you will gain fuller insight into the topic.

Conservative or Libertarian Focus

American Enterprise Institute

http://www.aei.org

Topics: Economics, foreign policy

Mission: "The American Enterprise Institute for Public Policy Research is dedicated to preserving and strengthening the foundations of freedom—limited government, private enterprise, vital cultural and political institutions, and a strong foreign policy and national defense—through scholarly research, open debate, and publications."

Cato Institute

http://www.cato.org

Topics: Economics,domestic and foreign policy, social policy

Mission: "Individual liberty, limited government, free markets, and peace."

Claremont Institute

http://www.claremont.org

Topics: Defense, domestic policy

Mission: "The mission of the Claremont Institute is to restore the principles of the American Founding to their rightful, preeminent authority in our national life. . . . [This] means recovering a limited and accountable government that respects private property, promotes stable family life and maintains a strong defense."

Competitive Enterprise Institute

http://www.cei.org

Topics: Consumer policies

Mission: "A non-profit public policy organization dedicated to the principles of free enterprise and limited government. We believe that consumers are best helped not by government regulation but by being allowed to make their own choices in a free marketplace. "

Heritage Foundation

http://www.heritage.org

Topics: Domestic and foreign policy

Mission: "The Heritage Foundation is a research and educational institute—a think tank - whose mission is to formulate and promote conservative public policies based on the principles of free enterprise, limited government, individual freedom, traditional American values, and a strong national defense."

Hoover Institution

http://www-hoover.stanford.edu

Topics: National security, economic policy, social policy

Mission: "The principles of individual, economic, and political freedom; private enterprise; and representative government were fundamental to the vision of the Institution's founder."

Hudson Institute

http://www.hudson.org

Topics: Domestic and foreign policy

Mission: "We demonstrate commitment to free markets and individual responsibility, confidence in the power of technology to assist progress, respect for the importance of culture and religion in human affairs, and determination to preserve America's national security."

Manhattan Institute

http://www.manhattan-institute.org

Topics: Urban, social policies

Mission: "The Manhattan Institute is a think tank whose mission is to develop and disseminate new ideas that foster greater economic choice and individual responsibility."

National Center for Policy Analysis

http://www.ncpa.org

Topics: Health care, taxes, Social Security, welfare, criminal justice, education, and environmental regulation

Mission: "The NCPA's goal is to develop and promote private alternatives to government regulation and control, solving problems by relying on the strength of the competitive, entrepreneurial private sector."

Pacific Research Institute

http://www.pacificresearch.org

Topics: Domestic and social policy

Mission: "The mission of the Pacific Research Institute (PRI) is to champion freedom, opportunity, and personal responsibility for all individuals by advancing free-market policy solutions."

Political Economy Research Center

http://www.perc.org

Topics: Environment, natural resources

Mission: "PERC—The Center for Free Market Environmentalism is the nation's oldest and largest institute dedicated to original research that brings market principles to resolving environmental problems."

Reason Public Policy Institute

http://www.rppi.org

Topics: Domestic, foreign policy

Mission: "Reason Public Policy Institute is a public policy think tank promoting choice, competition, and a dynamic market economy as the foundation for human dignity and progress."

Liberal or Progressive Focus

Center for Economic Policy Research

http://www.cepr.net

Topics: Social, economic policy

Mission: "Established to promote democratic debate on the most important economic and social issues that affect people's lives. "

Center for Law and Social Policy

http://www.clasp.org

Topics: Social, family policy

Mission: "Experts on a host of family policy issues, including welfare reform, workforce development, education and training, child care, child welfare, child support, reproductive health/teen parents, and couples and marriage policy."

Center for National Policy

http://www.cnponline.org

Topics: Economic analysis, equal opportunity, community studies and foreign policy

Mission: "Over the last two decades, CNP has contributed to policy debates on key issues of U.S. national interest, focusing activities in four program areas: economic analysis, equal opportunity, community studies and foreign policy."

Center for National Security Studies

http://www.cnss.org

Topics: Civil liberties, human rights

Mission: "The Center is the only non-profit human rights and civil liberties organization, whose core mission is to prevent claims of national security from eroding civil liberties or constitutional procedures."

Center on Budget and Policy Priorities

http://www.cbpp.org

Topics: Budget, taxes, welfare, health

Mission: "A non-partisan research organization and policy institute that conducts research and analysis on a range of government policies and programs, with an emphasis on those affecting low- and moderate-income people."

Century Foundation

http://www.tcf.org

Topics: Economics, domestic, foreign policy

Mission: "At The Century Foundation, we insist that the central answer to many of the troubling questions that Americans are likely to confront in this new century can be found in progressive ideas."

Economic Policy Institute

http://www.epinet.org

Topics: Economy, domestic policy

Mission: "The mission of the Economic Policy Institute is to provide high-quality research and education in order to promote a prosperous, fair, and sustainable economy. The Institute stresses real world analysis and a concern for the living standards of working people, and it makes its findings accessible to the general public, the media, and policy makers."

Progressive Policy Institute

http://www.ppionline.org

Topics: Economy, domestic and foreign policy

Mission: "Its mission is to modernize progressive politics and government for the Information Age. Leaving behind the stale left-right debates of the industrial era, PPI is a prolific source of 'Third Way' thinking that is shaping the emerging politics of the 21st century."

Russell Sage Foundation

http://www.russellsage.org

Topics: Labor, immigration, race relations, social policy

Mission: "The Foundation dedicates itself exclusively to strengthening the methods, data, and theoretical core of the social sciences as a means of improving social policies."

Neutral or Diverse Focus

American Assembly

http://www.columbia.edu/cu/amassembly/

Topics: International relations, arts policy, role of religion

Mission: "The Assembly's major objectives are: to focus attention and stimulate informed discussion on a range of critical U.S. policy topics, both domestic and international; to inform government officials, community and civic leadership, and the general public regarding the factual background and the range of policy options in a given issue; to facilitate increased communication among decision makers from the public and private sectors, as well as from institutions and organizations concerned with critical public policy issues; and to raise on a continuing basis the level and quality of public policy discourse on national and international issues."

Brookings Institution

http://www.brookings.edu

Topics: Business, defense, economics, education, governance, politics, science, technology, social policy

Mission: "The goal of Brookings activities is to improve the performance of American institutions and the quality of public policy by using social science to analyze emerging issues and to offer practical approaches to those issues in language aimed at the general public."

Center for Arts and Culture

http://www.culturalpolicy.org

Topics: Cultural policies

Mission: "Its mission is to enlarge the public vision of the centrality of the arts and culture in everyday life."

Center for Defense Information

http://www.cdi.org

Topics: Arms control, defense, military, foreign policy

Mission: "Its central aim is to educate the public and inform policymakers about issues of security policy, strategy, operations, weapon systems and defense budgeting, and to produce creative solutions to the problems of today and tomorrow."

Center for Public Integrity

http://www.publicintegrity.org

Topics: Public policy, politics

Mission: "The mission of the Center for Public Integrity is to provide the American people with the findings of our investigations and analyses of public service, government accountability and ethics related issues."

Center for the Study of Technology and Society

http://www.tecsoc.org

Topics: Cultural, social, biotechnology, defense policy

Mission: "The purpose of the Center for the Study of Technology and Society is to study and report on the important technological issues that affect society. Through original research and in-depth analysis, the Center will emphasize and clarify the point that advances in technology are neither inherently good nor inherently evil."

Consumer Federation of America

http://www.consumerfed.org

Topics: Pro-consumer policies

Mission: "An advocacy organization, working to advance pro-consumer policy on a variety of issues before Congress, the White House, federal and state regulatory agencies, and the courts."

Council on Foreign Relations

http://www.cfr.org

Topics: International relations, economics, globalization

Mission: "The Council on Foreign Relations is dedicated to increasing America's understanding of the world and contributing ideas to U.S. foreign policy."

Ethics and Public Policy Center

http://www.eppc.org

Topics: Domestic, foreign policy

Mission: "The Ethics and Public Policy Center (EPPC) was established . . . to clarify and reinforce the bond between the Judeo-Christian moral tradition and the public debate over domestic and foreign policy issues. Its program includes research, writing, publication, and conferences."

Independent Institute

http://www.independent.org

Topics: Social and foreign policy

Mission: "The mission of The Independent Institute is to transcend the all-too-common politicization and superficiality of public policy research and debate, redefine the debate over public issues, and foster new and effective directions for government reform."

Institute for Women's Policy Research

http://www.iwpr.org

Topics: Economic and social policy affecting women

Mission: "A public policy research organization dedicated to informing and stimulating the debate on public policy issues of critical importance to women and their families."

Joint Center for Political and Economic Studies

http://www.jointcenter.org

Topics: Public policy of interest to minorities

Mission: "The Joint Center for Political and Economic Studies informs and illuminates the nation's major public policy debates through research, analysis, and information dissemination in order to: improve the socioeconomic status of black Americans and other minorities; expand their effective participation in the political and public policy arenas; and promote communications and relationships across racial and ethnic lines to strengthen the nation's pluralistic society."

Marshall Institute

http://www.marshall.org

Topics: National security, environment

Mission: "Our mission is to encourage the use of sound science in making public policy about important issues for which science and technology are major considerations."

MRDC

http://www.mdrc.org

Topics: Social policy

Mission: "We are dedicated to learning what works to improve the well-being of low income people."

New America Foundation

http://www.newamerica.net

Topics: Economic, social, environmental and foreign policy

Mission: "The purpose of the New America Foundation is to bring exceptionally promising new voices and new ideas to the fore of our nation's public discourse."

Public Agenda

http://www.publicagenda.org

Topics: School and health care reform, national security, AIDS, crime, economic competitiveness and the environment

Mission: "The two-fold mission of Public Agenda is to: help leaders better understand the public's point of view on major policy issues; help citizens better understand critical policy issues so they can make their own more informed and thoughtful decisions."

RAND

http://www.rand.org

Topics: Military, social issues, foreign policy

Mission: "RAND (a contraction of the term research and development) is the first organization to be called a 'think tank.' In all of our work, we strive for the highest levels of quality, objectivity, and innovation."

Resources for the Future

http://www.rff.org

Topics: Environment, natural resources

Mission: "RFF conducts independent research—rooted primarily in economics and other social sciences—on environmental and natural resource issues."

Urban Institute

http://www.urban.org

Topics: Social and economic problems

Mission: "The Urban Institute is a nonprofit nonpartisan policy research and educational organization established to examine the social, economic, and governance problems facing the nation."

Appendix C

Proprietary Databases

This is a list of proprietary databases to which many libraries subscribe. Check with your local school, university, or public library for access. URLs are not included, since they may vary from library to library. While many databases can be of use for controversial topics, these were selected because they are issue-oriented or provide easy access to topical issues of the type covered in this book. Check with your local librarian for other useful databases.

Columbia International Affairs Online

Publisher: Columbia University Press

Description: Useful for international policy issues. Includes working papers from university research institutes, occasional papers series from NGOs, foundation-funded research projects, proceedings from conferences, books, journals, and policy briefs. Use the "course pack" section to find hot topics that are covered well.

CQ.com

Publisher: Congressional Quarterly

Description: In-depth analysis and legislative tracking of key issues on Capitol Hill. Access to issue briefs at additional cost. Includes a combination of proprietary analysis by CQ staff and government documents.

Issues and Controversies on File

Publisher: Facts on File News Services

Description: Provides researched essays written to give students a thorough review of all sides of a topical issue or controversy in today's news. Each essay includes a complete bibliography, contact information, and extensive links to related articles found throughout FACTS.com databases.

LexisNexis Current Issues

Publisher: LexisNexis Academic and Library Solutions

Description: Web-based access to more than 10,000 highly topical documents that lead to multiple perspectives on the issues of the day. Includes reports, conference proceedings, official documents, organizational newsletters, fact sheets, and briefing papers produced at all levels of government, academics, business, and industry but not published commercially.

SIRS Knowledge Source

Publisher: SIRS Publishing Inc.

Description: Includes full-text access to international news services and publications. The "database features" section includes a "suggested topics" area and a "leading issues" area.

Subject Index

Site Title Index

About the Authors

KAREN R. DIAZ is an Instruction Librarian at the Ohio State University Libraries, Columbus. She currently teaches online courses on research skills for college students. She has held positions as Web librarian, reference librarian, and online coordinator in academic libraries. Karen holds a Masters of Library Information Science from Louisiana State University. Other publications include articles and an edited book about online reference and research.

NANCY O'HANLON is currently an Instruction Librarian at the Ohio State University Libraries, Columbus, where she is responsible for developing and managing online information literacy programs. Nancy received an M.S. in Library Information Science from University of Illinois, Urbana, in 1983. In addition to holding various library positions at Ohio State, she was Associate Director of the Eisenhower National Clearinghouse for Mathematics and Science Education, and has also worked as a freelance Web developer. She has published a variety of articles on instruction-related topics.

CT 71x 34B